THE MUSIC OF JONI MITCHELL

THE MUSIC OF Joni Mitchell

LLOYD WHITESELL

OXFORD
UNIVERSITY PRESS
2008

OXFORD
UNIVERSITY PRESS

Oxford University Press, Inc., publishes works that further
Oxford University's objective of excellence
in research, scholarship, and education.

Oxford New York
Auckland   Cape Town   Dar es Salaam   Hong Kong   Karachi
Kuala Lumpur   Madrid   Melbourne   Mexico City   Nairobi
New Delhi   Shanghai   Taipei   Toronto

With offices in
Argentina   Austria   Brazil   Chile   Czech Republic   France   Greece
Guatemala   Hungary   Italy   Japan   Poland   Portugal   Singapore
South Korea   Switzerland   Thailand   Turkey   Ukraine   Vietnam

Published by Oxford University Press, Inc.
198 Madison Avenue, New York, NY 10016

www.oup.com

Oxford is a registered trademark of Oxford University Press

Library of Congress Cataloging-in-Publication Data
Whitesell, Lloyd.
The music of Joni Mitchell / by Lloyd Whitesell.
p.   cm.
Includes discography (p.), bibliographical references, and index.
ISBN 978-0-19-530757-3; 978-0-19-530799-3 (pbk.)
1. Mitchell, Joni—Criticism and interpretation. I. Title.
ML410.M6823W55 2008
782.42164092—dc22   2007043693

Publication of this book was supported by the Lloyd Hibberd Publication
Endowment Fund of the American Musicological Society

1 3 5 7 9 8 6 4 2

Printed in the United States of America
on acid-free paper

CONTENTS

ACKNOWLEDGMENTS

I am grateful to Fred Maus for encouragement at an early stage of this project. For conversations about method and generous advice about work in progress I would like to thank Udayan Sen, Daniel Sonenberg, and my colleagues David Brackett and William Caplin. An anonymous reader for the press was extremely helpful with suggestions for revision. Thanks go to my research assistants Heather White Luckow and Michel Vallières for their enthusiasm and insight in compiling a bibliography on the analysis of popular music.

Research for this book was carried out with the aid of an Internal Social Sciences and Humanities Research Grant from McGill University. Cynthia Leive and the wonderful staff at the Marvin Duchow Music Library offered abundant support. Les Irvin, of the Joni Mitchell Discussion List, gave invaluable help tracking down arcane details and materials. The two official Web sites are beautifully maintained treasure troves of information, making research a treat. I am grateful to Cathy Clarke of S. L. Feldman & Associates for help with permissions. A special thanks to Joni Mitchell for permission to reproduce her painting. Suzanne Ryan, Norm Hirschy, and the staff at Oxford University Press have been supportive and enthusiastic at every stage of the project. The book also received welcome assistance from the Lloyd Hibberd Publication Endowment Fund of the American Musicological Society.

I would like to thank the students in my graduate seminar on Joni Mitchell for the opportunity to share some of my ideas. Finally, thanks to Don McLean, Dean of the Schulich School of Music, McGill University, for working so untiringly to bring the artist herself to the Symposium on the Music and Art of Joni Mitchell at McGill, October 2004; to Howie Klein for smoothing the way; to David Brackett and Sarah Culpeper for their help in organizing the symposium; and to all the participants for making it a success: Line Grenier, John Kelly, Dan Levitin, Ann Powers, Jennifer Rycenga, Udayan Sen, Daniel Sonenberg, Greg Tate, and Jacqueline Warwick.

A portion of chapter 4 appeared as "A Joni Mitchell Aviary" in *Women and Music* 1 (Summer 1997): 46–54, and *The Joni Mitchell Companion: Four Decades of Commentary*, ed. Stacey Luftig (New York: Schirmer Books, 2000), 237–50. A version of chapter 5 appeared in *Popular Music* 21 (2002): 189–209.

ABBREVIATIONS

ALBUMS BY JONI MITCHELL

B	*Blue*
BOS	*The Beginning of Survival*
BSN	*Both Sides Now*
C	*Clouds*
C&S	*Court and Spark*
CMRS	*Chalk Mark in a Rain Storm*
DED	*Dog Eat Dog*
DJRD	*Don Juan's Reckless Daughter*
FR	*For the Roses*
H	*Hejira*
HSL	*The Hissing of Summer Lawns*
LC	*Ladies of the Canyon*
M	*Mingus*
MA	*Miles of Aisles*
NRH	*Night Ride Home*
S&L	*Shadows and Light*
SPG	*Songs of a Prairie Girl*
SS	*Song to a Seagull*
TI	*Turbulent Indigo*
TT	*Taming the Tiger*
WTRF	*Wild Things Run Fast*

BOOK

Luftig	Stacey Luftig, ed., *The Joni Mitchell Companion: Four Decades of Commentary* (New York: Schirmer, 2000)

THE MUSIC OF JONI MITCHELL

INTRODUCTION: POP SONG AND ART SONG

Joni Mitchell is now widely recognized as one of the foremost singer-songwriters of the late twentieth century. Since her career began in the 1960s she has produced fifteen original albums and a collaborative project with the great jazz musician Charles Mingus, as well as a number of concert albums and compilations.[1] By the 1990s she began to be marketed as a "classic" and was confirmed in her classic status by a series of tribute concerts and awards for artistic achievement.[2] Her songwriting, in its originality, creative integrity, stylistic adventurousness, and technical polish, has had great influence on musicians from many different backgrounds. Furthermore, her lyrical and musical output has acquired special cultural status as the representative voice of a self-exploratory intellectual bohemianism, shaped by the visionary ideals of the 1960s folksong revival, youth protest movements, and sexual revolution. In particular, her songs record a woman's response to those struggles and the prospects they have opened up. Mitchell is also unique in her perspective on the North American cultural landscape, as projected through a symbolic triangulation of the urban poles of New York City and Los Angeles with the prairies of western Canada. These aspects of her writing, as well as her depth of thought as a lyricist, have received some treatment by critics in the popular press.[3] Her musical craftsmanship, however, still lacks a full account.

This book is about music and poetry in the songs of Joni Mitchell. My subject is sound, syntax, design, and effect—how the songs are put together and how they work. I will not be judging the value of her music based on its influence, popularity, or exemplary nature as a chronicle of its times, though these are all topics worthy of consideration in their own right. Rather, I will be examining details of her craft, rummaging through her musical toolkit (her "box of paints," as she might put it) to establish a basis for judgments about the quality of her songwriting. I am not particularly interested in ranking Mitchell's work against that of other songwriters (to compete for the title of "the greatest" according to some presumed set of objective criteria). Nevertheless, I do feel compelled to point out that evaluation of her work has been affected by its placement within two predominant categories of cultural prestige: namely, on the disadvantaged side of the distinction between high and low art, and between male and female authorship. Prestige categories can operate as preconceptual filters, sorting artists into piles marked from the start as "superior" and "inferior" before engaging with their work on its own merits. Having been produced entirely within the context of a commercialized media industry, Mitchell's music risks being perceived as falling into a lower order of achievement in comparison with classical music. However, as Bernard Gendron has demonstrated, this general situation underwent changes in the 1960s, when certain popular musicians (notably the Beatles and Bob Dylan) began to acquire the status of serious artists rather than mere entertainers, and rock itself began to gain respect as a "legitimate art form."[4] Arriving on the heels of this advancement in status, Mitchell was able to overcome the lowbrow distinction to a limited extent. Already early in her career, critics were describing her music in terms of an art song aesthetic. For instance, Dan Heckman, reviewing *Blue* in 1971 for the *New York Times*, writes:

> I suspect this will be the most disliked of Miss Mitchell's recordings, despite the fact that it attempts more and makes greater demands on her talent than any of the others. The audience for art songs is far smaller than for folk ballads, and Joni Mitchell is on the verge of having to make a decision between the two.[5]

Late in her career (1996), Joni Mitchell was awarded the Polar Music Prize by the government of Sweden; in a rare leveling of status, the other recipient of the award that year was eminent classical composer and conductor Pierre Boulez. I will return to the distinction between high and low art below.

The privileging of male over female authorship occurs in both classical and popular music scenes. This is not the place to mount an extensive argument about male domination in the popular music business.[6] Suffice it to mention that Mitchell's 1997 induction into the Rock and Roll Hall of Fame came a full four years after she first became eligible, during which time her nomination had languished due to lack of support. Before her induction, music critic Stephen Holden had sharply criticized the Hall of Fame for its relative neglect of female musicians and their historical influence, citing this neglect as an index of gender bias in rock criticism at large.[7] I hasten to add, however, that my interest in promoting Mitchell's music arises not from any such perceived slights, but from its inherent quality. Mitchell herself has generally been dismissive of gender issues altogether. In the press conference in connection with the announcement of the Polar Prize, the interviewer solicits her thoughts on being the first woman to win the prize. Mitchell responds, "Oh, I don't like to think about that so much, this man-woman-man-woman thing. I wish we could get over that." When pressed, she adds,

> I try not to think about gender distinctions. It's kind of like [asking], "You are the first black to receive it—how do you feel about that?" I find it an isolating question and I hope there will come a day when this distinction is not made. I'm a musician and I leave gender aside. I'm an accomplished musician.[8]

While I would like to draw attention to the hierarchy of prestige within popular music, according to which women's intellectual production has been historically undervalued, I agree wholeheartedly with the view that Mitchell's accomplishment should stand or fall on its own merits, without respect to gender.

In concentrating on distinctions of style and musical craft, I hope to avoid setting up prestige categories of my own. In the chapters that follow, I don't mean to suggest, for example, that harmonic complexity in itself is aesthetically superior to harmonic simplicity or that complementary, closed melodic structures are superior to open-ended, dance-oriented formal processes. Rather, my aim is to develop a precise vocabulary by which to recognize her technical achievements for what they are and to identify a value system appropriate to them. Joni Mitchell's particular brand of songwriting is characterized by its conceptual depth, structural sophistication, stylistic dynamism, and aesthetic ambition. One can value her music for these traits without casting aspersions on other brands of songwriting, which may be recognized for their skill according to slightly different or even entirely different sets of priorities (such as rough immediacy, kinetic drive, effusiveness, accessibility, trendsetting).

The characteristics I have listed for Mitchell's music would seem to call for a value system traditionally associated with the world of high art. Mitchell herself, in numerous interviews, has appealed to the art concept as a way to convey her views on musical value.

> I was only a folk singer for about two years. . . . By that time, it wasn't really folk music anymore. It was some new American phenomenon. Later, they called it singer/songwriters. Or art songs, which I liked best. Some people get nervous about that word. Art. They think it's a pretentious word from the giddyap. To me, . . . the word *art* has never lost its vitality.[9]

Mitchell has asserted the importance of the classical music tradition in the formation of her tastes.[10] She has likened aspects of her songwriting to classical composition, claiming affinities with the expressive miniatures of German Lieder and the harmonic palette of Debussy—once even referring to herself as "a composer in the small, modern form."[11] Often, in light of her concurrent interests as a painter, she will refer to visual arts: she speaks of the song "Paprika Plains" [DJRD] as "the most experimental and bewildering piece [to compose], but it was always moving forward, always changing, much in the same way that Picasso paints.... He's always working toward his own satisfaction, that's his only criteria."[12] Another telling remark occurred off the cuff during a live concert in 1974 (captured on the *Miles of Aisles* album). As Mitchell adjusts her guitar tuning between numbers, fans compete for her attention, calling out a dozen different requests. This prompts the following philosophical observation:

> That's one thing that's always been a major difference between the performing arts to me and being a painter. Like, a painter does a painting and he does a painting, that's it, you know, he's had the joy of creating it, and he hangs it on some wall, somebody buys it, somebody buys it again, or maybe nobody buys it, and it sits up in a loft somewhere till he dies. But nobody ever says to him, you know, nobody ever said to Van Gogh, "Paint 'A Starry Night' again, man!"

These quotations indicate a personal creed favoring artistic ambition over populism, creative integrity over accessibility, and aesthetic value over market value. The last quoted remark also somewhat paradoxically upholds the ideal of the finished, durable artwork (the "masterpiece"), even within a context of live performance. In a more recent statement, Mitchell alludes to a similar concept while modifying it in an important way: "My music is not designed to grab instantly. It's designed to wear for a lifetime, to hold up like a fine cloth."[13] Here, her reference to textiles evokes a concept of art that is less removed from everyday life, one that acknowledges repeated use or enjoyment and allows more "give" to the work as it adapts to different listeners. We might bring all these various nuances together and suggest a "fine art" model for the appreciation of Mitchell's songwriting. The term "fine art" has the advantage of encompassing a broad range of practice in various media, including both high art and artisanal crafts.

In downplaying popularity and accessibility as creative goals, Mitchell is not announcing a willful intent to write difficult music. There is no question that her songs are designed to move and please listeners. Nevertheless, such an attitude ("art" before "pop") is maintained in tension with the reigning values of the popular music industry.[14] As Daniel Sonenberg has observed, Mitchell benefited from significant restructuring within the industry at the outset of her career. The increasing profitability of the long-playing record and rise of FM radio "reduced the demand on rock artists to attain instant stardom" and allowed for more breathing space to foster an original musical sensibility.[15] Mitchell and others were able to approach their music as both popular expression and fine art, thus bridging the gap between traditions commonly segregated into high and low forms. Mitchell was recognized at the time as a particularly strong proponent of such an approach. According to *New York Times* critic John Rockwell, her work in the 1970s established "her claim as the artist best able to link folk-rock with the older Western tradition of the art song."[16] Elsewhere, he says:

> The pop people have by now created their own artistic traditions and … their traditions have begun to merge, in some still vague and elusive sense, with the mainstream of high art. Today, there are a number of supposedly "pop" performers who are in no reasonable way distinguishable from "artists".… Joni Mitchell … is such an artist—as serious and experimental as they come.[17]

The label "singer-songwriter," one of the terms that evolved in response to the new approach, attempts to capture this sense of an intermediate aesthetic space. Defined neither entirely in commercial terms (as with "hit" or "star") nor in terms of high culture (as with "composer"), the new description plots a continuum between the dual poles of accessibility and artistry. But what does it mean to fall between the two traditions? What are the consequences of bridging high and low cultures? The meeting of Pierre Boulez and Joni Mitchell on equal footing at the Polar Music Prize press conference provided an occasion to address such questions. Boulez is asked about the possibility of breaking down barriers. He replies:

> Each time I meet journalists I am asked, why did you work with Zappa? That was the first time I broke down this imaginary but real barrier between the world of symphonic music and a music of another kind.… We in the kind of serious world have a lot of heritage and sometimes it is very heavy to assume that this heritage is yours and you have to continue in that direction. In the other world, you don't have this burden and they are more spontaneous and vital from this point of view and surely I think both worlds would have to benefit from each other. The vitality of the one world should be introduced in the world of classical music and vice versa. A kind of values should be introduced in the world of actuality [in the sense of *actualité*, current events]. I think this exchange should happen more often.

It is interesting to note Boulez's delicacy with labels. He uses a variety of terms for the world of art music (symphonic, classical, "kind of serious") while resisting specific terms for music of "another kind," other than the notion of the current music scene. He avoids the prestige labels of high and low culture altogether. Yet he does ascribe certain attributes to each world—spontaneity and vitality in the one case; seriousness, heritage, and an implicit set of "values" in the other. What might these unspoken values be?

If one were asked to list the stereotypical connotations of high art, the following descriptions would probably come to mind:

- serious, edifying
- profound
- complex, subtle
- carefully constructed
- enduring in value, establishing a cultural heritage

The stereotypical connotations of low or popular art would call up a contrasting list:

- entertaining
- vital, authentic
- simple, common
- spontaneous, immediate
- novel, topical in value

Furthermore, the comparative cultural status of the two categories has tended to confer evaluative weight, so that the traits of high culture are judged to be refined and aesthetically superior, those of low culture vulgar and aesthetically inferior. But it is not very difficult to expose this whole descriptive/evaluative grid as prejudicial. In the first place, none of the properties listed are exclusive to either culturally defined category: plenty of classical music idealizes simplicity and the common touch while some is deliberately vulgar; likewise, popular musicians are not categorically bereft of refinement, profundity, or careful attention to craft. In the second place, aesthetic superiority is not automatically conferred by cultural status; after all, there is no shortage of second- and third-rate classical composers. Popular music scholar Simon Frith puts it this way:

> To assert the value of the popular is also, necessarily, to query the superiority of high culture. Most populist writers, though, draw the wrong conclusion from this; what needs challenging is not the notion of the superior, but the claim that it is the exclusive property of the "high."[18]

In short, designations of "high" and "low" have to do with the question of prestige or cultural regard and are not to be equated with aesthetic distinctions. A range of attitudes toward creative expression can be encountered in both cultural spheres. Still, the first set of attributes above (especially the notions of edification, durability, and technical skill) has an established history of association with high art traditions, the second set (especially entertainment, immediacy, and accessibility) with popular traditions. It is possible to distinguish between approaches closer to an art model or a popular model without saying anything about relative superiority.[19] It follows that one can appreciate hybrid or intermediate forms like the singer-songwriter repertoire as popular expression or as fine art. When Mitchell praises Leonard Cohen's work for its "deeper thought," she is applying the fine art standard of profundity.[20] When Noel Coppage ends his review of *The Hissing of Summer Lawns* with these remarks—"I hope I've made it clear that this isn't much of a party record; you'll have to deal with it privately, as you would read a book. But it should keep you occupied for about as long as you want it to—and how often does 'popular' music do that?"[21]—he is suggesting a listening approach favoring seriousness and edification over immediacy and entertainment. Finally, John Rockwell, in a review of *Hejira*, argues for the careful construction and enduring value of Mitchell's music and in the process deems it worthy of the high cultural regard usually reserved for art song traditions:

> Like all of Miss Mitchell's work, *Hejira* is not for comfortable background listening. This is no boogie album, no soothing collection of pop tunes with handy hooks. Instead it is a series of personal statements couched in the idiom of sophisticated Los Angeles folk rock, but assembled with all the care of a Lied by Hugo Wolf. As such it is something not to be sampled casually and put aside, but to be savored seriously over the years.[22]

For a long time, representatives of high musical culture have looked on popular music with suspicion (when they haven't overlooked it altogether), despising it as lacking complexity, profundity, and the like. With the trend toward legitimation in the general culture as well as the rise of popular music studies in academia, such a viewpoint has become more difficult to maintain. But meanwhile, some champions of popular music for their part remain suspicious of the values associated with high musical culture. We should beware a sort of reverse discrimination, whereby structural complexity and technical sophistication are decried as elitist, pretentious, or ideologically loaded. Not all critics have been as approving as Coppage and Rockwell of the aesthetic ambition evident in Mitchell's career.[23] In the academic sphere, the analysis of complex structural relations is sometimes construed as a wholesale valorization of certain popular genres and styles over others. As popular music scholar David Brackett warns:

> Analytical work ... that uncritically accepts the basic tenets of Western music theory has tended to accommodate popular music to some notion of a canon of masterworks through either "legitimation" or "pluralism." "Legitimation" works by selecting music for analysis that contains a type of complexity that responds well to techniques designed for Western art music.... Sheet music or transcriptions are typically used to show sophisticated pitch relationships which, it is implied, are every bit as worthy of study as those found in the masterpieces.[24]

For my part, I agree that an uncritical attitude toward analytical precepts and the process of canonization is untenable. Nevertheless I hope that as listeners, we would be prepared to appreciate technical skill and subtlety wherever we encounter it, without enshrining it as a necessary standard of value.

What I offer, then, in this book is a set of analytical tools geared toward understanding Joni Mitchell's skill and achievement as a songwriter. Close musical analysis can unlock hidden aspects of song construction and lead to a more precise grasp of technical innovations and the idiosyncrasies of an original style. Analysis need not alienate listeners from the music they love. The incisive knowledge of the scholar can go hand in hand with the intimate knowledge of the fervent fan. In Brackett's words, analysis can compel the listener "to engage forcefully with the object of study, to learn it thoroughly and to hear it in new ways."[25] This endorsement, couched in the language of intellectual fascination, is not that far removed from the language of love. Along the same lines, I see no reason to divorce discussion of music's syntactic aspect (analysis narrowly defined) from its expressive, semantic, or cultural aspects (music criticism). These various aspects of musical meaning are wholly interrelated. My primary focus on analysis addresses a deficiency in the literature on Joni Mitchell; but wherever possible, I try to connect analytical detail to an awareness of the living musical experience in its power, beauty, and cultural reach.

In contrast to recent books by Richard Middleton, Allan Moore, and Ken Stephenson, whose concern is to elaborate a coherent theoretical system applicable to a wide range of popular music, my scope is more modest and pragmatic: the illustration of some useful concepts custom designed for a specific repertoire.[26] Some of the tools I use derive from traditional poetic criticism, some from the traditional analysis of art music. These have been adapted as needed to accommodate characteristics of style, form, and syntax peculiar to popular music traditions in general and Mitchell's music in particular. I have benefited from the growing body of scholarly literature devoted to the analysis of popular music. One question which has caused a certain amount of controversy in this field is the inherent suitability of analytical concepts originally designed for art music.[27] I hold with the view (articulated by John Covach, David Brackett, and others) that there are significant areas of overlap between various art music and popular music traditions[28] and that analytical techniques borrowed from art music can be useful as long as they remain flexible and sensitive to different generic conventions.[29] Such hybrid analytical practices, developed on an ad hoc basis, are especially appropriate to a songwriting approach that seeks to bridge traditions.

The objects of my analyses are sound recordings. That is to say, the primary material of study is aural experience rather than printed scores. In contrast to art song repertoire, which is conceived as abstractable from any particular performed version, the singer-songwriter repertoire more closely marries authorship and original performance; thus analysis entails sensitivity to authorial interpretations of songs as performed. For most songs I consider a single specific performance as captured and produced by Joni Mitchell in a definitive recorded version; in a few cases she has recorded more than one version. The commercially released songbooks are themselves generally transcribed by ear from recordings. However, even when they are carefully done, market-driven conventions often take precedence over faithful notation. For instance, songs may be transposed to avoid complex key signatures (true of Mitchell's early songs performed in F♯ and D♭), and piano accompaniments are frequently changed to incorporate the vocal line in the right hand. In Mitchell's early career, her guitar accompaniments were generally converted to standard tuning. In some of the songbook collections that do faithfully notate her alternate guitar tunings (namely, *Hits, Misses,* and *Joni Mitchell Complete {Guitar Songbook Edition}*), every song (even if originally performed on piano) is arranged willy-nilly for guitar performance. For such reasons, transcriptions in this book are my own, aided by reference to the published songbooks, whose reliability I have carefully checked against my own listening perceptions.[30] I have done my best to identify and describe sounds faithfully and with precision, but occasionally, certain musical details (e.g., meter, harmony, figuration) are ambiguous or obscured by sound layering. In such cases there may be more than one valid interpretation of the phenomena. Questions of performance technique (such as inquiry into Mitchell's extensive use of alternate guitar tunings and fingerings) are not my subject here.

In the chapters that follow, I offer a survey of Mitchell's output, with many discussions of individual songs; but I have organized the material by topic rather than chronology. This allows for variety in analytical approach (each chapter exploring different parameters, such as poetic voice, harmony, melody, and large-scale form) as well as in analytical focus (different sections concentrating variously on single songs, entire albums, themes recurring between albums, and style periods). Instead of attempting to cover every song, I delve into different aspects of her songwriting craft by way of selected illustrative examples.

In chapter 2 I present an overview of Mitchell's dynamic stylistic evolution from 1966 to 1998 according to four distinct periods. In the first period she takes an acoustic folk aesthetic as the point of departure for various explorations into intricate poetic structure, rhapsodic expression and idiosyncratic instrumentation. The second period, initiated by the album *Court and Spark* and climaxing with the *Mingus* collaboration, is marked by a dramatic shift toward jazz stylings, an integral backup band, and highly polished production. The third period (representing Mitchell's least-known work) mingles forays into mainstream upbeat pop with brittle synthesized soundscapes and a tone of political indignation. The fourth period, tinged with nostalgia, returns to a largely acoustic palette, while fusing aspects from previous periods. I illustrate salient aspects of each period—such as poetic style, changing vocal production, genre references, melodic writing, instrumental timbre, and figuration—by discussing representative songs. This overview introduces many of the topics that will receive extended treatment in subsequent chapters as well as providing a general chronological framework for the individual analyses in the remainder of the book. The chapter ends by focusing on one of Mitchell's signature songs, "Woodstock," which unfolds its own distinct narrative of changing sound and style as it has traveled with her throughout her career.

Chapters 3 and 4 share an emphasis on the lyrics to the songs. In chapter 3 I explore a particularly vivid aspect of Mitchell's songwriting and performing style: the colorful array of lyrical voices and personalities she brings to life. My discussion pays special attention to details of poetic technique. In the first section of the chapter, I make reference to an extensive range of song lyrics to suggest the flexibility and nuance to be found in Mitchell's creation of fictional personae. After systematically mapping out categorical distinctions of poetic mode, representation, syntax, diction, and vocal performance, I illustrate their use through the analysis of an entire poem. In the second section of the chapter, I highlight five character types of special importance in her work.

Chapter 4 takes a more sweeping view of poetic themes. I focus on a favorite thematic preoccupation—personal freedom—as explored by way of potent symbols of confinement, the journey quest, bohemianism, creative license, and spiritual liberation. Here analyses of individual songs are mustered with an overarching goal in mind: to demonstrate the complexity and profundity of Mitchell's poetic-musical thought, her provocative coupling of personal and universal concerns, and her rhetorical assurance in articulating and engaging with some of the pressing cultural issues of her generation.

In chapter 5 I turn to musical detail work, considering the extent of Mitchell's harmonic innovation, an aspect that clearly sets her apart from her songwriting peers. My harmonic analyses are carried out in conjunction with poetic and expressive interpretation. Through a representative survey, I demonstrate how her songs fall under five broad categories of harmonic organization: modal, polymodal, chromatic, polytonal, and pedal point. Mitchell's work is especially impressive for its thoroughgoing exploration of alternatives to single key structures and the major/minor system. In conversation, she has equated this experimental harmonic practice ("chords of inquiry") with the musical articulation of a critical perspective.

In chapter 6 I study the structural intricacy underpinning Mitchell's melodic writing. The first section of this chapter introduces vocabulary basic to popular song form and shows how she devises variations on the standard forms. The second section examines the internal structure of formal sections, highlighting Mitchell's nonformulaic approach to phrase construction. Phrase proportions are often irregular, due to devices such as harmonic extension and metric disruption. Phrases commonly relate to one another through audible patterns of parallelism, contrast, and complementarity; I introduce a concise method of diagramming such relations. I also spend some time clarifying the principle of hierarchic cadences and complementary pairings (what Allan Moore calls the "open/closed principle"), an issue plagued by terminological confusion.[31] This principle, crucial to Mitchell's melodic style, has not yet been carefully theorized in popular music studies. In the third section of this chapter I turn to the expressive effects made possible through the sculpting of melodic contour. Along the way I characterize two dramatic paradigm shifts in her approach to melodic writing, one occurring in the mid-1970s and another in the early 1980s.

Chapter 7 places individual songs in the context of larger formal spans, tackling the question of coherence at the level of the album. From her beginnings Mitchell was interested in trying out both song collections and song cycles, that is, loose groupings of diverse characterizations (*Clouds, Ladies of the Canyon*) as well as "concept" albums organized by connecting frameworks (*Song to a Seagull, Blue*). I analyze large-scale form in three albums, pondering just what kind of unity is at stake. Elements to be considered include recurrent imagery, thematic and motivic interconnections, consistency of expressive tone, narrative and tonal planning, and visual design. The centerpiece of the chapter is a comparison of two consecutive albums from the late 1970s whose cyclic characters could not be more different. Where *Hejira*'s songs of the open road are tightly interlinked in theme and consistent in sound, the double-LP *Don Juan's Reckless Daughter* is multifarious, sprawling, and contradictory. By way of a coda, chapter 8 reflects on the significance of a high-profile collective tribute to Joni Mitchell released on the Nonesuch label in 2007.

Though analytical terminology is handled in a cumulative fashion, I have tried to make it practicable for readers to approach individual chapters out of order according to their interests. The flow of the book would have been more streamlined had I reduced the sheer number of songs discussed. But I have preferred to err on the side of variety and inclusiveness, in the hopes of extending the book's usefulness as a compendium as well as a preliminary study. Some songs make multiple appearances under different rubrics (e.g., "I Had a King," "The Dawntreader," "Song to a Seagull," "Woodstock," "Amelia"). Readers comparatively new to Mitchell's work may wish to begin by learning a limited number of songs and tracing a progress through the book by way of these stepping stones.

The analyses that follow do not pretend to be comprehensive. By no means have I covered everything of note regarding Mitchell's harmonic language, thematic resonance, or my other chosen topics. Moreover, many fascinating musical aspects touched on in passing—such as rhythm, timbre, instrumental figuration, studio production, and mixing—deserve extended consideration in their own right. But in developing substantial scholarly inquiry into the areas of style, voice, theme, harmony, melody, and large-scale form, I have had four broad goals in mind: discovering initial points of entry into a rich and relatively uncharted body of popular song; laying the groundwork for future analytical inquiry; providing practical models of analysis for use in the classroom; and establishing a basis for evaluating Joni Mitchell's stature as a songwriter. Given my earlier caveats about cultural prestige, I realize that this last aim bears an ironic similarity to the Great Man approach toward music history, used so effectively to exclude women (and other classes of people) in the past. In focusing on one remarkable artist's individual achievement, my intent is not to wedge her into a position of rank or bury her under a weight of symbolic importance. I would rather view this project in terms of a visit to a busy workshop, with an emphasis on the appreciation of skill, ingenuity, design, polish, and knowledge of materials. But in moments of musically induced weakness, I have been known to refer to her as a genius.

2

SOUND AND STYLE

Joni Mitchell is one of those modern artists who maintain a constant sense of adventure and unpredictability in their work, treating style not as a dependable personalized manner but as a changing field of possibility. She likens herself to Miles Davis and Pablo Picasso in this regard.[1] The towering influence of both figures derives in part from their dramatic stylistic experimentation over the course of long careers. Picasso's path from the postimpressionism of his youthful contemporaries through primitivism, cubism (analytical and synthetic phases), and classicism was impetuous and marked by sudden ruptures. Davis, "the innovator of more distinct styles than any other jazz musician," restlessly explored new approaches from cool jazz to modal playing to fusion, while refusing to define his creative impulse by any single approach.[2] Mitchell herself has covered ample ground, moving from folk roots through inventive encounters with jazz, world music, and synthesized pop. Her protean character as a songwriter means that any two fans may cherish completely contradictory mental images of her music. This fact was brought home to me with a jolt when I attended Mitchell's performance at the New Orleans Jazz and Heritage Festival in the spring of 1995. Mitchell was playing a solo set at one of the large open stages. Only one week earlier, she had acquired a new electric guitar fitted with a Roland VG-8 controller to facilitate her multiple alternate tunings.[3] She began the set with "Sex Kills," a searing social critique released on *Turbulent Indigo* the year before. The stern persona adopted in her recent work together with the unexpected aggressive electric sound struck me with the excitement of a new stylistic venture. However, one thirty-something female fan near me listened for about twenty seconds before spluttering, "I can't take this," and elbowing her way out of the crowd. (Mitchell recalls the moment: "I started with 'Sex Kills,' playing this diabolical kind of Jimi Hendrix/fuzztone sound, just for the hell of it, and I think a lot of people were quite annoyed.")[4] On the other hand, after the concert, as I joined a small group of admirers in search of the backstage exit area, it was hard not to notice an undaunted spirit of the sixties frolicking on the grass in full wizard costume (robe and conical hat) while clutching a Joni LP.

Clearly, Joni Mitchell's audience is a heterogeneous bunch. There are "universal" Joni fans who have stayed with her for the whole trip as well as devotees of favorite periods in her career. In this chapter, I want to convey a sense of the breadth of her style by sketching the overall arc of her musical evolution. But I also plan to outline a succession of loose stylistic periods to use as a framework for later discussion. I freely admit that this periodic grouping is my own interpretation; others may well hear things differently. Nor do I mean to imply that the music within each period is stylistically static or homogeneous. Mitchell's invention is typically multidimensional and open to all sorts of byways. Nevertheless, we can point to common preoccupations spanning several albums and contributing to a cumulative sense of direction.

I hear Mitchell's work from 1966 to 1998 as falling into four distinct periods, defined according to the studio albums released between the following dates: 1968–1972 (five albums), 1974–1979 (five albums), 1982–1988 (three albums), and 1991–1998 (three albums).[5] The beginning of each successive period is signaled by an album announcing a bold new departure in sound and style: in 1974 the album is *Court and Spark;* in 1982, *Wild Things Run Fast;* and in 1991, *Night Ride Home.* I have chosen specific songs to illustrate the stages in Mitchell's musical journey.

FIRST PERIOD (1966–1972)

Mitchell wrote her first song, "Day after Day," in 1964 when she was twenty. She started writing her own material in earnest the following year after forming a folksinging duo with husband Chuck Mitchell and after the traumatic experience of giving her daughter up for adoption.[6] However, the earliest songs she chose to include on commercial recordings ("Night in the City," "Song to a Seagull" [both *SS*], "I Think I Understand" [*C*], and "The Circle Game" [*LC*]) date from 1966. The year 1966 thus marks the start of Mitchell's official published work.[7] All four of her first albums include songs written while she was on the touring circuit during the two years before her recording career was launched in 1968.

With the opening number on her debut album, "I Had a King" (1968, *SS*), Mitchell was in effect introducing herself as a recording artist to a wider audience. Presented simply as a solo for voice and guitar, the song evokes the ambience of the waning folk scene in its quiet presence, its strophic form, and its troubadour imagery.[8] Mitchell's voice modulates between tones of fragile simplicity and bardic solemnity. But these seemingly modest resources reveal great artistry and expressive power. The song's medieval dress of castles and carriages is merely a threadbare overlay for its real setting—a shabby pocket of some modern city. Lingering wisps of premodern fantasy are exposed as romantic illusions in the ugly light of a marriage breaking apart. Within the verse, rhymes are arranged to form a densely interlocking structure. Verse 1 is the most rigorously constructed:

I had a king in a tenement **castle**			a		
Lately he's taken to painting the **pastel** walls **brown**			a	b	
He's taken the curtains **down**				b	
He's swept with the **broom** of contempt	c	d			
And the **rooms** have an **empty ring**	c	d			e
He's cleaned with the **tears** of an **actor**	f	g			
Who **fears** for the **laughter's sting**	f	g			e

Note how the end rhymes of lines 1, 4, and 6 are paired with internal rhymes in the subsequent lines, nested within different end rhyme pairs. Such a highly worked attention to rhyme is common in Mitchell's songs from the late 1960s.[9] Here, the ornate verbal patterning chimes with the deliberately precious metaphorical conceit. Elsewhere, Mitchell is able to turn the same technique to quite different expressive effect. In a song like "Willy" (*LC*), for example, the leapfrogging rhymes are more vernacular and liquid (verse 2: "real ... peal ... bells, tell ... spell ... real, lose ... blues ... feel"), as if swept up in the tumbling current of passion. In "I Had a King" one can point to a further effect of the poetic structure. The added end rhyme on the second poetic line creates asymmetrical lengths in the first half of the verse (with lines of eleven, thirteen, and seven syllables—or 4 poetic "beats," 5 beats, and 3 beats), and Mitchell adheres to this in her musical setting, constructing a melody in irregular phrase groups of two, three, and three bars.

The guitar sets up a pattern of running eighths. At first, Mitchell spins out a filigree of arpeggiation across a two-octave span, with some interesting knots in the middle range. But at the poem's emphatic reversal in line 2 ("pastel walls *brown*"), she begins to give the guitar a multivoiced texture, with a certain independence between bass parts, upper melodic figures, and chordal punctuation. (JM: "When I'm playing the guitar ... I hear it as an orchestra: the top three strings being my horn section, the bottom three being cello, viola, and bass—the bass being indicated but not rooted.")[10] In the second half of the verse, the chord changes are knit together by internal voices slowly and wistfully falling by seconds (Ex. 2.1). Though the accompaniment is composed out, Mitchell occasionally alters the strophic pattern in response to special moments in the poem (as in verse 2, when she adds chordal accents to catch the syncopation of "become that kind"). Many musical elements work together to assert the song's central idea of refusing to be trapped (more on the theme of entrapment in chapter 4). The accompanimental rhythm, for instance, presents its own drama—passages of gentle burbling motion crossed by groups of ominous strong accents. Rhythm conjoins with gradations in timbre, as in the chorus, where the guitar's soaring melody repeatedly falls to a forceful downbeat, the rhythmic constraint emphasized with a percussive touch. The treatment of register in the interaction between voice and guitar is also dramatic: at first, the voice is tangled in the middle stretch of the guitar line, then at line 4 the guitar recedes as the voice reaches into a flutier soprano. In the chorus, the hopefully rising vocal lines ("I can't go back there anymore") dovetail with plunging descents in the guitar. All of these tensions are made cogent by the conflicted harmonic implications at work. The song cannot decide on its mode: each verse begins with an immediate shift from an A major to an A minor chord, while each chorus concludes with a shift from minor to major. In between, many of the ominous accents occur on open, quartal harmonies (chords built of fourths; Ex. 2.1). The chorus's rising vocal lines do all cadence on A major, only to be checked every time by the plunging guitar arrivals on suspended chords (i.e., chords in which the middle note of a triad [1,3,5] is replaced by a dissonant note [1,4,5 or 1,2,5 or 1,2,4,5]). For its final cadence, the song returns very fittingly to

EXAMPLE 2.1. "I HAD A KING," GUITAR ACCOMPANIMENT, SECOND HALF OF VERSE

All examples are notated as heard (i.e., no octave transposition in guitar).

an open, undecided Asus2 (for an explanation of the chord symbols used in this book, see the Appendix). In this, her debut song, Mitchell evokes the ingenue persona of a sunnier folk repertory while setting her within a darkly textured, charged drama of internal conflict, frustration, and self-assertion.

By the time of "The Arrangement" (1969, *LC*), reference to folk models is no longer pertinent. Regarding its genre, this song combines two types common to Mitchell's work as a whole: the character portrait and the statement of social critique. From this perspective, "The Arrangement" fits in well on the album *Ladies of the Canyon*, which includes many portraits (often combined with love poems: "Conversation," "Willy," "Rainy Night House," "The Priest") as well as two of her most famous "statement" songs ("Big Yellow Taxi" and "Woodstock"). The kind of portrait painted here is notable for its archetypal quality. The person being pleaded with ("You could have been more") could be a particular man known to the songwriter but equally seems to stand for a whole generation of consumers settling for a shallow life. The song was written for piano, like five other songs on the album. A turn to piano writing in 1969 reflects the availability of the instrument in her new home with Graham Nash in the Laurel Canyon neighborhood of Los Angeles (the canyon of the album's title).[11] Mitchell's piano style is typified by a rhythmic matrix of steady rocking figures in the left hand, with harmonic fill and chordal accents in the right. Her right-hand chords fit easily in the hand and are often triadic, but their relation to the left hand's harmonic root is complex, with plentiful use of "slash chords" (so termed from the lead sheet notation, where they are written as upper triad then bass note separated by a slash: e.g., G/A, or "G over A"). The first three chords in this song's prelude, for instance, are all such chords: G/A, D/E, and C/D (Ex. 2.2). Once the voice enters, the piano takes a supporting role with little melodic interest. (Other piano songs like "My Old Man" [*B*] feature melodic licks in counterpoint with the voice.) The modal irresolution between Aeolian and Dorian and the absolute pervasiveness of suspended chords (including the final cadence) recall the harmonic ambiguities of "I Had a King" (modes will be explained in chapter 5).

In other ways, "The Arrangement" looks forward to musical directions taken up in the following album, *Blue*. (In 1974, Mitchell judged: "There's a song called 'The Arrangement' which seemed to me as a forerunner and I think has more musical sophistication than anything else on the album.")[12] The rhapsodic possibilities inherent in solo piano accompaniment are explored in the metrically free instrumental prelude and coda. Mitchell's delivery of the text is highly erratic in rhythm—now rushing headlong, now drawing out a single word (especially true in the B section; see the formal divisions marked below). Her voice ventures into a raw, dangerous volatility. The melodic design is similarly reckless, with moody troughs and peaks and abrupt shifts in register. The

EXAMPLE 2.2. "THE ARRANGEMENT," PIANO PRELUDE

poem, while maintaining a scheme of interlocking rhymes, no longer projects an unwavering sense of structural control. For one thing, there is a whole series of important line-ends that remain unmatched by rhyme.

A section:

You could have been **more**	a	
Than a name on the **door**	a	
On the thirty-third **floor** in the *air*	a	x
More than a credit **card**	b	
Swimming pool in the back**yard**	b	

A section:

While you still have the **time**	c	
You could get away and **find**	c	
A better life, you know the **grind** is so *ungrateful*	c	x
Racing **cars**, whisky **bars**	b	b
No one cares who you really **are**		b

B section:

You're the keeper of the **cards**	b	
Yes I know it gets **hard**	b	
Keeping the wheels *turning*	x	
And the wife she **keeps the keys**	d	d
She's so **pleased to be**	d	d
A **part** of the *arrangement*	b	x

The unrhymed x phrases spill across the underlying pattern with words that don't attempt to fit. These phonic lapses serve to underscore the speaker's point, echoing the dissociated quality of a life on the thirty-third floor *in the air*, the pointlessness of keeping the wheels *turning*, the hollowness of the whole *arrangement*. Formally, the song is unusual in being through-composed, that is, in inventing a unique design that doesn't follow a traditional strophic or verse-chorus format. The B section sounds like a bridge at first, because of its fresh harmonic direction, but in fact it is integrally needed to complete the rhyme scheme (the "cards/hard/part" rhyme answering the end of the A sections) and cadential structure. It is not a chorus because it never repeats; instead there is a return to a modified, expanded A section, where the voice, already pushing to the edge of a wail, finally dissolves into raw "la la" vocalization.[13] (The complete form can be expressed as **AAB A'+coda**.) All elements of the composition, in fact, are minutely sensitive to the turbulent emotional detail.

SECOND PERIOD (1973–1980)

In the mid to late seventies, Mitchell's career reached its zenith. Over a period of seven years, she released four studio albums (including one double LP), two concert albums (both double LPs), and a collaborative project with Charles Mingus. Three of these albums peaked within the top five on the U.S. charts (*C&S* and *MA* at no. 2, *HSL* at no. 4), and with the song "Help Me" she had her only Top Ten single (at no. 7). Her music received more airplay than at any other time in her life, as her songwriting reached new levels of maturity and sophistication. While *Court and Spark* is the breakaway album that most clearly sets a new course, *For the Roses* (at the end of the first period in my scheme) is unmistakably transitional. Many characteristic ingredients of the second period style already make an appearance there. These include multipart instrumental arrangements incorporating winds and percussion, strong jazz inflections (notably Tom Scott's woodwind solos on "Cold Blue Steel and Sweet Fire" and "Barangrill"), a new polish in vocal performance, and ambitious formal innovations (e.g., the episodic "Blonde in the Bleachers" and the complicated interludes in "Let the Wind Carry Me" and "Judgement of the Moon and Stars (Ludwig's Tune)"—an homage to Beethoven).

For *Court and Spark*, however, Mitchell used an integral backup band for the first time, engaging members of Tom Scott's jazz-rock fusion group the L.A. Express. The sound of the album is anchored by the core group of drums, bass, electric guitar, electric piano, and winds, with the addition of special instruments including trumpet, chimes, and clavinet. In fact, each song is conceived with its own unique combination of instrumental resources in mind. One example of a striking coloristic touch can be heard during the coda to "Car on a Hill," where Mitchell's acoustic piano transmutes by sleight of hand into electric piano, silvered by guitar harmonics and swathed in eerie Doppler wails in the horns. Another effect occurs at the end of the chorus in "Trouble Child," where the Malibu surf is evoked by electric guitar arabesques and cymbal crescendi over pauses in the rhythmic groove. In "Down to You," Mitchell introduces a fully orchestral excursion (bringing in strings, horns, bassoon, oboe, clarinet, and harp). This album shows signs of a new interest in large-scale form: a terse, idio-syncratic piano fanfare at the opening; elaborate interludes in "Car on a Hill" and "Down to You"; segues linking the fourth and fifth songs ("People's Parties" and "The Same Situation") and the final two songs ("Trouble Child" and "Twisted"). (The same formal techniques will be greatly developed a few years later in *DJRD*; see chapter 7.)

The hit song "Help Me" (1973, *C&S*) provides a good basis for more extensive comments on the second period style. Here, Mitchell's steady guitar strumming is thoroughly blended into the mix; drums set a suave beat; electric piano and electric guitar fill in and warm the texture; mellow flutes and heckling reeds enter on the breaks. As befits the glossy production, Mitchell's voice is sweet and beau-tifully modulated, her passion tastefully restrained.[14] Jazz inflections are evident in harmony, melody, and rhythm. Harmonically, the song maintains an almost continuous string of seventh chords. The sense of key is elastic; swerves to new local tonics occur by third relations, or by planing through whole steps.

A   E5   GM7
Help me, I think I'm falling in love again.

GM7   FM7
When I get that crazy feeling I know I'm in trouble again.

    FM7
I'm in trouble 'cause you're a rambler and a gambler and a sweet-talking ladies' man.

    CM7 GM7   CM7 A CM7 DM7 B♭M7 FM7 G A
And you love your lovin' but not like you love your free—dom.

A reduced harmonic analysis would read as follows (bold letters indicate shifts to new local tonics):

A—G pivot—F (IV in C)—G pivot—**D**—**F**—**A**

(G is a pivot chord because it belongs to several of the keys involved [A Mixolydian, D, and C], and is used to shift between keys.) Note how the first three chords in the harmonic reduction plane down through whole steps; the last three chords are related by thirds.

EXAMPLE 2.3. "HELP ME," CADENCE FOR
INSTRUMENTAL BREAK

Over a harmonic progression which is rhythmically deliberate and unvarying across verses, the melody is more freely constructed, following similar contours in each verse while allowing for a degree of variation in rhythm and pitch.[15] Mitchell also punctuates the verse with witty metric disruptions. The meter is laid back and foursquare until the final words, "your freedom," where it gets into a pileup of dotted eighths and misses a beat. Then, at the end of the instrumental break, there is a syncopated threefold cadential figure. On the first two times through, the syncopation causes an anticipation of the cadential downbeat; on the last time, Mitchell simply drops a beat so the cadence and the barline finally line up (Ex. 2.3).[16] Throughout her second style period, Mitchell combines characteristic elements of her musical language—for example, extended harmonies, modal/tonal complexity, flexible melodic phrasing, and syncopated rhythmic hooks—so as to evoke an affinity with jazz. This affinity is often an unobtrusive blend, but at times overt jazz stylings rise to the surface, from momentary vocal ornaments or slides, to improvised instrumental solos, to songs that present a full jazz pastiche. *Court and Spark* ends with such a stylization: Mitchell sings a cover of Annie Ross and Wardell Gray's "Twisted," accompanied by a classic small combo of drums, bass, and trumpet. Subsequent jazz stylizations include "Centerpiece" (by Johnny Mandel and Jon Hendricks, *HSL*), "Blue Motel Room" (*H*), and of course most of the songs on *Mingus*.

The poem for "Help Me" is atypical: a breezy pop-romantic morsel, in standard strophic form plus bridge, though it is interesting in the way its colloquial language is pressed into an exaggeratedly schematic form (note the dual refrains at the beginning *and* end of each verse, a gerund in the second phrase ["feeling"/ "hoping"/"going"] matching those in the refrains ["falling," "lovin'"], and close repetition in the third phrase ["I'm in trouble ... I'm in trouble"/"hot hot"/"flirting and flirting"]). Mitchell's oeuvre is sprinkled with such unique experiments. More representative of the poetry of this period is the song "Amelia" (1976, *H*). Its tone is an attractive blend of the conversational with the poetic. Thus the diary-entry sound of lines such as "I wish that he was here tonight" flows comfortably into the lyricism of "A ghost of aviation/She was swallowed by the sky." In its structural rhythm the poem is discursive, drifting through a series of impressions as the poet muses on her burden of wanderlust and disillusionment. The song's open-ended, lengthy multiverse form is especially prevalent on this album, dedicated to evocations of road travel (see chapter 7). (Mitchell had used it first in the five-verse "For the Roses" [*FR*] and the six-verse "Don't Interrupt the Sorrow" [*HSL*].) Where the artifice of the first-period poetry was typically manifest in decorative verbal detail, now it operates primarily at the level of the image. Rhyme schemes become plainer, while the deployment of imagery becomes more challenging and complex. Here is verse 1 of "Amelia."

> I was driving across the burning desert
> When I spotted six jet planes
> Leaving six white vapor trails across the bleak terrain
> It was the hexagram of the heavens
> It was the strings of my guitar
> Amelia, it was just a false alarm

The opening image of vapor trails sets the poem's mood of loneliness in open space. It introduces the central themes of travel and transience—but only implicitly. Rather than beginning with a fanciful image conveying a particular poetic interpretation (as in "I had a king in a tenement castle"), Mitchell begins with a Wordsworthian observation of the world around her. But then, far from clarifying the significance of her observation, she reconfigures it by way of metaphoric substitutions, left uninterpreted. The image of the hexagram suggests arcane metaphysical meanings deliberately resistant to understanding. This skywriting then transforms into a symbol of the poet's own songwriting and thus her inner world; but the purport of this new metaphoric likeness is just as much of a riddle. The substance of her vision is somehow both impossibly distant and as near as the car seat next to her. (Such a dreamlike elasticity of dimensions will continue throughout the poem.) The refrain offers little help in closing the sequence of thought. It takes an oblique turn, changing to an apostrophic address (to Amelia) without warning, and coming to a despondent conclusion that doesn't clearly follow what came before.

Speaking generally, if the first-period poetry is characterized by an intricate decorative surface, that of the second period prefers to stir up rich conceptual resonances. We might borrow terms from art criticism and describe this as a shift from linear to painterly thinking. The distinction derives from Heinrich Wölfflin, who differentiates an interest in outline, surface, and clearly defined objects, on the one hand, from an interest in "the apprehension of the world as a shifting semblance," on the other, where objects merge in unbounded space.[17] Such a conceptual distinction is suggestive not only for Mitchell's poetic development but for her treatment of melody and instrumentation as well. Early melodies (especially before 1970) are conceived as chiseled intervallic designs in fairly precise rhythmic coordination with accompanimental figures. In contrast, a typical second-period melody is a more plastic contour, allowing for a lot of give in its alignment with the background. Early instrumental figuration (especially guitar) typically lays down a decorative line. In the second period, however, Mitchell takes full advantage of backing performers and studio production to create "aural landscapes in which the singer loses, rediscovers, and surrenders herself."[18] The sound of "Amelia," for instance, is anchored by a stable underlying guitar pattern; but Mitchell consciously softens the outlines of her guitar by doubling it loosely. Over and around the strangely reverberant guitar background the vibraphone and lead guitar are applied like daubs of paint, creating bell-tone highlights and a swarm of subliminal "voices" that bend, croon, and soar. Here, Mitchell uses her instrumental resources to create an ambient sound environment, emphasizing musical space and texture. The added instruments are also free to respond to transient moments in the text, as each verse calls up its own set of sonic impressions.

THIRD PERIOD (1981–1988)

The two projects marking the culmination of Mitchell's second period (*DJRD* and *M*), her most ambitious in concept and execution, received mixed reviews, including some stinging rebuffs from prominent critics.[19] Her insistence on following her own uncompromising path had made her cutting-edge in the 1970s; at the end of the decade it left her open to critical and commercial desertion. In the 1980s she transformed herself again, now regrouping in a turn to mainstream pop and absorbing innovations from recent pop trends, especially new wave. At the same time she pulled back to a more leisurely pace of work, producing a new album only every three years. While recording *Wild Things Run Fast* she met bassist Larry Klein, and the two embarked on a fruitful, long-term collaborative relationship (Klein went on to co-produce all Mitchell's subsequent albums through *Travelogue*, except *TT*). Nevertheless, the third period represents a low point for Mitchell's music in terms of exposure (*Dog Eat Dog*, for instance, remains the only album for which a songbook was never produced). In the 2003 reissue of this material, she dubs the decade the "Lost Years," recounting her personal efforts to save the albums from oblivion.[20] Following the career watershed of *Mingus*, Mitchell's continued musical development in the 1980s attracted comparatively little public attention, while her work projected an increasingly public voice.

Wild Things Run Fast (1982) is a highly accessible album, cast mainly in conventional pop styles and forms. Conceptually, it works with nothing as controversial as the bold stylistic compounds and high literary conceits found on the previous two albums. In fact, *Wild Things* contains an atypical number of happy, enjoyable songs without lofty artistic goals. The pull of jazz is still evident—for instance, in the shuffle beat of "Moon at the Window" and "Be Cool," the blues-based progression in the latter song, and the flexible, meandering vocals of "Love." But there are also several rock 'n' roll songs (the title song, "Baby, I Don't Care," "You Dream Flat Tires," "Underneath the Streetlight"), a contemporary pop ballad ("Chinese Café"), a song harking back to Tin Pan Alley ballad form ("Moon at the Window"), and even two songs in rhythm and blues (R&B) style ("Ladies' Man," "Man to Man"). (JM: "'Ladies' Man' [is] a song that Aretha Franklin could have sung. In fact, there's two little catches in my vocal that are out of admiration for her.")[21] Significantly, instead of the jazz covers found in the second period, this album features a cover of Leiber and Stoller's tune "Baby, I Don't Care" (released in 1959 by Elvis Presley). In fact, Mitchell opens the album with a nostalgic tribute to the pop hits from her youth, fragments of two of which ("Will You Still Love Me Tomorrow?" and "Unchained Melody") are embedded in the song.[22] As usual, Mitchell's treatment of familiar genres is rarely formulaic; she handles conventions with originality and sophistication. In "Be Cool," for example, she gives the shuffle beat a surprising twist by weaving it into a hemiola (two-against-three) cross-rhythm which aligns with the *backbeat* and thus undercuts the downbeat (see Ex. 2.4).[23] Meanwhile, the chord changes in "Be Cool" offer a fresh take on the standard blues progression (Ex. 2.5). Mitchell expands the form from 12 bars to 16 by elongating the dominant section of the third phrase while replacing the standard dominant chord with a more piquant major II (E major in the key of D).[24] Mitchell also enhances her pop sound with style markers adopted from new wave groups such as the Police and Talking Heads: for example, the repeated-note bass line in "Wild Things Run Fast," the striking minimal instrumentation at the end of the same song, the reggae groove in "Solid Love," and the importance of synthesizers in the mix for much of the album. In fact, according to Mitchell, the Police were an explicit model in the making of this album:

> I love that band, and they were definitely a factor. My appreciation of their rhythmic hybrids and the positioning and sound of their drums was one of the main things calling out to me to make this a more rhythmic album. I was in the Caribbean last summer, and they used to play "De Do Do Do" at the disco. I love to dance, and anytime I heard it, boy, I didn't care if there was no one on the floor, I was going to dance to that thing because of those changes in rhythm. You get into one pattern for a while and then WHAM, you turn around and put a whole other pattern into it. My feet got me into that record.[25]

EXAMPLE 2.4. "BE COOL," INTRO

Small notes indicate an alternative way of hearing the rhythmic groupings, cutting across the meter.
Note that the prominent chords line up with beats 2 and 4 (marked by arrows), rather than the downbeat.

EXAMPLE 2.5.

A. STANDARD BLUES PROGRESSION

B. "BE COOL," CHORD CHANGES

a.
	I		I		I		I	
	IV		IV		I		I	
	V		IV		I		I	

b.
	V		V		I		I	
	IV		IV		I		I	
	II		II		II		II	
	IV		IV		I		I	

"You Dream Flat Tires" (1982, *WTRF*) is one of Mitchell's true rock 'n' roll songs.[26] She lets the rhythm section drive the song with its heavy beat and hyperkinetic bass; the point is musical impact and energy rather than intellectual subtlety. The poetry is an unrefined concoction of graphic images, romantic musing, and raw snippets of conversation, all nailed down by the repetitive refrain, which hardly holds up as a poetic line but sounds great as a "hook," or memorable musical figure (Ex. 2.6). In fact there is an abundance of hooks, from the flashy intro, to the catchy repartee in the bridge, to the major-mode vocal loops in the coda. Guest vocals are added by Lionel Richie, at that time just entering the high point of his success as a mainstream pop artist. Once again, the song's conventional aspects are given clever turns. The bass sets up the rock beat as a speeding compound duple; when the drum first enters, it marks a hemiola cross-rhythm without any reference to the downbeat for an unsettling few moments. The combination of slipped rhythmic gears and frenzied angular bass motion captures the key image of a car spinning out of control before the vocals even start. Harmonically, the song doesn't venture beyond i, iv, and v (Dm, Gm, and Am)—until the refrain, which suddenly veers on a wild chromatic path from Am11 through Cm11 and Fm11 back to D. Formally, Mitchell follows a matter-of-fact alternation between verse and bridge—until the last verse, which cuts short after two lines and elides into an instrumental break and coda.

Other mannerisms in "Flat Tires" reflect a new set of tastes which will hold sway over the third period. First is the tone of bravado mixed with aggression, shared by the whole band but coming to the fore in Mike Landau's lead guitar, whose solo licks crack like a whip. In comparison, Mitchell's voice here is laid-back. More attention-grabbing is the unusually cocky, strutting voice she affects for "Underneath the Streetlight," which looks forward to future vocal affecta-

EXAMPLE 2.6. "YOU DREAM FLAT TIRES," REFRAIN

tions. Second, Mitchell emphasizes the ends of certain phrases by brutally cutting off the sound. In "Flat Tires" this can be heard at the end of the intro and most notably at the end of the song, where it sounds as if the vibrations of the final phrase are abruptly sucked into a vacuum. Such a penchant for dry cadences with little or no reverberation will extend through the decade (for other examples on *WTRF*, see "Solid Love" and "Streetlight"). Third, like many songs on the album, this song makes important use of backing vocals in repetitive verbal riffs (notably in the coda: "Flat tires, love, love is precious . . ."). Finally, on this album (though not on this song) Mitchell starts to experiment with a new terseness in her poetry. The new direction is most evident in "Wild Things Run Fast," about which Mitchell relates: "I wrote this for the discipline of saying something in short, fragmented sentences, which is basically what pop writing always was. It was more of an exercise to see if I could do it, to say something in a minimalist way. I failed" (i.e., she was unable to quell her characteristic lyric pattern of "paragraphs," or connected thoughts).[27]

By the next album (*Dog Eat Dog*), however, Mitchell had become much more practiced at a verbal style of end-stopped, compressed lines (especially notable in "Fiction," "Tax Free" [both poems responding to music by Larry Klein], and "Impossible Dreamer"; see Ex. 6.20). This is in keeping with a remarkable change in tone and subject matter, emblematized in Mitchell's cover art. Compared to the relaxed self-portrait on *Wild Things* (Joni in a comfortable leaning posture, hand in pocket, shoes kicked off), the photographic image on *Dog Eat Dog* shows her with both fists raised, eyes clamped shut and mouth open in a yell, surrounded by howling or snapping wolves. This image stamps an album dominated by social and political protest as no Joni Mitchell album had been before.[28] The title song, "Dog Eat Dog" (1985, *DED*), decries social attitudes of rampant greed and hypocrisy in language that modulates between sharp colloquial harangue ("you can lie, cheat, skim, scam") and the rolling cadences of scripture ("People looking, seeing nothing").[29] Mitchell's voice is taut, clipped, and deliberately constricted, her phrasing often rigidly tied to an implacable strong beat. The groove is pieced together from a number of interlocking rhythmic parts, forming a rather inflexible whole. In fact, the concept of mechanization guides the entire sound design. Brittle percussive effects (including an extremely sharp backbeat) are slotted into a matrix of synthesized harmony. There is a very quick decay in keyboard and drum, deliberately exaggerating the sense of an artificially constructed performance space. Drums are either sampled or kept fanatically uniform. Stitched into the rhythmic underlay is a persistent syncopated vocal sample of the primary refrain ("dog eat dog"), leached of its vowel qualities. It's difficult to tell whether the consonantal enhancement is due to electronic alteration or the result of mixing with other sounds, so intimately has the human merged with the machine.

Yet the chilly surfaces in this song are posed against warmer musical resonances: full-bodied backup harmonies, unabashed major-mode cadences, moments of thawing, even tenderness, in Mitchell's vocal. The scriptural reference in the coda is amplified by the harmonic gesture there, which settles on a series of plagal cadences (IV-I, common as a benediction: "Amen"), thus dissolving the foregoing anger into an elegiac perspective. The strong polarities kept in play make for a complex expressive utterance. Meanwhile the grooves and timbres of 1980s pop still animate the musical style, though Mitchell bends them to an overt ethical purpose. In its marriage of accessible pop style with a strong ethical orientation, her music in this period resembles concurrent work by the Police and U2.

FOURTH PERIOD (1989–1998)

On the release of *Night Ride Home* in 1991, Geffen Records took out promotional advertisements reading: "Her work has become a standard by which others are compared. Once again, the standard is raised. The much anticipated new album from an artist whose sound has inspired a generation of listeners and influenced a generation of musicians." By this stage in her career Mitchell was being marketed as a classic. The album received enthusiastic critical attention, again with an emphasis on her seasoned status as a writer as well as the retrospective aspects of her work. Stephen Holden, in a *New York Times* interview, highlighted her age (47) and the perspective that comes with "middle-age resignation." Linda Sanders, in *Entertainment Weekly*, concluded that Mitchell had synthesized "various musical styles from every phase of her career" so successfully that the album "sounds like the distilled essence of everything she's done before."[30] The 1990s also ushered in a period of official acclaim, in the form of prestigious awards for artistic achievement, beginning with *Billboard* magazine's Century Award (1995). Inaugurated in 1992 to recognize established but underappreciated songwriters for the excellence of their "still-unfolding body of work," Mitchell was the fourth person to receive this honor (after George Harrison, Buddy Guy, and Billy Joel).[31] The Century Award was followed by a number of accolades in quick succession, including Sweden's Polar Music Prize, the Canadian Governor General's Performing Arts Award, and a Lifetime Achievement Award from the National Academy of Songwriters (all 1996) as well as induction into both the Songwriters' Hall of Fame and the Rock and Roll Hall of Fame (1997). However, at the same time as her importance was being affirmed by her peers, the press, and cultural agencies at home and abroad, Mitchell's career as a songwriter came to a standstill in 1998 with the release of *Taming the Tiger*, her last collection of new songs until *Shine* (2007).

The opening song, "Night Ride Home," from her 1991 release (*NRH*) was actually written in 1988, the same year as the release of *Chalk Mark in a Rain Storm*. Nevertheless, in its eventual recorded incarnation, Mitchell clearly unveils a renovated sound for the 1990s. The busy layering of her late-1980s studio work is gone; instead an uncluttered texture allows for maximal exposure of the guitar figuration. The rhythmic groove, laid down by guitar and hand drums, is simple and relaxed. In its reinstatement of acoustic timbres, showcasing of intricate guitar work, and elegant, chiseled melodic design (see Ex. 6.21), the song represents a return to values from Mitchell's earliest style period. A digital sample still provides an ostinato, but here it's a chirping cricket, a sound that reaches beyond the confines of the studio to evoke a peaceful natural space. Mitchell's voice is showing its late huskiness, but it is relaxed and honeyed in tone. The poem likewise is relaxed, a summer nocturne celebrating a moment of quiet harmony and beauty. Pedal steel guitar is added sparingly for painterly highlights and spatial resonance, as in second-period style. Meanwhile the harmonic palette explores a relatively new direction for Mitchell in its consistent unmixed major mode and its generous use of major dominant chords at the cadence, which in the context of her previous harmonic usage is a turn to a simpler, more classical idiom.[32]

The song is not a love song per se but includes reference to a comfortable partnership ("I love the man beside me") as integral to the ambience of peace and fulfillment. In general, the fourth period is characterized by its seasoned perspectives on love, spiritual aspiration, and the adventures of youth. The personal storm and stress of earlier periods has largely given way to greater authority and self-possession. The sociopolitical causes so starkly exposed in the third period are now sometimes diffused into mythical presentiments of apocalypse. Examples of the latter include "Passion Play" (based on the story of Zacchaeus from the Gospel of Luke) and "Slouching towards Bethlehem" (based on W. B. Yeats's poem "The Second Coming") from *NRH*, "The Sire of Sorrow" (based on the Book of Job) from *TI*, and "Taming the Tiger" (based on William Blake's poem "The Tyger") from *TT*.[33] This scriptural/metaphysical genre exists alongside protest songs similar to those from period 3 (such as "Sex Kills," "The Magdalene Laundries," and "Not to Blame," all from *TI*). Character portraits remain a favorite genre, as always. Finally, there is a proliferation of retrospective vignettes from her childhood and teenage years (on *NRH*, these include "Cherokee Louise," "Come In from the Cold," and "Ray's Dad's Cadillac"). "Cherokee Louise," a memory of a childhood friend who was sexually abused, is especially interesting in its integration of the portrait, nostalgic, and protest genres. Stylistically, Mitchell synthesizes elements from across her career, each song carefully and individually crafted. Certain songs are marked by particularly unique or refined touches in timbral design, such as the combination of oboe, omnichord, and Latin percussion in "The Only Joy in Town," or the percussive guitar hockets (hiccup-like interjections), special "tribal" drum sound, sirens, and vocal glissandi in "Slouching towards Bethlehem" (both *NRH*).

In "Harlem in Havana" (1998, *TT*), the possibilities for unique sound design are expanded by means of Mitchell's new digital guitar. This album was the first to appear after she acquired the Roland VG-8, which came equipped with a variety of sound patches to affect the guitar's timbral output. This song is particularly adventurous with the sonic palette of the instrument (Mitchell refers to it in special terms as a "guitar orchestra" in the liner notes to this and one other song). The first sound produced bears no resemblance to a guitar, sounding more like a kind of malleted keyboard, especially brittle and metallic, with very salient upper partials. In its next overlay, the guitar adopts the tones of a calypso drum band, as befits the poem's Afro-Cuban reference. As verse merges with refrain, the instrument has a third incarnation as a raunchy quasi-horn section, with a lot of fuzz. All this sonic experimentation builds to a roaring climax, but when the dust clears in the interlude, it's evident that the bones of the performance are set down by a classic jazz combo (bass, drums, sax), with a shuffle beat and free vocal phrasing to match. The poem here belongs to the nostalgia genre: a story of carnies coming to Mitchell's prairie town, she and her teenage friends sneaking in wideeyed to the burlesque show. The song's subtle wit rests in the distance between the youthful and the adult perspectives (conveyed in words and music, respectively). The poem deliberately captures a naive, limited frame of reference in the girls' first thrilling experience of sophistication: their brush with "snakey" black music, gender-bending performers, moral rebellion, and interracial romance. Meanwhile, Mitchell's music makes use of all the formidable resources built up over a lifetime of romance with the black muse. In its complex gapped shuffle groove, seasoned jazz manner, digitally minted sound layers, and iridescent shifting harmonies, the song is an expression of Mitchell's style at its most ultra-cool. The adult musician looks back with knowing fondness on the moment when she first fantasized about being "on the inside."

RETROSPECTIVE PROJECTS

For nearly ten years following *Taming the Tiger*, Mitchell discontinued songwriting.[34] Instead, her musical energies were taken up in producing various compilations and reinterpretations of her existing body of work. To some extent this was a response to pressure from record companies for marketable "Greatest Hits" anthologies; but in many of these projects Mitchell took the opportunity to shed new light on her work as a whole, through unexpected juxtapositions, thematic concepts, or new musical arrangements. The first compilation, *Hits*, appeared in

1996; Mitchell insisted on a companion anthology, *Misses*, of personal favorites she wished to rescue from neglect.[35] In *Both Sides Now* (2000), Mitchell debuted as a big-band-style crooner, covering popular standards from the 1920s to the early 1970s (including two of her own) in lush orchestral arrangements. This unique project was followed by no less than five compilations in the years 2002 through 2005: a hits anthology (*Dreamland*), two thematic collections (*The Beginning of Survival* and *Songs of a Prairie Girl*), a box-set reissue of the four albums made for Geffen, and the ambitious *Travelogue*, in which twenty-two of her songs from across all periods receive expansive orchestral treatment.

The periodic framework outlined in this chapter does not represent the views of the composer; it is my own schema, devised according to explicit criteria laid out here. It is helpful for making general distinctions of style and sound but shouldn't take on a life of its own. I would not want the artificially sharp borders between periods to blind us to strong musical ebbs and continuities across those borders. Moreover, there are other ways besides periodization to make connections within a catalogue of over 150 songs, and make sense of a creative time span of thirty-odd years. To illustrate one such countervailing path, I would like to follow one of Mitchell's most famous songs, "Woodstock," as it has traveled with her throughout her life. Among the small number of early favorites Mitchell continued to perform in live appearances from the 1970s through the 1990s, this song was unique in that she chose to thoroughly redesign its sound, not once but twice. These changes in sound can be mapped consistently onto the periodic framework. But if the framework is laid aside, Mitchell's revisions of the song suggest a distinct evolutionary narrative with a different set of turning points and a continuing dialogue between the present and the past.

Mitchell wrote the song in August 1969 as the original Woodstock Festival was taking place. However, she never actually made it to the festival herself.

> Crosby, Stills, Nash and myself all went to the airport. Woodstock had been declared a national disaster area, so we were informed that we couldn't get in and get out. I had to do *The Dick Cavett Show* the following day, so I left the boys there, thinking they were going someplace else. But they rented a helicopter. I felt left out. I really felt like the Girl. The Girl couldn't go, but the Boys could. I watched everything on TV. But I don't know if I would have written the song "Woodstock" if I had gone. I was the fan that couldn't go, not the performing animal. So it afforded me a different perspective.[36]

In its first incarnation (released on *LC*, 1970), despite lyrics flush with utopian dreams of peace and renewal, Mitchell conceives the song as a lament for solo voice and keyboard in E♭ Dorian. Bluesy keyboard passages introduce and close the song. The vocal melody repeatedly aims upward for a tonic octave peak, only to end by groveling in its lowest range (Ex. 2.7a). Mitchell creates a special mystical aura through extreme vibrato in the electric piano, pentatonic harmony (including exposed parallel fourths), dirge-like rhythms, and sobbing, sibylline backup vocals at the end of every refrain. The long wordless vocal coda captures the song's contradictory emotional crux: having finally attained the melodic highpoint, Mitchell allows her voice to go painfully raw as it gulps and throbs with loss. Perhaps not surprisingly, this introverted original version was eclipsed in popularity by the joyous Crosby, Stills, Nash & Young cover (1970, *Déjà Vu*), which casts the song in blues G major with a rock beat, departs from the original melody to hover around the octave peak, and replaces the cadential downward drift on "garden" with an ecstatic upward melisma (Ex. 2.7b).

The evolution of Mitchell's own conception of "Woodstock" can be traced from its subsequent appearances in her concert tours, as recorded on albums and videos available in commercial release. The first concert album, *Miles of Aisles*, captures a tour undertaken in 1974 with the L.A. Express; the expanded musical horizons due to that collaboration are palpable in striking new arrangements of songs such as "The Last Time I Saw Richard" as well as new songs such as "Jericho" (which would not be released in a studio version until three years later). "Woodstock" closes side 1 of the double LP. The new arrangement is full of funk attitude: drums and bass set down a leisurely beat while the rest of the band fills in with varying degrees of nervous energy. The electric piano, formerly a conduit of melancholy, now chimes in with offhand splashes of color. Mitchell's voice coasts above all this at its own deliberate pace, her vocal manner noticeably lighter than in the 1970 version. The song has been transposed down from E♭ to B, bringing the melody within comfortable vocal range and relaxing the level of tension. Nevertheless, the melody remains very close to the original, and the effect is strangely double-faced, the voice retaining some of its former gravity and passion while the band steps out with a very danceable, ebullient sound. Where the refrain was once marked by melodic collapse, the voice now rises at this point and takes on its sternest tones, as the entire band joins in a strongly marked cadential progression (Ex. 2.7c).

This rock-band version of "Woodstock" seems to have been the brainchild of a particular moment (and in fact it hasn't dated well). In contrast, the next version for electric guitar, first showcased in a 1979 tour (with Pat Metheny, Lyle Mays, Jaco Pastorius, Michael Brecker, Don Alias, and the Persuasions), proved much more enduring. The corresponding concert album, *Shadows and Light* (1980), includes this song as its closing number—the only number in which Mitchell performs alone.[37] Where the keyboard version was drenched with desire for the

EXAMPLE 2.7. "WOODSTOCK," CHORUS, FOUR VERSIONS

a. From *Ladies of the Canyon* (1970)

(continued)

EXAMPLE 2.7. (CONTINUED)

b. Crosby, Stills, Nash & Young, from *Déjà Vu* (1970)

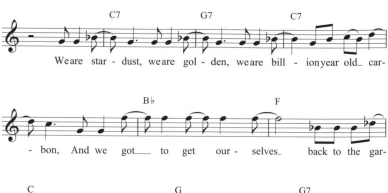

We are star - dust, we are gol - den, we are bill - ion year old_ car-

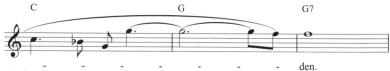

- bon, And we got___ to get our - selves_ back to the gar-

- - - - - - - den.

state of innocence, the guitar version has a chilled, understated beauty, everything crystalline and in place. The key is a comfortable C Aeolian; gravity and passion have now completely given way to a cool jazz voice, breathy and streamlined. Where melodic phrases in the original tended to linger and trail off well after the harmonic resolution, now phrases are trimmed and punctuated clearly. On guitar, Mitchell adapts the piano's distinctive parallel-fourth motion (originally employed to evade triadic harmony) into a stepwise countermelody with a sense of rhythmic precision.[38] She accentuates the rhythmic profile by slapping the strings on the occasional backbeat and by marking the melodic highpoint ("we're golden") with a pair of high chimed chords.

In short, Mitchell has reconceived the song by classicizing it. A few specific comparisons of structural detail will help to illustrate the prevailing aesthetic. The 1970 version used aspects of harmony and scansion to imbue its phrase structure with a sense of urgent yearning. For instance, the subdominant chord that has such prominence mostly occurs in suspended form ($A\flat$-$D\flat$-$E\flat$), implying a resolution to an $A\flat$ triad without revealing whether that chord would be major or minor. For this reason the mode of the song remains unclear (Dorian? Aeolian?) until the very end of the refrain ("garden"), when the triadic quality of the chord is revealed in passing as $A\flat$ major (i.e., Dorian). In particular, the first section of the refrain ("We are stardust") prolongs the sense of harmonic tension by sounding the $A\flat$sus chord for four continuous bars (Ex. 2.7a). During this passage, the melody climbs to its highpoint, but without the support of harmonic resolution it collapses again. In contrast, the 1979 version makes use of a simpler harmonic palette overall, based solely on clear iterations of i, iv, and v—all definitely minor in quality (Ex. 2.7d). (The one exception is the F/G chord at the end of the refrain, which admits a brief flicker of modal ambiguity.) The inclusion of a dominant chord allows for more stable progressions. In the crucial first section of the refrain, Mitchell aims for a completely different effect, defusing the tension by loosening the phrase structure from four bars to five

EXAMPLE 2.7. "WOODSTOCK," CHORUS, FOUR VERSIONS

c. From *Miles of Aisles* (1974)

d. From *Shadows and Light* (1979)

while changing the harmony so there is actually a strong cadence at this point (iv–v–i), coinciding with the melodic highpoint arrival.[39] Meanwhile, where the original performance emphasized urgency by placing the words "And we *got to*" at the point of tonic arrival, in the later version these words are passed over very quickly before the first beat of the new bar. A final telling change occurs in the treatment of the concluding word "garden": originally charged with emotion due to its collapsed range and its prolongation over three bars, in the later version the word is quickly declaimed, leaving room for a coolly commentative hum on a three-note turn. The lavish sorrow of the original cadence is here condensed into this restrained melodic tag with a final note (F) that cuts ambivalently across the tonic C minor.

The refashioning of "Woodstock" from an emotionally raw to a highly aestheticized form is multiply significant at this point in her career. She reminds listeners of her authorship of this iconic song, already known as a rock classic. At the same time, by putting an entirely new stamp on it, she reclaims it to some degree from the associations acquired in its well-known CSNY incarnation. By foregrounding her aesthetic treatment she spotlights her technical skill as a composer and arranger rather than her emotional prowess or immediacy. The unveiling of this arrangement also comes at the end of a decade of tremendous popular success and progressive musical exploration, thus confirming a kind of arrival at a peak of creative power. Stylistically, by reference to a cool jazz persona, she acknowledges her own individual journey to maturity through a dialogue with jazz. Finally, in thematic terms, it is certainly significant that 1979 marks the ten-year anniversary of Woodstock and the song's genesis. Mitchell's musical revision can be seen as adopting a new perspective on the social ideals captured in the song. In her polish and detachment, Mitchell measures a retrospective distance from the utopian groundswell of the youth movement and its exuberant, messy festivals. Even in a short ten years, those ideals of radical social change had been notably compromised by apathy, self-interest, commercial success, and exploitation. In Mitchell's new, chilly "Woodstock" the ideals of spiritual and earthly renewal are not abandoned, but they take on an ironic poignancy in light of the intervening evidence of all-too-human failings.[40]

In essence, it is this solo guitar arrangement that Mitchell returns to for the next twenty years. The concert video *Refuge of the Roads* (from a 1983 tour) closes with "Woodstock." Only a few changes have been made since 1979, including a striking vocal descent on "we're golden," and a return to the original melisma on "garden." Fifteen years later, her concert video *Painting with Words and Music* (1998) also closes with "Woodstock."[41] Mitchell's singing voice has passed into its late state of repair, very husky and short of breath. This version of the song is still based on the 1979 arrangement, though she has tinkered with the figuration and mellowed the sound. Her playing is less percussive, omitting the slaps and accented chimes. The guitar ritornello is longer, ringing yet another change on the pentatonic, parallel-fourth motif. The accompanimental track is treated more loosely throughout, open to spontaneous variations. She mixes in figural touches strongly reminiscent of her 1994 song "Sex Kills," and even mixes in temporary shifts to a major tonic. In a tiny but resonant detail, where the 1979 and 1983 recordings remain open-ended, fading out on a harmonic loop, Mitchell uses her new guitar break to bring the latest version to musical closure. Here is a clear case where the evolution of general composerly style and the treatment of a single signature song tell different stories. Despite the major stylistic shifts Mitchell undertook in the 1980s and 1990s, her concept of "Woodstock" preserves the retrospective tone and classicized image formed at the peak of her career.

Mitchell returned to the song yet again in *Travelogue* (2002), her two-disc farewell project (as she conceived it at the time) featuring selections from her catalogue in lush orchestral arrangements by Vince Mendoza. In this collection, "Woodstock" is given no prominent position (the choice for closing number is one of her earliest, "The Circle Game," sentimental anthem to the passing years). It is transposed down even further (to A!) to accommodate a sinking vocal range. Mendoza's arrangement takes off from the original keyboard version, turning its pentatonic riffs into nebulous string clusters. After an extensive meditative prelude, drums and horns enter, setting up a constant, quasi-military thrum as background for the voice. Sparkling harp highlights complete the timbral scheme. The success of the orchestrations on this album I find hard to gauge. In terms of pure sound, they are pleasurable immersions into a technically polished, vast symphonic space. As arrangements, they tend to be unimaginative, never straying too far from the revered original figuration. In expression, they are consistently grandiose, occasionally lugubrious. This can come across at times as an ill fit with the art-song scope of the material as well as with Mitchell's small weary voice. At times, however, the orchestral pomp allows for a dreamlike expansion of a song's original limits. As for "Woodstock," the song's carefully judged marriage of homespun narration and visionary cosmology is overborne by the epic orchestral gestures. The thrumming march is impressive and ominous, but uncomfortably ambiguous in its signification—as if at this distance, the global warmongers and the gathering crowds of countercultural pilgrims blur together in memory.

Even in this introductory survey, one encounters numerous signs that Joni Mitchell is consciously seeking to bridge cultural traditions. Such signs show up in the authorial discourse around her music: for instance, when she situates her work in the context of high art figures (Picasso, Yeats, Beethoven) as well as figures from popular music (Jimi Hendrix, Aretha Franklin, the Police); or when she uses terms from art music (orchestral resources) to describe her approach to the guitar; or when she freely intermingles ideals associated with fine art (sophistication) and popular entertainment (infectious dance rhythms). They show up, of course, in her composition of music and lyrics: song forms range from conventional to through-composed; instrumental breaks can be well-spun hooks or rhapsodic arabesques; lyrics bubbly or gravid; chord changes down to earth or twisting through strange dimensions. "I Had a King" and "Amelia" make bids for art-song status in their consistent high-mindedness and dense working of materials. "Help Me" and "You Dream Flat Tires" are engaging pop songs, crafted with wit and originality but without pretense. Other songs perch elsewhere along the continuum. Accordingly, analysis of Mitchell's songwriting needs to be diversified in its vocabulary and flexible in its aesthetic register. The following chapters set out to explore the details of such an approach, beginning with poetic technique.

3

VOICES AND PERSONAE

VOCAL PRESENCE

Well before she began her career as a songwriter, Joni Mitchell was already painting and writing poems. She credits a charismatic seventh-grade teacher with her
discovery of poetry as an art form: "He encouraged us to write in any form that
we liked. Even at that age I enjoyed poetry, the structure of it, the dance of it, to
essays or any other form."[1] Her song lyrics on the whole are distinguished by their
literary quality; self-consciously so to begin with and more comfortably assimi-
lated as she matures. It might be surprising to learn, therefore, that Mitchell has
typically written lyrics to fit her music, rather than the other way around. In an
early interview, she explains, "I get the melody first and then I write out three
sets of lyrics before I'm satisfied. Usually I think the melody is too pretty for the
lyrics."[2] As this statement suggests, such a method does not preclude painstaking
attention to verbal design, and for the most part, her lyrics exhibit their own aesthetic integrity when considered outside their musical context. For these reasons,
in the following discussion I will refer to Mitchell's lyrics as poems—keeping in
mind their special dimension as poems designed to be sung.[3]

Is there such a thing as a typical Joni Mitchell poem? There are many poems
in which she shows off her skills as a raconteur, such as "Barangrill" (*FR*) and
"Furry Sings the Blues" (*H*), with their wealth of anecdotal detail, or "Free Man
in Paris" (*C&S*), with its vivid character impersonation, or "Dry Cleaner from Des
Moines" (*M*), with its easy bantering tone.[4] There are those in which she molds
poetry out of spontaneous conversation, whether chatty commonplaces ("All I
Want" [*B*]), furrowed-brow monologue ("Lesson in Survival" [*FR*]), or impassioned unburdening ("River" [*B*]). Yet Mitchell can take just as much pleasure
in constructing verbal artifice: the free play of words and images is salient, for
instance, in the sequentially intermeshed stanzaic structure of "Roses Blue" (*C*)
(where the final word or phrase of each verse becomes the opening phrase of the

next), the Beat verbal collisions of "Cold Blue Steel and Sweet Fire" (*FR*), or the hallucinatory metamorphic symbolism of "The Jungle Line" (*HSL*). One favored genre is the individual portrait, with an eye for colorful particulars of time and place, and sharp, often biting observation of character (as in "The Last Time I Saw Richard" [*B*], "Shades of Scarlett Conquering" [*HSL*], or "Otis and Marlena" [*DJRD*]). On the other end of the spectrum, however, one finds poems that deal in anonymous, archetypal emotions, as if in conscious imitation of a timeless folk repertory ("The Fiddle and the Drum" [*C*], "The Circle Game" [*LC*], and "The Silky Veils of Ardor" [*DJRD*]).

Such a range of poetic endeavor calls for a plural analytical approach. In chapter 4 I will explore a cluster of overarching themes inspiring sustained treatment amid the diversity of tone and voice. In this chapter I have chosen to focus on her control over certain effects basic to the poetic utterance, namely, the illusion of speaking voices and poetic personae. This will allow me both to survey the range of effects at her disposal and to identify distinguishing features of her literary style. The concept of "voice" is a well-used metaphor with an array of overlapping connotations. In literary criticism it has a technical meaning, indicating the set of conventions by which fictional speakers are dramatized or implied in a text. In less technical parlance, "voice" can refer symbolically to the distinctive personality of an individual creative artist or suggest the expressive force of a social identity more broadly (representing a Canadian "voice," for example, or a female "voice" within a male-dominated industry). In music the word has a literal referent (the organ of sound production) as well as a common metaphorical use, denoting any melodic entity ("voices" in a contrapuntal texture). In addition, music scholars have recently begun to test the value of the literary-critical concepts of "persona" and "voice" (understood as referring to dramatic agents or fictional sources of utterance) for the experience of music, with or without words.[5] Song, as an amalgam of music and poetry, is susceptible to every one of these connotations; thus if we use "voice" as an analytical concept, we will need to clearly distinguish its competing layers of metaphor.

In this chapter I intend to focus on "voice" in its literary-technical sense, indicating the vivid fictional characters and implied speaking presences in Mitchell's poetry. In the medium of song, these fictional voices are performed in real time; thus their dramatization depends on the skillful handling of the singing voice as a way to embody poetic constructs. Since the early 1990s, Mitchell has often spoken of vocal performance in terms of dramatic impersonation. When discussing her songwriting goals as a middle-aged woman, she says, "What I'd like to do is experiment and create roles for myself."[6] When asked about her use of guest singers on the album *Chalk Mark in a Rain Storm*, she explains, "I'll need another voice to deliver a line, because [the songs] are like little plays."[7] When asked whether she ever considers returning to her early songs, she replies, "I never wanted to be a human jukebox. I think more like a film or a dramatic actress and a playwright. These plays are more suitable to me. I feel miscast in my early songs. They're ingenue roles."[8] Given the vivid character portrayals for which she has always been known as a performer, it's remarkable that such theatrical metaphors do not appear explicitly until late in her career.[9] She explores this realization in more detail in a radio interview:

> I've been thinking [recently] about something Faye Dunaway said years back. It was at a time when actresses were complaining that there were no good roles for women, and there weren't. All the roles were written by men, and they were basically decorative parts and tits and ass; and she said to me, "Joni, you're lucky because you can create your own roles." And I hadn't thought of it really that way, you know, I hadn't focused on it as a role. You know, I just thought they were songs. But really she's [right], they're little plays, and I'm the playwright and I am the actress, and I've written some songs, like "Cold Blue Steel and Sweet Fire," that I didn't have the right voice for, I don't think, although maybe it's interesting the way it was. But I think that would be a good song for a man with more grit in his voice to sing, to bring out the darkness of it, the soliloquy.... As long as I can genuinely get into [the old material] and find something as an actress, so to speak—because they are very theatrical, these songs—to bring to the role, I have no problem with playing the old songs.[10]

The metaphor of dramatic roles is useful in that it emphasizes the importance of vocal delivery while maintaining a clear distinction between the singer-songwriter and the personae she brings to life. But it is potentially confusing in that it collapses a host of poetic effects into the single mode of dramatic representation. Some of Mitchell's poems are indeed framed as drama, but many are better understood as narrative or lyric poems. Sometimes she foregrounds her narrative or lyric personae as animated characters, while at other times they figure as subtle background presences. We need more precision in our descriptive language to account for the whole spectrum of effects in order to appreciate Mitchell's rhetorical command and versatility. In the first section of this chapter, I will introduce a set of categories designed to distinguish the various literary and performative elements that together create the illusion of fictional voices. The second section will survey five specific persona types characteristic of Mitchell's work. I will be charting the categorical distinctions in succession, referring to a dense fabric of examples taken from her entire output. The categories will prove useful conceptual tools in the more sweeping view of poetic themes undertaken in chapter 4.

Some readers may prefer to skip the first section of this chapter to begin with, returning to it as needed to clarify specific categories as they arise.

Mode

The first aspect to consider is the general manner in which a poem addresses its audience. What kind of communicative relation is presumed between the poetic speaker and her hypothetical listeners? This involves distinctions between various imaginary speech situations. While in actual terms, Mitchell's songs were all intended for oral performance (either live with an actual audience present or simulated in recorded form with little authorial control over the listening situation), in fictional terms, they present themselves according to four different modes of artistic enunciation: dramatic, narrative, lyric, and political. These modes can be distinguished by the different roles they assign to the singer as well as to the implied audience. In the following classification I am using terms common to discussions of poetic genre, without subscribing to any particular system.[11] It is not my project in this book to theorize songwriting genres in any systematic way, nor to worry too much about airtight classification by genre category. I will be referring to established musical and poetic genres and subgenres pragmatically as they figure in my chosen examples. But for the moment my analytical lens is trained on the dynamics of audience address as fictionally presented within the encompassing medium of sung poetry.[12]

Dramatic

Poetry in the dramatic mode consists of words spoken directly by fictional characters, thus resembling a scene or monologue from a play. Scenes may feature a single character, or several; the singer impersonates different characters as they appear. The audience is placed in a kind of spectator role (but without the visual component), observing the drama from the other side of a virtual proscenium. (A possible term for this special auditory role would be "closet spectator," by analogy with so-called closet drama, i.e., unstaged dramatic reading.)

An early example of dramatic address is found in "The Pirate of Penance" (*SS*), for which the names of the speaking characters are labeled explicitly in the printed poem. The main character is Penance Crane, a woman living in a harbor town. Initially she sounds detached from the tale she relates, of a pirate who has had his way with a cabaret dancer and then stolen off at dawn. But as the song continues it becomes clear that Penance is personally involved. She bursts out as if in answer to unseen accusers: "It isn't true I hardly knew him." Eventually we learn that a murder has taken place (but who is dead?); Penance protests her innocence. Meanwhile, the Dancer also has a speaking part, recalling her rendezvous with the pirate and implicating Penance in the past events. The dialogue of the two characters overlaps in performance; Mitchell distinguishes the voice of the Dancer through a slower, more languid speech pattern, and by mixing her vocal part low, as if she is speaking from a distance.

A late example occurs in "The Sire of Sorrow (Job's Sad Song)" (*TI*), a reworking of Job's dramatic dialogues from Scripture. In the Bible, Job's long diatribes alternate with responses and reproach from his three friends. Mitchell condenses these responses into a chorus of "Antagonists" whose interspersed comments are harsh and comfortless. Both of these songs represent the dramatic mode in its pure form: the entire poem is cast in direct speech, the only speakers being characters in the drama. In other songs, Mitchell introduces dramatic speech by means of a framing narrative voice. Thus in "Raised on Robbery" (*C&S*), an introductory section (four lines long) describes the setting and main characters, ending in "She says ..."; the body of the song (four verses) then adopts the voice of the "lady in lacy sleeves" trying to pick up the man in the hotel lounge. A similar introduction occurs in "The Beat of Black Wings" (*CMRS*), though in this case the framing narrator is present in the dramatic scene and speaks in the first person ("I met a young soldier"). In "Free Man in Paris" (*C&S*), the narrative frame is reduced to two words ("he said"); otherwise the song is a monologue spoken by the unnamed music business executive. When such speaking characters occupy the body of the song and the introduction is minimal, the effect is comparable to that of dramatic address (though impure in mode). (Some well-known examples of purely dramatic songs include the Shangri-Las' "Leader of the Pack," the Rolling Stones' "Sympathy for the Devil," Cat Stevens' "Father and Son," Queen's "Bohemian Rhapsody," and the character songs that make up the Who's *Tommy*.)

Narrative

In this mode, the singer takes the role of storyteller while the listener is positioned as the recipient of the story (sometimes called the "narratee"). Thus a narrative song implies a direct communicative role between listeners and singer, who is understood as telling the story *to them*. (A dramatic song, by contrast, presents fictional characters who speak to each other and are overheard by the audience.) Some songs from the folk revival scene make this relationship with the audience quite explicit, as in Bob Dylan's "North Country Blues" (1963), which begins with the familiar ploy: "Come gather 'round friends/And I'll tell you a tale." But even when the invitation is not put into words, the intent is still to draw listeners in with the lure of a well-told tale. So, for instance, when Mitchell begins a song "He comes for conversation/I comfort him sometimes," she sets up an intriguing situation while only gradually revealing the full circumstances of the story. There are myriad examples of narrative songs in Mitchell's work: stories of troubled love affairs (as in "Conversation" [*LC*]), reminiscences of childhood ("Cherokee Louise" [*NRH*]), comic vignettes ("Dry Cleaner from Des Moines" [*M*]), and quasi-mystical encounters ("Woodstock" [*LC*]). Narrating voices may signal their presence to a greater or lesser degree: they may be implicit or dramatized, objective about described events or personally involved in them. (Such distinctions will be considered below under "Syntax.")

Lyric

Lyric poetry is generally understood to convey "a state of mind or a process of perception, thought, and feeling" from the perspective of an expressive subject.[13] As for the audience presumed by lyric poetry, I quote literary critic Northrop Frye: "The lyric is ... preeminently the utterance that is overheard. The lyric poet normally pretends to be talking to himself or to someone else: a spirit of nature, a Muse, ... a personal friend, a lover, a god, a personified abstraction, or a natural object."[14] In contrast to dramatic poems (also "overheard" by the audience), lyric poems are typically spoken in a voice that approximates the voice of the poet. Thus when Wordsworth, in his poem "I Wandered Lonely as a Cloud," writes: "For oft, when on my couch I lie/In vacant or in pensive mood," we are invited to take these words as the thoughts of the poet himself rather than those of a fictional character. The same is true of statements such as this one, from Mitchell's song "Amelia" (*H*): "Maybe I've never really loved/I guess that is the truth/I've spent my whole life in clouds at icy altitudes." But not all lyric speakers are autobiographical in this way; some may be conventionalized or invented poetic personae.[15] "A Chair in the Sky" (*M*) is a lyric song taking the persona of Charles Mingus.

The purely lyric utterance entails a scene of reflection rather than one of dramatic action. The audience is granted special access to the thoughts of the poetic persona, as vocalized in an imaginary monologue or a one-sided dialogue. For the most part, "Amelia" gives the impression of solitary contemplation; but in the refrain closing every verse, Mitchell addresses Amelia Earhart as a kind of personal muse. Another poem addressed to a muse is "Impossible Dreamer" (*DED*); the unnamed dreamer represents the spirit of political visionaries such as Martin Luther King, Jr. Many of Mitchell's lyric songs are addressed to lovers ("Woman of Heart and Mind" [*FR*], "Blue" [*B*], "Jericho" [*DJRD*]), some to personal friends ("Song for Sharon" [*H*], "Chinese Café" [*WTRF*]). "Song to a Seagull" (*SS*) is spoken to a seabird, representing a romanticized "spirit of nature" (in the tradition identified by Frye). In "Sweet Bird" (*HSL*), the apostrophized bird figure is a personified abstraction representing lost youth. (Compare Paul Simon's "The Sound of Silence," also addressed to a personified abstraction: "Hello darkness, my old friend.")

Political

Political poetry aims to communicate a set of ethical beliefs or highlight an urgent social problem. It also appeals to a collective audience by affirming shared values or rallying listeners to a common cause. Sometimes such lyrics will imply group singing, where individuals merge in a communal "we" (as in the traditional "We Shall Overcome"); though it is rare for Mitchell to relinquish her individuality in this way. When the issue is specific and the goal of agitation is overt, this is known as a protest song. But political poetry can take more indirect forms. Thus songs such as Bob Dylan's "Blowin' in the Wind" and John Lennon's "Imagine," while advocating political causes, employ nonspecific, even mythicized images and a rhetoric of metaphysical questioning rather than activism. (Of course, such songs have certainly been *used* as protest songs by groups of activists.) Mitchell's political songs cover a number of different issues, including war ("The Fiddle and the Drum" [*C*]), the environment ("Big Yellow Taxi" [*LC*]), poverty ("Banquet" [*FR*]), the media ("Fiction" [*DED*]), aboriginal rights ("Lakota" [*CMRS*]), and spousal abuse ("Not to Blame" [*TI*]). In "The Fiddle and the Drum," the poet first addresses a soldier, trying to persuade him to relinquish warfare. The second half of the poem repeats the plea, this time addressed to "America," the poet now adopting a communal voice: "We have all come/To fear the beating of your drum."

Some of Mitchell's political songs move in and out of a lyric voice. Thus in "Banquet," the verses speak in general terms of social inequity; the bridge section, however, turns to a lyric perspective: "I took my share down by the sea." There are other hybrid modes as well: "The Beat of Black Wings" (*CMRS*) is a quasi-dramatic song (with a narrative frame, as discussed above) with a strong anti-war message. This brings up the possibility of mixing modes, a common practice in Mitchell's work and in fact common in poetry generally. Canonic lyric poems routinely incorporate narrative passages. The Wordsworth poem alluded to earlier begins with such a passage ("I wandered lonely as a cloud ... When all at once I saw ..."), crucial to the effect of lyric reflection at the poem's end. One type of hybrid is even recognized as its own subgenre: the so-called dramatic lyric (a favorite genre of Robert Browning), which captures the lyric utterance of a single speaker, caught in "an identifiable situation at a dramatic moment" and often interacting with other characters.[16] The speaker may be the poet, as in "Carey" (*B*), set in a particular locale in Crete as a conversation with a friend as the two prepare to go out for the evening; or "Off Night Backstreet" (*DJRD*), addressed to an unfaithful lover and calling him on the carpet for his actions. Or the speaker may be a fictional character, as in "Two Grey Rooms" (*NRH*), based on a gay man's unrequited love and the lengths to which he goes to observe the object of his infatuation; or "The Magdalene Laundries" (*TI*), spoken by a pregnant girl committed to a Catholic house of charity and dramatizing a particular moment ("Peg O'Connell died today"). (General examples of dramatic lyrics include songs in which the singer is in the process of writing a letter [as in the Jenkins/Mercer song "P.S. I Love You"], conversing on the telephone [Jim Croce's "Operator"], or seducing a lover [a recurring genre for Prince].) Numerous songs move freely between modes of address as I have defined them here. Thus the modes should not be considered fixed and globally controlling but miscible and interactive.

Representation

A second basic aspect of poetic technique concerns broad questions of representation—how the poet chooses to depict specific fictional worlds. This may seem at first glance to have little to do with "voice," since the verbs commonly used to describe this aspect ("depict," "portray") invoke visual metaphors, more appropriate to painterly rather than vocal personae. But the topic does have a bearing on the implied presences in poetry: first, poetic representation, being verbal, is often attributable to the various lyric, narrative, or dramatic voices (*speaking* presences) we have already distinguished. Second, modes of representation involve different perceptual filters, determining what kinds of observed or intellectual detail dominate the poetic (and the listeners') perspective and thus contributing to the effect of a *perceiving* presence. Third, the depicted worlds furnish the situations in which the poems' *characters* find themselves. I will briefly discuss four representational categories important in Mitchell's work.

Realistic

Many poems take place in the everyday world. Reality is represented through the description of ordinary physical and social surroundings, human actions and emotions. "Barangrill" (*FR*), for instance, is set in a truck stop. The poetic speaker (a blend of lyric and narrative) describes her observations of the commonplace scene: the conversation and attire of the waitresses, the personal charm of the gas station attendant as well as her own concurrent thoughts and yearnings. (Compare the similar lyric/narrative mode and realistic representation in Paul Simon's "Homeward Bound.") In "Help Me" (*C&S*), a lyric speaker expresses familiar feelings of vulnerability at the beginning of a love affair. She offers no details concerning the physical setting, but her descriptions of emotion, character, and actions (dancing, talking, flirting) depict common experiences from real life.

Mythic

In contrast, some poems describe their settings and actions in terms more picturesque, idealized, or mysterious than everyday life. Thus in "The Dawntreader" (*SS*), the lyric speaker refers to clothing as "satins" and money as "silver." The seaside setting evokes images of mermaid colonies and brilliant underwater treasure. The human encounter at the heart of the poem may well have been inspired by an actual occurrence, but it is poetically cast as a romantic fantasy, filtered through an idealized archaic outlook that suggests magical access to a world of dreams. (Compare David Crosby's "Guinnevere.") The song "Blue" (B) works in a similar way to portray a contemporary human relationship in terms of romanticized seafaring imagery rather than realistic detail. Specific negotiations over personal commitment are transformed into the poetic plea: "Crown and anchor me/Or let me sail away." (Thus the explicit reference to drugs ["acid," "needles"] and guns has a harsh, intrusive effect.) I use the term "mythic" for this category to indicate the typical recourse to collective, primal symbols (castles, mermaids, lost Edens, and the like).

Aesthetic

In certain poems, real-world referents seem less important than the aesthetic qualities of the verbal constructions. An interest in decorative or conceptual artifice is foregrounded to the point where connections to represented objects become tenuous. In "Cold Blue Steel and Sweet Fire" (FR), for instance, the actual details of the situation (a drug addict in need of a fix) are subsumed in a kind of verbal free play. People and things lose their real names and sprout fanciful titles. Words surrealistically cluster and combine according to their textural properties:

> Underneath the jungle gym
> Hollow-grey-fire-escape-thief
> Looking for Sweet Fire
> Shadow of Lady Release

(Compare the verbal free play in songs such as Dylan's "Subterranean Homesick Blues," Paul Simon's "Mrs. Robinson," and David Bowie's "Jean Genie.") In this representational category, the emphasis is on verbal and symbolic patterning rather than closeness to objective reality. Symbols tend to be newly invented, rather than taken from the collective repository of myth. Thus the song "Electricity" (FR) expands on an ironic metaphor whereby romantic attraction is portrayed as faulty wiring, held together by makeshift repairs:

> The masking tape tangles
> It's sticky and black
> And the copper
> Proud headed Queen Lizzie
> Conducts little charges
> That don't get charged back
> Well the technical manual's busy

"The Jungle Line" (*HSL*) is a virtuosic display of metaphoric substitution, in which images of modern Manhattan jazz clubs dreamily disconnect and merge with images suggesting an African American racial memory, overseen by a disembodied, ambiguously raced primitivizing presence (identified with the painter Rousseau).

Philosophical

Finally, some poems are primarily taken up with philosophical discourse. They expound on metaphysical principles and the basic conditions of existence rather than the details of particular lives. To this category belong the songs "Love" (*WTRF*), a reworking of Paul's famous sermon from I Corinthians, chapter 13, and "Shadows and Light" (*HSL*), a lesson in Manichaean dualism. On a less exalted level, the personal details at the heart of "Down to You" (*C&S*) are framed by passages contemplating the transience of fortune and desire.

Syntax

One of the most overt ways to create the illusion of poetic speakers is through clues indicating grammatical person. Many lyric and narrative poems are spoken in a voice explicitly claiming the first-person "I." Some poems flesh out the sense of an immediate speaking situation by addressing a second-person "you." Other poems, however, avoid such overt clues, treating the speaking voice as an implied presence. One common technique in such cases is for the implicit poetic speaker to describe a scene or story entirely from the perspective of a third-person central character. In this subsection I will discuss different syntactical constructions of voice and perspective and their rhetorical effects.

Explicit speakers

FIRST-PERSON SUBJECT The explicit personalized voice is common coin in the singer-songwriter genre, revealing a historical link to the Romantic lyric poem. Given this extended exploration of the expressive possibilities of first-person utterance, we can expect to find a rich and complex field of signification within this grammatical category. One distinction to note at the outset is whether the speaker is identified as *singular* or *plural*. The plural "we" is less common and thus a special case, suggesting a folky inclusiveness, or occasionally, more eccentric groupings (as in the Beatles' "Yellow Submarine"). A famous example of the plural subject expressing a common human condition occurs in the chorus of "The Circle Game" (*LC*): "We can't return we can only look behind/From where we came." A more eccentric community is portrayed in "Sisotowbell Lane" (*SS*): "We have a rocking chair/Each of us rocks his share."

As for the singular speakers, some seem to be *autobiographical* while others are clearly *fictional roles*. The "I" voice in "A Chair in the Sky" (*M*) belongs to Charles Mingus (as Mitchell imagines him); in "The Magdalene Laundries" (*TI*), it is a fictional unwed mother who speaks. On the other hand, all of the songs on the album *Hejira* use an "I" virtually identical with the songwriter herself, recording her thoughts and preoccupations at the time of writing and referring to autobiographical details. There are also cases when the line between fiction and autobiography is blurred. "The Priest" (*LC*), for instance, relates a fraught romantic encounter with great immediacy; but without extratextual information there is no way to verify whether Mitchell is recalling something from her own experience or projecting herself into an intriguing fictional role.

In many songs, the first-person subject speaks in soliloquy, as if to herself. Such a *reflexive address* is evident in "River" (*B*), with its stream of reminiscence, hand-wringing, and internal remonstration:

> I'm so hard to handle
> I'm selfish and I'm sad
> Now I've gone and lost the best baby
> That I ever had
> I wish I had a river
> I could skate away on

A later example, less "confessional" in tone but still presented as interior monologue, is "The Only Joy in Town" (*NRH*): "I want to paint a picture/Botticelli style/Instead of Venus on a clam/I'd paint this flower child." Equally numerous, however, are those songs using *second-person address*, that is, direct speech to an explicit "you." Direct dialogue can create a vivid sense of spontaneous emotions and possibilities, as in "All I Want" (*B*): "Do you want to take a chance/on maybe finding some sweet romance with me baby/Well, come on." Or it can present a more measured, ruminative conversation, as in "Chinese Café" (*WTRF*): "Caught in the middle/Carol, we're middle class/We're middle aged." But in either case it is less self-enclosed than the reflexive voice. Second-person address captures the poetic speaker interacting with another person and thus gestures toward a dramatic scene, whether of seduction, accusation, or long-distance correspondence ("For the Roses" [*FR*], "Song for Sharon" [*H*]).

Some first-person (reflexive) speakers focus their attention on another central character, not as a second-person addressee but as a third-person object. ("The Priest" and "The Only Joy in Town" are examples.) Thus in "Conversation" (*LC*), the speaker doesn't directly enact the conversation of the title but rather tells a story about her unrequited love for a married man, in the third person: "I only say hello/And turn away before his lady knows/How much I want to see him."

In such cases, the speakers may be *dramatized* or *undramatized*. This distinction originates with narrative theorist Wayne Booth, who explains how "many novels dramatize their narrators with great fulness, making them into characters who are as vivid as those they tell us about," while other narrators, even if explicitly presented as "I," are "given no personal characteristics whatever."[17] (While Booth is discussing narration, I believe the distinction is also applicable to lyric voices. In any case, lyric and narrative modes are often inextricably combined in Mitchell's poetry.) The narrator in "Conversation" is fully dramatized, relating her personal involvement in the situation. Likewise, in "Furry Sings the Blues" (*H*), Mitchell sketches a third-person portrait of a singer (Furry Lewis) fallen on hard times while at the same time including precise details about her visit to his house (she came by limo, bringing gifts), her observations of the neighborhood, and her feelings about Furry's music. On the other hand, the first-person speaker in "Roses Blue" (*C*) is exiguous, taking up the story of a character who has lost her way in occult practices ("I think of Rose, my heart begins to tremble") without confiding any significant details about her own personality or involvement in the situation. The emphasis here is on the third-person object rather than the speaker. Another example of an undramatized speaker is found in "Marcie" (*SS*). In fact, this song has no explicit speaker until the final verse, when a first-person voice unexpectedly appears: "Marcie leaves and doesn't tell us/Where or why she moved away." The songwriter neglects to reveal any more about this shadowy "us."

SECOND-PERSON SUBJECT In a limited number of songs, Mitchell casts the reflexive speaking voice in the second person. That is, the subject of the poem speaks of herself as "you" rather than "I." This syntactic move is striking in its divergence from everyday linguistic usage; nor does it have any obvious precedent in nineteenth-century lyric poetry. Instead, the immediate influence is the poetry of Leonard Cohen, specifically the song "Suzanne" that uses the device throughout ("Suzanne takes you down/to her place near the river").[18] Early examples from Mitchell's work include "Michael from Mountains" (*SS*), "Little Green" (*B*), and the unreleased song "The Wizard of Is" (1966). Whereas first-person songs are typically set in the past tense, second-person songs are in the present: "Michael wakes you up with sweets/He takes you up streets and the rain comes down." Thus in temporal terms they have a special immediacy, even as in psychological terms they create a unique doubling or mirroring effect. The listener is given the same kind of access to the speaker's thought processes as in first-person poetry, but the speaker addresses herself through a poetic convention as another person: "You want to know all/But his mountains have called so you never do——."[19] In one sense, this reinforces the self-enclosed, reflexive aspect of the speaking situation (soliloquy), but in another sense, by using the typically outward-directed second person, the songwriter makes it easier for the listener to identify with her subjective experience and enter into that psychically enclosed space of reflection. The only other Joni Mitchell songs using this device are "Barangrill" (*FR*) and possibly "Down to You" and "Trouble Child" (both *C&S*), though these are ambiguous (they will be discussed below under the second-person focal category).

Implicit speakers

THIRD-PERSON FOCAL CHARACTER There are many poems in which the speaker does not lexically introduce herself as an "I" or "you" but remains an implicit linguistic presence. In Mitchell's poetic practice, virtually all such poems are focalized through a central character: that is, the narrative or scenic situation is described from that character's perspective, following his or her actions and thoughts. (The term "focalization" originates with Gérard Genette.) [20] This does not mean that the speaker and the character are the same; we should recognize the distinction between the experiential *perspective* of the character and the poetic *voice*, which may reveal a certain distance from the focal character through irony or other forms of commentary.

In "Blue Boy" (*LC*), the scene is focalized through a love-smitten lady, whose self-abasing worship of a unresponsive lover eventually turns her to stone, in a reversal of the Galatea myth. The poem unfolds by way of the lady's thoughts and perceptions:

> She would wake in the morning
> Without him
> And go to the window
> And look out through the pain
> But the statue in her garden
> He always looked the same

In this case one does have the impression that the poetic speaker has wholeheartedly projected herself into the lady's tragic perspective. It is hard to detect any verbal clues of perceptual distance; and in performance, Mitchell abandons herself to a painful emotional vulnerability. The situation is very different, however, in "Shades of Scarlett Conquering" (*HSL*). The poem still presents the experiential focus of a central character, this time haughty and vain:

> She comes from a school of southern charm
> She likes to have things her way
> Any man in the world holding out his arm
> Would soon be made to pay

But the poetic voice constantly distances itself from the latter-day Scarlett's attitudes and behavior. From the first, her emotions are portrayed as false and theatrical ("Mimicking tenderness she sees/In sentimental movies"). The implied speaker conveys a tartly ironic tone, disguising a criticism of the self-centered heroine as a compliment: "It is not easy to be brave/[...]/To carry the weight of all that greed." The song "Sunny Sunday" (*TI*) presents a third possible relation between voice and perspective. Here the narrative voice remains rather detached from the solitary main character, reporting her odd actions (shooting a pistol at the streetlight) but not her feelings. There is only one moment when we gain access to an inner thought: "That one little victory, that's all she needs!" At the same time, the speaker mostly refrains from commentary or critique: only one literary simile betrays an external commenting presence: "She dodges the light like Blanche DuBois." This type of objective speaker is more distant than the empathetic voice of "Blue Boy," yet less obtrusive than the critical voice of "Scarlett."

In general, third-person focal characters are taken to be fictional, but there are a few exceptions where the "she" of the poem refers to an autobiographical persona. One clear example is "Ladies of the Canyon" (*LC*), which makes reference to the bohemian enclave of Laurel Canyon, Mitchell's home at the time, while painting a stylized self-portrait. Mitchell's various talents as visual artist, homemaker, and songwriter are personified as three separate archetypal female characters. Another example, "Cactus Tree" (*SS*), is less precise in its autobiographical references, but in the context of the personal geography set out in the album, the "lady in the city" suggests Mitchell's own perspective. Though it's told in the third person, we understand the central conflict between romance and independence to express the songwriter's own dilemma. Once again, by casting her portrait in the third person, she translates personal traits into archetypes: the poet as heartbreaker and rolling stone. Note that this poem's refrain uses an obtrusive voice, commenting ironically on the choices made by the protagonist: "she's so busy being free." Thus her internal conflict is not only thematized but it is also expressed structurally in the distance between Mitchell-as-focal-character and Mitchell-as-poetic-speaker.

SECOND-PERSON FOCAL CHARACTER In a limited number of songs, the scene is focalized through a character addressed as "you." Even though there is no explicit "I" persona, the second-person address strongly conjures up an implied speaker. An example is found in "Judgment of the Moon and Stars" (*FR*), focalized through famous composer Ludwig van Beethoven. The poetic voice empathizes with the composer's frustration due to his loss of hearing: "Cold white keys under your fingers/Now you're thinking/'That's no substitute.'" The poem ends with an extended exhortation as if in direct dialogue with the composer: "You've got to shake your fists at lightning now/You've got to roar like forest fire." A similar device is used in "Blonde in the Bleachers" (*FR*), whose focal character is a "Rock 'n' Roll man": "She follows you home/But you miss living alone/You can still hear sweet mysteries/Calling you."

Note that second-person address can appear in three different speaking situations, according to the syntactic categories I have outlined: first-person subject, second-person subject, and second-person focal character. The latter two (lacking "I" pronouns) are distinguishable by whether the pronoun "you" refers to the poet herself or a fictional character whose perspective guides the discourse. Given that autobiographical experience tends to be aestheticized and fictionalized when cast in poetic form, one can see how such a distinction may blur, and Mitchell exploits this unique ambiguity in two songs (both from *C&S*).[21] "Down to You" is a wry meditation on the transience of love and moral certainty. It starts out sounding like a second-person monologue, the poet talking to herself (or possibly using "you" in the general sense of "one"): "Things that you held high/And told yourself were true/Lost or changing as the days come down to you." But then she begins to address what seems like another character: "Constant stranger/You're a kind person/You're a cold person too." Is this stranger a focal character or is the poet still speaking to herself as an object of self-analysis? The following (bridge) section turns from abstract thoughts to concrete anecdotal detail: "You go down to the pick up station/Craving warmth and beauty/You settle for less than fascination/A few drinks later you're not so choosy." This passage can be read either as a focalization through a fictional (male?) character, or as a less-than-flattering personal confession (in second person). The syntax allows either reading.[22]

"Trouble Child" also maintains a grammatical illusion of contradictory perspective: either second-person subject or second-person focalization. There are few clues pointing strongly one way or the other. The main character is apparently hospitalized for reasons of mental health:

> Up in a sterilized room
> Where they let you be lazy
> Knowing your attitude's all wrong
> And you got to change
> And that's not easy

Our access to his or her thoughts means either that the "trouble child" is engaged in a soliloquy or that an empathetic voice has charge of the discourse. At the end, it sounds like the poetic voice is finally establishing a bit of distance to comment on the situation: "Well some are going to knock you/And some'll try and clock you/You know it's really hard/To talk sense to you." But this could conceivably still represent an interior voice driven to argue with itself. And in fact such a reading, where the exasperated subject is "breaking" down into separate components, is made likely by the segue into the next song, "Twisted," a humorous first-person take on the same scene of psychoanalysis and split personality.

Diction

Poetic speakers are characterized through the things they talk about, but they are also characterized through their vocabulary. Even undramatized or implicit speakers may reveal a tangible persona by their choice of words. One broad distinction to be made is whether a speaker chooses to employ everyday language or some form of heightened, "poetic" language. Some poems are deliberately homespun. "Morning Morgantown" (*LC*), for instance, is about simple pleasures in an idyllic town. The speaker suggests an innocent, fresh persona through her consistent use of utterly common words: "We'll rise up early with the sun/To ride the bus while everyone is yawning/And the day is young/In morning, Morgantown." The speaker in "Woman of Heart and Mind" (*FR*) also uses thoroughly ordinary diction, but the effect is different. Worldly wise, she is using bluntness to cut through bullshit:

> Is it all books and words
> Or do you really feel it?
> Do you really laugh?
> Do you really care?
> Do you really smile
> When you smile?

She also descends for a moment into vulgar speech to make a point:

> Nothing seems to keep you high
> Drive your bargains
> Push your papers
> Win your medals
> Fuck your strangers
> Don't it leave you on the empty side

In another variation on everyday speech, there are songs in which Mitchell cultivates a colloquial manner to create an especially approachable persona. This is the case with "Big Yellow Taxi" (*LC*) and its casual contractions: "Don't it always seem to go/That you don't know what you've got/Till it's gone." She uses colloquialism to portray the working-class woman looking for a pickup in "Raised on Robbery" (*C&S*): "You know you ain't bad looking/I like the way you hold your drinks/Come home with me honey/I ain't asking for no full length mink." But she has also used it to express complex emotions in terms that are down to earth.

In "The Same Situation" (*C&S*), the character is in an existential quandary, but her words are familiar and unintimidating:

> With heaven full of astronauts
> And the Lord on death row
> While the millions of his lost and lonely ones
> Call out and clamor to be found
> Caught in their struggle for higher positions
> And their search for love that sticks around

In "Be Cool" (*WTRF*), there is no explicit speaker, but the colloquial diction creates a strong impression of one: "Don't whine/Kiss off that flaky valentine/You're nobody's fool."

But of course, while adept at the common touch, Mitchell is well known for the intellectual aspects of her verse—both in its subject matter and in her ease with sophisticated turns of phrase. In "Hejira" (*H*) she takes the everyday stuff of love trouble and voices her thoughts through a hyperarticulate persona: "In our possessive coupling/So much could not be expressed/So now I am returning to myself/Those things that you and I suppressed." In "The Boho Dance" (*HSL*), the speaker's freedom to move between bohemia and the glamour set is expressed verbally as well, with unpretentious phrases like "hard-time," "working cheap," and "runs in her nylons" jostling with lexical sophisticates such as "affectation," "stricken," and "capsulized."

The turn to a markedly poetic language can take several forms. It can introduce an archaic register, as in "Nathan La Franeer" (*SS*), where calling a taxi becomes "I hired a coach," and urban commotion is described as "the bedlam of the day." The second verse of "Rainy Night House" (*LC*) contains a striking temporary modulation to archaic diction: "You are a holy man/On the FM radio/I sat up all the night and watched thee/To see, who in the world you might be." "Holy man" is already evocative of premodern religious imagery, but by importing "thee" into the contemporary discourse, the speaker imbues the moment with a special aura of veneration, as if setting a halo above her lover's face.

Poetic language can be a matter of stylization, employing more formal cadences than everyday speech, as in the first verse of "Little Green" (*B*):

> Born with the moon in Cancer
> Choose her a name she will answer to
> Call her green and the winters cannot fade her
> Call her green for the children who have made her
> Little green, be a gypsy dancer

Here contractions are avoided, phrases are repeated for their melodic effect, and the consciously artificial address creates a strong sense of ceremony. In this case the formalized language is a sort of response to the trauma of giving up a child for adoption, with the poem taking the form of a letter of farewell, a bittersweet keepsake for the lost child. Stylized language can also result from elaborately constructed imagery, as in "Love or Money" (MA): "Vaguely she floats and lacelike/ Blown in like a curtain on the night wind/She's nebulous and naked/He wonders where she's been." In "Don Juan's Reckless Daughter" (DJRD), Mitchell employs an extended symbolic pattern whereby she casts herself and her romantic partner as the opposing poles of a dialectical pair, which transmutes dizzyingly into other dual images—eagle/snake, airplane/train, reason/desire:

> We're going to come up to the eyes of clarity
> And we'll go down to the beads of guile
> There is danger and education
> In living out such a reckless life style
> I touched you on the central plains
> It was plane to train my twin
> It was just plane shadow to train shadow
> But to me it was skin to skin

Though the vocabulary is unassuming here, the image structure is complex, moving through multiple layers of abstraction, while the verbal cadences have a high density of internal rhyme and recursive patterning.

There are cases where stylization is exaggerated for a special effect. For instance, in "Songs to Aging Children Come" (C), psychedelic apparitions and stilted language go hand in hand ("Does the moon play only silver/When it strums the galaxy/Dying roses will they will their/Perfumed rhapsodies to me"). "Don't Interrupt the Sorrow" (HSL) toys with deliberately opaque imagery and obscure contortions of grammar:

> A room full of glasses
> He says "Your notches liberation doll"
> And he chains me with that serpent
> To that Ethiopian wall

In this poem, one of Mitchell's thorniest, the main characters are engaged in personal combat over a woman's proper place. Some of the male chauvinist's statements sound like defective English, brutally stripped of connective particles. But even the female speaker's lines come across as dangerously disconnected, as if outrage is making it hard for her to marshal her thoughts ("Don't interrupt the sorrow/Darn right/In flames our prophet witches/Be polite").

Of course ordinary and poetic diction do not remain segregated. Some of the most interesting effects arise from counterpoint between the two. Thus "The Wolf That Lives in Lindsey" (*M*) plays with a tonal ambiguity. Diction is fluid, passing quickly from high-flown to veristic:

> There lives a wolf in Lindsey
> That raids and runs
> Through the hills of Hollywood
> And the downtown slums

The interpenetration of poetic register creates a double image: does the poem's language aestheticize degraded subject matter (crime and moral corruption) or does it attempt to bring a lofty philosophical disquisition down to earth? The inconstant tone resonates with the poem's portrayal of glamorous amorality. In "Dog Eat Dog" (*DED*), on the other hand, the passage from low to high is sudden and complete. The body of the poem employs harsh confrontational diction ("you can lie, cheat, skim, scam/Beat 'em any way you can"), only to pass into a coda of stylized lyricism ("People looking, seeing nothing/People listening, hearing nothing"). "Blue Motel Room" (*H*) contains a line where the conversational tone switches briefly and campily into mock-poetic image construction:

> I know that you've got all those pretty girls coming on
> Hanging on your boom-boom-pachyderm
> Well, you tell those girls that you've got German measles
> Honey, tell 'em you've got germs

As part of the discussion of diction, I want to call attention in passing to the variety of specific types of utterance (e.g., emotional expression, reminiscence, self-scrutiny, statements of decision) that together constitute poetic speech.[23] The monologue spoken by the wheelchair-bound Charles Mingus in the first verse of "A Chair in the Sky" (*M*) moves from past-tense narration setting the scene ("The rain slammed hard as bars"), to lyric reflection in the present ("I'm waiting for the keeper to release me"), reminiscence, then wistful reincarnational fantasy, borrowing the diction of marketing hype ("Next time/I'll be bigger!/I'll be better than ever!"), to end with present-tense narration ("But now Manhattan holds me"). The modulation between different types of utterance (or different "speech acts") and the rhythm of that movement can be exploited for its own effect. "A Chair in the Sky" sets up a very regular, formalized rhythm, changing utterance about every four lines. In contrast, "See You Sometime" (*FR*) is a casual jumble of distinct utterances, helping to create the illusion of spontaneous speech. The poem opens with questions suggesting an imaginary dialogue ("Where are you now/Are you in some hotel room"). Then comes a direct accusation, followed by the revelation that an actual telephone conversation has been taking place:

> Why do you have to be so jive
> O.K. hang up the phone
> It hurts
> But something survives
> Though it's undermined
> I'd still like to see you sometime

From "O.K." on, the phone connection is cut off and the conversation is definitely imaginary. The rest of the poem moves randomly between lyric expression ("I'm feeling so good"), narrative ("I run in the woods"), declarations of will ("I'm not ready to/Change my name again"), and friendly persuasion ("Pack your suspenders/I'll come meet your plane").

In "Little Green" (B), the verses consist of narration, stylized self-address ("Choose her a name"), and farewell wishes to the lost child. But the chorus is linguistically suspended in a highly refined utterance that is hard to describe:

> Just a little green
> Like the color when the spring is born
> There'll be crocuses to bring to school tomorrow
> Just a little green
> Like the nights when the Northern lights perform
> There'll be icicles and birthday clothes
> And sometimes there'll be sorrow

The first two lines are neither narration nor expression, not even a complete sentence—just an isolated thought unfolding a single poetic image, deepening the significance of the chosen name. The next line is a masterstroke of understatement: ostensibly limited to a precise objective detail about the turning of the seasons, it trembles with the subtext of future moments the speaker will never share. The final line is exquisitely ambiguous. Its imprecise, ongoing future tense disguises a very fresh wound. And who is it spoken to? Into the air apparently, conveying a parental wish to pass on hard-won knowledge, from a disappearing speaker whose despair is spun into perfectly balanced verbal designs.

Performance

Appreciation of the impact of the speaking presence in moments such as these is not complete without considering the manner of vocal performance. When Mitchell sings "there'll be sorrow" (especially in the final chorus), her emotions are very restrained. Only for a brief moment, just before the cadence, does she give a hint that her vocal tone, and therefore her calm facade, is in danger of breaking. Such an emotionally controlled persona is in stark contrast to the naked vulnerability of the voice in a song like "Blue Boy" (*LC*), where the verses ultimately dissolve into extravagantly broken moans. In general, Mitchell's singing voice responds sensitively to poetic shape and detail. But apart from the projection of textual particulars, one can suggest general categories of vocal production through which the singer brings diverse personae to life. The following attributes are not meant to be rigorously distinct from one another; rather, they explore different nuances in the embodiment of vocal personae.

Vivid versus *impersonal* in character

In a song like "Raised on Robbery" (*C&S*), Mitchell employs vocal histrionics to portray the main character. Her brash personality is conveyed through a bright, forceful vocal tone and suggestive, flamboyant slides. The vocal persona in "Talk to Me" (*DJRD*) is equally vivid: hyperactive, full of chatter, mercurial, and lightly self-mocking. On the other hand, a song like "The Dawntreader" (*SS*) aims for a hauntingly impersonal effect by maintaining a mysterious languid monotone for long melodic stretches. The singing voice in "Sweet Bird" (*HSL*) is also generally subdued, as befits the poem's supramundane, bird's-eye perspective (see the discussion of this song in chapter 4).

Intense versus *detached* in expressivity

Like a face in cinematic closeup, Mitchell's voice in songs such as "Willy" (*LC*) acts as a living vehicle of emotion. Subtle expressive nuances are communicated through constant changes in pressure, vocal purity, and fullness of tone. Even words not explicitly concerned with feelings ("Willy is my *child*, he is my *father*") are infused with the sounds—the sobs, swoons, and tender breaths—of emotional intensity. "Last Chance Lost" (*TI*), about the fallout from a divorce, is a later example of an intensely expressive performance. In contrast, the vocal persona in "Marcie" (*SS*) holds herself aloof from the plight of the focal character, maintaining a steady composure even through phrases that invite expressive comment ("Marcie's sorrow needs a man"). Likewise, in "Cold Blue Steel and Sweet Fire" (*FR*), the trauma of the junkie ("Bashing in veins for peace") does not register in the cool, nonchalant singing voice.

Controlled versus *unstable* in manner

This dichotomy is well illustrated by the contrasting vocalities in "Little Green" and "Blue Boy," introduced above. A controlled persona is also audible in the trim, streamlined voice Mitchell uses in the 1979 version of "Woodstock" (discussed in chapter 2). In still another instance, "Dog Eat Dog" (*DED*), the taut, compressed vocal delivery gives a strong impression of anger held in check. On the other hand, a dangerously volatile persona is especially prominent on *Ladies of the Canyon* and *Blue*. In songs like "The Arrangement" (*LC*), Mitchell's voice climbs to a wail, veering in and out of control as if skating an emotional precipice.

Natural versus *artificial* in elocution

In songs such as "Chelsea Morning" (*C*), Mitchell projects artlessness by avoiding a cultivated vocal tone and by approximating the flexible declamation of everyday speech. (Later examples include "Cherokee Louise" [*NRH*] and "The Crazy Cries of Love" [*TT*].) But on the same album, in "Songs to Aging Children Come" (*C*) she adopts a highly unnatural vocal style, with extreme range and exaggerated warble. One of the dramatic characters in "The Pirate of Penance" (*SS*), the Dancer, also sounds artificial in her rhythmic uniformity and eerie lack of inflection. In a later example, "The Beat of Black Wings" (*CMRS*), the voice of the Vietnam veteran is performed as a distorted series of vocal tics, expressive of his personality disorder.

Naive versus *sophisticated* in tone

The vocal persona in "Morning Morgantown" (*LC*) is fresh, innocent, and unpretentious. Mitchell sings with a limpid tone and warm, exuberant energy, completely free of vocal bruises or scuffmarks. In "The Circle Game" (*LC*) she matches the childlike lyrics with a voice that sounds timid, impressionable, and wide-eyed. By her second period, however, she is drawn to suave, knowing personae. For the cynical vignettes in "Edith and the Kingpin" (*HSL*) and "Otis and Marlena" (*DJRD*), Mitchell's voice is arch, cool, and well-dressed. Her melodies quirk and tail off in an urbane manner. Coy vocal slides and vibratos sound like ironic winks at the listener. Mitchell reaches a pinnacle of cool sophistication in the breathy, sometimes cocky jazz voice she cultivated for the album *Mingus*.

Polished versus *raw* in timbre

In certain performances, Mitchell foregrounds the beauty of her voice as an aesthetic object. Expressive power is secondary to timbral sweetness, purity, and technical confidence. Such a polished persona makes an appearance in "Both Sides Now" (*C*). Similarly, the emotional trouble of "Trouble Child" (*C&S*) is filtered through an aestheticized singing voice. Vocal tone is relaxed, lulling, lustrous; final nasal consonants are lingered over for their sensory effect. Other songs sacrifice beauty for expressive power. The impassioned monologue in "The Last Time I Saw Richard" (*B*) does not shy away from vocal cracks or impurities. Forays into the high register are piercing and exposed. In the third period, harsh, forced timbres are often used to convey political indignation. This is audible in songs such as "Fiction" and "Ethiopia" (both *DED*). Note that the quality of Mitchell's voice alters materially over time as it is cured by age and tobacco, deepening in register, becoming increasingly husky, and losing flexibility. But this dramatic metamorphosis is a separate issue from the topic under discussion of how she uses her voice. In the late albums *TI* and *TT*, though her instrument is audibly autumnal, Mitchell generally avoids deliberately raw vocal timbres, while she imparts special polish to the song "Last Chance Lost" (*TI*).

Combined Analysis

In the foregoing discussion my concern has been to develop as many conceptual levers as possible for the analysis of musicopoetic voice. The distinctions will not all be applicable with the same frequency. Some of the categories deal in precise technical terminology (such as syntax) while others (diction, performance) call for a more impressionistic or sensory descriptive language. We are now in a position to try out the foregoing categories in the analysis of an entire song. I hope to illustrate how the concepts, laid out systematically so far, may be applied organically as they arise, the better to discern a song's subtle rhetorical effects.

My example is "The Tea Leaf Prophecy" (*CMRS*), from Mitchell's third period. This song follows a very clear verse-chorus form. There are also backing vocal chants with their own distinct text, first appearing in the intro and later laid over the chorus. With a scenario deriving from the circumstances under which Mitchell's parents first met during World War II, the poem is cast as a third-person narrative, focalized through "Molly McGee" (based on her mother, Myrtle McKee); thus it is autobiographical at a remove.[24] The verses relate a fortune-teller's prophecy of marriage, which comes true despite the scarcity of eligible men. Molly is characterized through colorful quoted speech, as well as through access to her thoughts:

> Oh these nights are strong and soft—
> Private passions and secret storms
> Nothin' about him ticks her off
> And he looks so cute in his uniform

In a few short strokes the empathetic narrator portrays a woman who is lively and pragmatic, yet with emotional depths. In fact, taken by themselves, the verses resemble a nostalgia piece from the viewpoint of a narrator curious about her own origins. But such a straightforward perspective has already been deflected by the background vocals as the song opens: "Study war no more/Lay down your arms." These recurring lines open up the poem's conceptual and temporal horizon by referring to another prophecy, from the Old Testament (Isaiah 2:4) as paraphrased in a traditional spiritual, thus posing a mythic frame of reference.[25] They also put the listener on alert by using a political mode of address. In relation to this widened frame, the narrative of Molly's whirlwind engagement takes on a more portentous shading: the detail of her attraction to a man in uniform (in the line quoted above) is a humanizing touch but presented in such a way as to emphasize the trifling, accidental impulses often lying behind momentous decisions. And before the line is quite finished, the singer is overtaken by the admonitory backing vocals reminding us of the wider theater of war and its potential costs.

Strange things happen as we pass between verse and chorus. The rate of poetic declamation is augmented; now it takes twice as long to declaim one line. There is a corresponding shift in represented time, from the singular events of the verse to the time-lapse, seasonal recurrence of the chorus:

> She plants her garden in the spring
> She does the winter shoveling
> Tokyo Rose on the radio
> She says she's leavin' but she don't go

The elliptical dimensions of the chorus disturb the realistic chronology of the verses, while zooming out from scenic detail to discern a well-worn routine. Molly in this archetypical aspect represents a woman missing her chance to break out of predestined roles; the narrator casts a critical eye. The effect of diverging perspectives (two views of Molly, two narrative distances) is heightened by the backing vocals, interwoven between the lines and split into two layers: one a collective monotone ("Study war no more"), one solo and strident ("Lay down your arms"). One suggests melancholy and inertia, one righteous indignation.

The words of successive choruses are not wholly identical, but vary to reflect changing circumstance as the main character is increasingly identified in terms of her family. Chorus 2 comes after the wedding (now "he" does the shoveling), chorus 3 after the birth of a child ("The three of 'em laughin' 'round the radio"), but the overall routine remains the same. The arrival of the child is unnarrated; we learn of it indirectly in verse 3, which abruptly breaks into the dramatic mode. The narrator disappears for the time being to be replaced by Molly's voice, addressing her baby:

> "Sleep little darlin'!
> This is your happy home
> Hiroshima cannot be pardoned!
> Don't have kids when you get grown

> Because, this world is shattered
> The wise are mourning—
> The fools are joking
> Oh—what does it matter?
> The wash needs ironing
> And the fire needs stoking"

This is an eccentric lullaby, to say the least. The sudden burst of outrage against the bomb creates a blaring clash of utterances, detonating amid the warm nest and derailing the unself-conscious normality of home life. In a flash, that distant fallout has reached western Canada and deformed the realistic picture of motherly contentment. (What mother has ever forbidden her newborn to continue the family line?) Molly's voice frays as it becomes a mouthpiece for the narrator's anxieties—a narrator who despairs of the future, who perhaps remains childless. (At the time of writing, Mitchell had not yet been reunited with her daughter.) In a significant off-rhyme, the "darlin'" of the lullaby rings false with "pardoned." Instead, the latter word conjures up the ghost of another rhyme, namely the "garden" Molly busies herself with every spring, a consolation as well as a self-imposed limit. Note also the strangely reflexive second-person address—the poet imagining herself as "you," tiny auditor of an urgent primal message while in fact putting words in her mother's mouth. This points up another idiosyncratic feature of the poem. Its syntax is strung with second-person warnings, but each "you" is different. "Lay down your arms" takes in a general audience; "You'll be married in a month" is Molly's own special heirloom; while "Don't have kids when you get grown" reflects back on the poet, both personally and in her broader role as representative of the baby boom. This fracturing of person further elaborates the idea of divergent perspectives.

In "Tea Leaf Prophecy," Mitchell arranges deceptively ordinary material into a structure with unforeseen complexity of tone and voice. As the choruses continue, time speeds forward:

> She plants her garden in the spring
> They do the winter shoveling
> They sit up late and watch the Johnny Carson show
> She says "I'm leavin' here" but she don't go

A nostalgia piece twists into antinostalgia; a charming cameo is set within a critique of postwar inertia. The narrator's empathy for Molly's close-knit situation is repeatedly questioned by reference to a wider frame—and by recognition of the poet's own utterly different viewpoint, as a woman who managed to leave.

SOME RECURRING TYPES

From the foregoing discussion the reader will have an impression of the incredibly diverse repertory of speaking personae Mitchell has brought to life in her poetry. Among this collection of dreamers, wags, and knaves, certain character types stand out as favorites; I will highlight five of these. Where the first part of this chapter concentrated on finely tuned distinctions of poetic voice, this section will take a more holistic view, describing typical character roles shared by numerous songs and explored from different angles over time. Together, these five types represent Mitchell's most well-known personae as a writer and performer. Noteworthy strokes of poetic skill will be highlighted along the way.

The Ingenue

We have already encountered the callow, wide-eyed girl in "Morning Morgantown" (*LC*). Her youthfulness is conveyed through naive vocal tones, simple diction, and a visual/emotional filter that paints the town in glowing colors. But not all ingenue songs are upbeat; the key feature is their intensity of response to life's pleasures or pains, as if experiencing them for the first time. In "All I Want" (*B*), the speaker's exuberance results in phrases that gush out in a stream of insistent repetitions and volatile emotions:

> I am on a lonely road and I am traveling
> traveling, traveling, traveling
> Looking for something, what can it be
> Oh I hate you some, I hate you some
> I love you some
> Oh I love you when I forget about me

Expression is naively direct, trading in sincerity ("All I really really want") rather than suave versifying. Even the simplest actions ("I want to talk to you, I want to shampoo you") trigger steep highs and lows. Nor does the speaker shy away from clichés in her confessional outpouring. On the other hand, an ingenue persona does not preclude verbal deftness or intelligence. Take the following passage at the end of verse 2:

> Applause, applause—Life is our cause
> When I think of your kisses my mind see-saws
> Do you see—do you see—do you see
> how you hurt me baby
> So I hurt you too
> Then we both get so blue

There is a charming gaucherie in the first line with its puffed-up theatrical parlance. But then, as the musical section comes to a cadence (on "see-saws"), Mitchell fashions a brilliant, witty link to the following section through a multiple pun. The first syllable of "see-saw" unexpectedly evokes a rhyme in "Do you see." Following the established pattern of excited repetition, this phrase stutters upward three times as if mimicking the rocking rhythm of a seesaw. Emotionally as well, a similar gesture is enacted in the quick lurch from joy to pain.

Where "All I Want" is a paean to love, in "Nathan La Franeer" (*SS*), the ingenue is an urban waif, fleeing from the city ("You feed it all your woes/The ghostly garden grows"). Her voice is unfailingly earnest. The very premise of the song is melodramatic, casting a simple taxi ride to the airport ("from confusion to the plane") as a litany of alienation. From her taxi window, the fugitive glimpses garish images from a Bosch painting ("I saw an aging cripple selling Superman balloons"). Her complaint intermittently unfurls in expansive, limber poetic lines:

> Through the tunnel tiled and turning
> Into daylight once again I am escaping
> Once again goodbye
> To symphonies and dirty trees

Sentiments such as these are ingenuous in their appalled recoiling from everyday grime and human traffic and their need to imbue commonplace incidents with allegorical urgency.

"The Gallery" (*C*) is a metaphorical tale of an artist's model sung in a giddy, nimble voice. The speaker is one of those ingenues who profess a premature world-weariness ("I gave you all my pretty years/Then we began to weather"), similar to the jaded youth in "The Circle Game" (*LC*) ("So the years spin by and now the boy is twenty/Though his dreams have lost some grandeur coming true"). The tale unfolds from the first bloom of love through disillusionment and separation to a kind of wry détente. Especially felicitous is the treatment of the chorus, which by the simplest of alterations effects a complete reversal of meaning. In its first appearance, the narrator quotes the artist, who has "gotten into a funny scene," assuming the mantle of an ascetic:

> "Lady, don't love me now, I am dead
> I am a saint, turn down your bed
> I have no heart," that's what you said
> You said, "I can be cruel
> But let me be gentle with you"

Though the situation is not entirely clear, it appears that her lover, the artist, has mortified his flesh and is asking her to deny her own sexual desires ("turn down your bed"). She portrays this demand as a power play of cruel condescension. But by the final chorus, the artist has undergone a crisis in his religious convictions and comes flying back "like some lost homing pigeon":

> "Lady, please love me now, I was dead
> I am no saint, turn down your bed
> Lady, have you no heart," that's what you said
> Well, I can be cruel
> But let me be gentle with you

The tables are turned. The artist renounces his sainthood and pleads abjectly for physical warmth and affection ("turn down your bed"). The lady, in return, accepts him back graciously even as she chides him with his own words of condescension. Mitchell's vocal tone at this clinching moment is masterfully complex, managing to be sexy, shrewd, mildly mocking, and self-congratulatory all at the same time.

The Mystic Bard

For the mystic persona, the phenomena of the physical world are keys to a cosmic reality. To the narrator in "Woodstock" (*LC*), for instance, a fellow human being is a "child of God," a potential seeker of truth. Solid bodies dematerialize into carbon from ancient stars. The lyric speaker in "The Dawntreader" (*SS*) likewise conveys a mystical vision of the world around her:

> Peridots and periwinkle blue medallions
> Gilded galleons spilled across the ocean floor
> Treasure somewhere in the sea and he will find where
> Never mind their questions there's no answer for
> The roll of the harbor wake
> The songs that the rigging makes
> The taste of the spray he takes
> And he learns to give
> He aches and he learns to live
> He stakes all his silver
> On a promise to be free
> Mermaids live in colonies
> All his seadreams come to me

From the outset, this poem plunges us deep into a fantasy construction. The actual details of setting and character are dreamily indeterminate, so that the identities of "he," "they," and "me" are never precisely drawn. Scenic descriptors

("roll," "wake," "rigging," "spray," "pilings") are chosen above all for their phonetic beauty and romantic resonance. The language is image-centered to such a
degree that syntactic logic is suspended; each line begins a new thought before
the last one resolves, in the lulling rhythm of overlapping wavelets. Together,
the effect is one of immersion in a sensory flow and openness to archetypal quest
imagery (more on the theme of quests in chapter 4). Just as crucial to the bardic
persona is Mitchell's vocal delivery: somber, subdued, and mysterious, spoken
with a trance-like languor.

In contrast to the romantic mystique of "Dawntreader," "Shadows and Light"
(*HSL*) is more austere, speaking in riddles like an oracle: "The perils of benefactors/
The blessings of parasites." Such paradoxical images tell of primal forces locked
in struggle: "Hostage smiles on presidents/Freedom scribbled in the subway." The
poetic discourse climbs to a metaphysical plane, patterning the successive verses
around the figures of "devil," "god," and "man." At issue are "the everlasting laws/
Governing day and night": laws that dictate fundamental oppositions while con-
founding clear duality. Another oracular voice makes an appearance in "Don Juan's
Reckless Daughter" (*DJRD*), this time borrowed from Native American shamanistic teachings:

> Out on the vast and subtle plains of mystery
> A split tongued spirit talks
> [...]
> And he says:
> "Snakes along the railroad tracks"
> He says, "Eagles in jet trails ...
> Coils around the feathers and talons on scales ..."

Mitchell's attraction to mystic personae is evident as well in her late-period adaptations of classic visionary poems by W. B. Yeats ("Slouching towards Bethlehem"
[*NRH*]) and William Blake ("Taming the Tiger" [*TT*]).

The Torch Carrier

Mitchell's work is filled with love songs of various kinds. These include love-
in-the-bud ("Tin Angel" [*C*], "Help Me" [*C&S*]), the idyll ("Morning Morgantown"
[*LC*], "My Old Man" [*B*]), furtive love ("Conversation," "The Priest" [both *LC*]),
spats ("Don't Interrupt the Sorrow" [*HSL*], "Off Night Backstreet" [*DJRD*]),
the song that cuts the lover down to size ("The Gallery" [*C*], "Woman of Heart
and Mind" [*FR*]), and the philosophical meditation on love ("Both Sides, Now"
[*C*], "Sweet Sucker Dance" [*M*], "Be Cool" [*WTRF*]). One special kind, the torch
song, pours out sadness over lost or unrequited love. The torch persona is wholly

absorbed in her grief and desire, which push her to extravagant declarations of chagrin (as in "River" [*B*]: "Oh I wish I had a river/I could skate away on") and abasement (as in "Blue Boy" [*LC*]: "Like a pilgrim she traveled/To place her flowers/Before his granite grace/And she prayed aloud for love/To waken in his face"). But she's still not over it, and her affirmations of love are just as extravagant. Here is the first verse of "Willy" (*LC*):

Willy is my child, he is my father
I would be his lady all my life
He says he'd love to live with me
But for an ancient injury
That has not healed
He said I feel once again
Like I gave my heart too soon
He stood looking through the lace
At the face of the conquered moon
And counting all the cars up the hill
And the stars on my window sill
There are still more reasons why
I love him

It's not enough to say "Willy is my lover"; her love is too hungry for more powerful expressions and plants him in every possible position above her, beneath her, as if he formed her entire family and provided her every need. But Willy is not as wholehearted as she is. The image of the "conquered moon" is extremely bittersweet, bringing up age-old romantic associations (where she is the one "conquered" by love), while souring them by implied reference to the moon landing (where the romantic mystique of the moon has been exposed and violated by cold science). The phrase "conquered moon" echoes the earlier "ancient injury," both evoking the idea of a damaged love played out over a vast canvas. But the speaker's words after this traumatic central passage show that she has not really been listening; she has been "counting all the cars," optimistically tallying her love (while absorbing and transforming the syllables of "conquered"). Again she insists on the inadequacy of words to express her feelings ("There are still more reasons"), and the ultimate rhyme on "still" shows she has not given up hope. It all comes down to the unadorned essential statement ("I love him"), standing outside the rhyme scheme and unaltered by any setbacks.

"A Case of You" (*B*), set in a dimly lit bar, proclaims itself a torch song right away ("Just before our love got lost ..."). But—no surprise—the chorus reveals that the speaker is still under the influence:

Oh, you are in my blood like holy wine
You taste so bitter and so sweet
Oh I could drink a case of you, darling
And I would still be on my feet

The idea of confessional outpouring, key to the genre, is thematized in the song: "part of you pours out of me/In these lines from time to time." "These lines" refer to the song's poetic/melodic lines, of course, as the speaker is writing or performing them. But they also encompass the graphic lines of her visual art, since she identifies strongly as an artist in this poem (sketching her lover's face in verse 1, introducing herself as "a lonely painter" in verse 2). What is being poured out is thus her unrequited emotion as well as its embodiment in art and alcohol. In fact, one of the beautiful things about this poem is how a handful of vivid images bleed and flow into one another. In verse 3, the outpouring comes from a wound ("Go to him, stay with him if you can/But be prepared to bleed"); this bleeding then flows right into the dizzy blood of the chorus. Love figures in metaphors of bleeding and tasting; but in proximity to the visual art imagery, it is refigured as "drawing" ("I'm drawn to those ones that ain't afraid"). Meanwhile, the paint-box resonates with the liquor case and the TV screen in a motif of feeling boxed-in ("I live in a box of paints"), for which the antidote is the outpouring of the soul.

As a final example of the genre, I'll mention the lovely "Blue Motel Room" (*H*), which handles the torch persona with lightness and wit. Mitchell finds unexpected humor in the self-absorbed conventions of the torch song:

I've got a blue motel room
With a blue bedspread
I've got the blues inside and outside my head
Will you still love me
When I call you up when I'm down

The hopeful word "still" is pivotal here, as in the other examples. But the obsessive mirroring of an internal melancholy is portrayed in this case as slightly ridiculous, given the humble setting and the overdone color scheme. And in the last line, love's tumultuous highs and lows are reduced to a comical seesaw of "up" and "down."

The Free Spirit

Of primary significance in Mitchell's work are the many personae who chafe at being tied down. They speak to a wide field of potential restraints on one's freedom, including monogamy, restrictive social roles, and pressure to settle down in one place. (The overarching theme of freedom will be explored in much more detail in chapter 4.) One common expression of personal freedom is the simple pleasure of relaxing and going out on the town, as in "Carey" (*B*):

> Come on down to the Mermaid Café and I will buy you a bottle of wine
> And we'll laugh and toast to nothing and smash our empty glasses down

The spirit of uninhibited revelry is often linked to dance music, as in "Let the Wind Carry Me" (*FR*): "staying up late/In my high-heeled shoes/Living for that Rock 'n' Roll dancing scene"; or "Cotton Avenue" (*DJRD*): "Poor boys'll be hanging around outside in the street/They got all the latest words/They're dancing to the latest beat/While they're hustling and sizing you/On Cotton Avenue." The liberatory ethos of rock is the theme of "In France They Kiss on Main Street" (*HSL*). All three verses are dedicated to the excitement of the downtown strip, with its dance halls, pinball arcade, and sexual possibility ("Young love was kissing under bridges/Kissing in cars, kissing in cafés"). But though most of the poem riffs on pleasures of the moment ("I'd be kissing in the back street/Thrilling to the Brando-like things that he said"), along the way it articulates a critique of suburban values, as conformist and inimical to the vitality of rock:

> And I told him "They don't take chances
> And they seem so removed from romance"
> "They've been broken in churches and schools
> And molded to middle-class circumstance"
> And we were rolling, rolling, rock 'n' rolling

Besides the carousal song, another common expression of the free-spirit persona is the "rolling stone" or rambler song. Though before Mitchell's time it was typically a male preserve, she takes to this genre wholeheartedly, again and again extolling the mystique of rootlessness. Here are examples from three adjacent songs on *For the Roses*: "And you want to get moving/And you want to stay still" ("Barangrill"); "I know my needs/My sweet tumbleweed" ("Lesson in Survival"); "I'm a wild seed again/Let the wind carry me" ("Let the Wind Carry Me"). As in the male-authored version of the genre, the urge to ramble can get in the way of romantic commitment. This dilemma is the burden of the early song "Cactus Tree" (*SS*):

> She will love them when she sees them
> They will lose her if they follow
> And she only means to please them
> And her heart is full and hollow

Like a cactus tree
While she's so busy being free

The carousal song typically expresses joy in friendly company, while the lonely pleasures of the rambling song are often tinged with melancholy, as in "California" (*B*) or "Hejira" (*H*). There is plenty of time for lyrical reflection, as in verse 3 of "Hejira," which returns to the conflicted question of settling down:

We're only particles of change, I know, I know
Orbiting around the sun
But how can I have that point of view
When I'm always bound and tied to someone
White flags of winter chimneys
Waving truce against the moon
In the mirrors of a modern bank
From the window of a hotel room

Note how the last quatrain of the verse veers off at a tangent, as if the self-scrutiny and logically constructed argument of the previous lines has suddenly become too much, motivating an escape into purely visual images. At first the pictures have no clear angle of reference to the speaking subject, who seems to have disappeared from the discourse, relentlessly first-person until now. But as the images are traced to their origin we come back to the speaker's subjective location. The first person remains unvoiced at the end, however. We could interpret this striking discursive shift as an escape from active deliberation into passive perceptions—except that the image sequence turns out to be a neat illustration of the present mental quandary, expressed in a different medium (surrendering to romance [the moon] versus losing oneself in anonymous travelscapes). The final quatrain translates the verbal reflectiveness of the previous sentences into spatial reflection, as the image of snow-clad chimneys is reframed by the opaque glass panels of the bank, and then again by the transparent hotel window. This double filtering imposes layers of separation between the lyric speaker and the open vistas she takes as her backdrop, while the precisely composed succession of images sets up a chain of symbolic associations concerning the snug and the chilly, the mobile and the frozen, the eternal and the transitory.

The Critic

My final example of a recurrent persona is the critical observer. At various times, such a persona will train an analytic eye on a romantic partner, a third-person character, or the speaker herself. The critical persona in the romantic context makes for a rather cerebral kind of love song, as in "Strange Boy" (*H*):

> What a strange, strange boy
> He still lives with his family
> Even the war and the navy
> Couldn't bring him to maturity

Nor does the speaker hold back or mute her judgments, even when they cut to the bone, as in "Woman of Heart and Mind" (*FR*):

> I am a woman of heart and mind
> With time on her hands
> No child to raise
> You come to me like a little boy
> And I give you my scorn and my praise

We have already sampled the continuation of this song above, as an illustration of blunt, scathing diction. (Such a scathing second-person address brings to mind the similar persona well explored by Bob Dylan in songs like "Positively 4th Street" and "Like a Rolling Stone.")

Other songs employ caustic observation in the service of third-person vignettes. "Otis and Marlena" (*DJRD*) is a contemptuous send-up of Miami resort culture and the foibles of the idle rich. Marlena, the focal character, is portrayed as vacuous and bloodless ("white as stretcher sheet"), a specter amid the tanned, enhanced bodies at her hotel. Bored, she looks down at the pool, whose denizens are described in terms of circus performers and frying meat:

> She taps her glass with an emery file
> Watching three rings in the sun
> The golden dive, the fatted flake
> And sizzle in their mink oil
> It's all a dream
> She has awake
> Checked into Miami Royal

Another such vignette is sketched in "Edith and the Kingpin" (*HSL*). A powerful man makes an official visit to a small town; the pageantry that greets him on his arrival is belittled as "Sophomore jive/From victims of typewriters." His eyes light on Edith; the girls he has overlooked retaliate by attempting to undermine her confidence and filling her ears with venomous gossip:

One by one they bring
His renegade stories to her
His crimes and his glories to her
In challenge they look on
Women he has taken grow old too soon
He tilts their tired faces
Gently to the spoon

In the end, Edith finds herself in his bed. But instead of being dominated or used up, she discovers an inner affinity with her unscrupulous, dangerous new lover: "She says—his crime belongs." The final image pits the two in a deadlock of mutual respect and mistrust, like vipers at bay:

Edith and the Kingpin
Each with charm to sway
Are staring eye to eye
They dare not look away

Mitchell's poetic speakers are by no means immune from self-scrutiny. The penchant for critical examination of one's own motives, shortcomings and inner conflicts is a defining trait of her lyric poetry. It haunts the disillusioned speaker in "Both Sides, Now" (*C*):

But now it's just another show
You leave 'em laughing when you go
And if you care, don't let them know
Don't give yourself away

It worries the torch singer in "River" (*B*): "I'm so hard to handle/I'm selfish and I'm sad/Now I've gone and lost the best baby/That I ever had." (Note that more than one persona type can figure in a single song—here, torch and critic.) Even when autobiographical, her judgments can be stingingly harsh, as in "People's Parties" (*C&S*): "I'm just living on nerves and feelings/With a weak and lazy mind/And coming to people's parties/Fumbling deaf dumb and blind." In fact, the airing of unflattering imperfections acts as a stamp of authenticity in the confessional genre.

But the self-critical persona is not limited to raw exposure; it can also develop structures of great elegance. "Song for Sharon" (*H*), an imaginary conversation with a childhood friend, is one such poem. Given its length (ten verses), my discussion here will be very selective (further discussion of the song will be found in chapter 7). The poem is populated with many characters and shuttles back and forth in time and place. But the central thread is the deep-seated yearning for love, especially as glamorized in the image of the new bride:

> When we were kids in Maidstone, Sharon
> I went to every wedding in that little town
> To see the tears and the kisses
> And the pretty lady in the white wedding gown
> And walking home on the railroad tracks
> Or swinging on the playground swing
> Love stimulated my illusions
> More than anything

Here in verse 7, the speaker delves into her psychological history in a tone that is not at all distressed, but relaxed, clear, expansive, and mellifluous. The neuroses that surface elsewhere in the poem never disturb its beautiful surface, even when the speaker's penchant for self-examination is itself the object of criticism: "And the power of reason/And the flowers of deep feelings/Seem to serve me/Only to deceive me" (verse 9). In the final verse, she comes to a kind of closure by weighing the sacrifices she and her friend have made against the very different lives each has built:

> Sharon you've got a husband
> And a family and a farm
> I've got the apple of temptation
> And a diamond snake around my arm
> But you still have your music
> And I've still got my eyes on the land and the sky
> You sing for your friends and family
> I'll walk green pastures by and by

The couplets proceed in a series of regular, parallel exchanges ("you" then "I"), but the psychological undercurrents are convoluted. The first line has the impact of revealing belatedly that Sharon is happily settled down, thus suggesting a subtext of marriage envy motivating the entire poem. The speaker (Joni) is highly critical and ironic about her own situation and accomplishments while apparently offering consolation to Sharon (implying that Sharon suffers from a corresponding career envy). The ostensible linguistic parallels are not really symmetrical: the two "stills" in mid-verse have very different connotations. In Sharon's case, she "still has" a bird in the hand, a musical talent she can call on for her own and her family's enjoyment. Joni, however, has two in the bush—she's "still got" unfulfilled desires for happiness and a patch of land. Sharon's attributes are present tense and rooted in space ("still"), while Joni's are in motion and wishfully future tense.

Mitchell creates an equally expansive seven-verse structure in "Amelia" (*H*). This poem is especially remarkable for its multifaceted voice that elegantly harmonizes a spectrum of personae all central to Mitchell's work: the traveler ("I was driving across the burning desert"), the torch carrier ("I wish that he was here tonight"), the mystic ("Like Icarus ascending/On beautiful foolish arms"), the artist ("It was the strings of my guitar"), and the critic turned inward ("Maybe I've never really loved").

There is a story Joni Mitchell has told numerous times and with different nuances, about the origins of her own voice as a singer-songwriter, in which she credits the electrifying influence of Bob Dylan:

> I wrote poetry, and I had always wanted to make music. But I *never* put the two things together. Just a simple thing like being a singer-songwriter— that was a new idea. It used to take three people to do that job. And when I heard "Positively Fourth Street," I realized that this was a whole new ballgame; now you could make your songs literature. The potential for the song had never occurred to me—I loved "Tutti-Frutti," you know. But it occurred to Dylan.[26]

We know from Mitchell's subsequent career that this early conversion experience did not cancel out her love of rock 'n' roll. The Dylanesque model of serious poetic ambition merely took its place alongside the Little Richard model, in an expanded understanding of what words in pop songs can accomplish. In another retelling of her first encounter with the seminal Dylan song, she includes specific details about technique: "When I heard that—'You got a lotta nerve to say you are my friend'—I thought, now that's poetry; now we're talking. That direct, confronting speech, commingled with imagery, was what was lacking for me."[27] It is certainly telling that the galvanic spark, as she describes it, is delivered by way of a vivid scenario of direct speech, a haughty, critical persona, and a caustic voice. The literary potential of songwriting was opened up for Mitchell when she glimpsed the versatility and power of all those vocal presences yet to be created. Now we're talking.

4

THEMATIC THREADS

One reason Joni Mitchell's body of songs deserves to be regarded as a coherent oeuvre rather than a miscellany of occasional pieces has to do with the musico-poetic themes running through her work in extended threads of correlation and reflection. Counted among her favored themes are substantial matters that have not ceased to occupy poets of every rank and generation: the untamable currents of love, the cost of personal independence, the stern vows of an artistic calling, spiritual perplexity, the journey quest, the terms of interracial conversation, and the charting of a mythic homeland. Characteristic of her poetic gift is the ability to couple personal incident with general human concerns in tones that blend playfulness with intellectual density.

To give a sense of the depth and texture of Mitchell's thought, I have chosen to explore a specific thematic strand—personal freedom—as she develops its ethical implications in diverse symbolic and poetic registers. The word "free" and its cognates flash forth at prominent moments in her songs like a golden thread catching the light: "She's so busy being free," "He was playing real good, for free," "Try and get my soul free," "I was a free man in Paris," "Freedom scribbled in the subway," "A prisoner of the white lines on the freeway." Together with related chains highlighting words like "wild," "dance," and "dream," such occurrences form a highly visible set of verbal motifs spanning her entire career. As further evidence of the absolutely central importance of the theme, one can note how Mitchell frames her first album, *Song to a Seagull*, with two songs devoted to the question of personal freedom. The opening song, "I Had a King," relates the protagonist's escape from a suffocating marriage; the closing song, "Cactus Tree," evokes the more spacious horizons, as well as the emotional costs, of her ongoing quest. The two scenarios stand for the two poles she is compelled to negotiate in her search for self-fulfillment: the perils of domesticity and the perils of rootlessness. By countering the irresistible, open-ended urge for independence with a difficult, unresolved yearning for love, Mitchell sets up a lasting internal controversy at the core of her musical expression.

To tease out the different tributaries of this grand theme, I will consider specific examples under the following topics: cautionary tales of confinement, chronicles of the ongoing quest, declarations of social nonconformity, invocations of creative license, and visions of spiritual liberation. Mitchell introduces all five of these topics on her first album.

TRAPS

We have already considered "I Had a King" in some detail in chapter 2. There I pointed out how the song's central idea of refusing to be trapped was dramatized musically, in scenarios of rhythmic constraint, melodic entanglement and release, and harmonic suspension. In chapter 5 I will emphasize the role of the double pedal point (lower tonic pedal, upper dominant pedal) in creating an especially constrained voice-leading situation. Here I will expand on significant details relating to the theme at hand and broaden the context for the song's configuration of symbols in connection with other songs from the first period.

The specific trap described in "I Had a King" is a bad marriage. The husband is (indirectly) portrayed as an artist—or perhaps it would be better to say that his social character is represented through aesthetic activities (painting, acting, singing). But in every case his form of expression is depicted as ugly, mean, or false. His perversion of the aesthetic impulse, or the speaker's failure to respond to him in such terms, is a strong sign of the death of love. (The following song on the album, "Michael from Mountains," provides a counterexample: when the protagonist is with Michael, every ordinary scene takes on the bright artifice of paintings or puppet shows; even the film of oil in rain gutters shows "taffeta patterns," magically rearranged at Michael's touch.) Mitchell expresses the sense of confinement not only through imagery (empty rooms, the enclosing grove) but through form and representation. The poem continually stages an ill fit between mythic and realistic representation, with material from postindustrial life ("drip-dry," "salt-rusted") showing through the threadbare medieval trappings and exposing their aura of fantasy as inadequate. Furthermore, the poem opens with a structural ill fit: the second line overshoots the expected rhyme on "pastel" to introduce a new end rhyme on "brown." This trick with the rhyme scheme conveys the speaker's disillusionment by embedding an initial rhyme pair ("castle/pastel") from the realm of romantic fantasy within an ultimate pair ("brown/down") that contradicts those conventions. (Similarly, in verse 3, the initial pair "carriage/marriage" is rebuffed by "too soon.")

In verse 2, the emphasis is on the ill fit of an antiquated gender role.

> He lives in another time
> Ladies in gingham still blush
> While he sings them of wars and wine
> But I in my leather and lace
> I can never become that kind

The putative king despises his freethinking queen, preferring the role of unquestioned hero. The "gingham" suggests a reduced female position (lower than royalty), as in the accepted image of the demure unassuming housewife. In contrast, the speaker's "leather and lace" is shorthand for a sense of experimentation in women's roles, in search of a personal style in which toughness and tenderness can coexist. Right from the start of the poem, the speaker signals her unease with the role of romantic "lady" in her unconventional locution: "I had a king." Given the connotations of monarchic privilege, we would expect a more submissive turn of phrase: "I was wed to a king," or "A king took me as his lady." But here, the speaker claims the role of lyric subject for herself, shouldering the king into the object position. The clash between the poem's competing subjects is only resolved in the chorus, when she repudiates the man and asserts her own agency ("I can't go back there anymore").

In other songs of the period, Mitchell continues to treat the archaic image of the "lady" as a tempting but dangerous myth. The male romantic lead in "The Gallery" (C) is another artist figure. At first, the female speaker admires his portraits of "ladies," but the mystique palls as she is reduced to a domestic role, dusting and keeping house. As in "I Had a King," the speaker chafes at being "left to winter here," while her lover is free to travel. His attempts to maintain power over her are baited with the empty title of "Lady." The speaker's ambivalence about the mystique of sentimental fantasy does not result in as strong a critique as we saw in the previous poem. The archaic language is less assuredly undermined; the woman herself is compromised in choosing to stay and wait for her man. But she does effect a stinging reversal in the third chorus when she turns his own words against him, asserting the hitherto masculine right to withhold or grant her favor (see the discussion under "The Ingenue" in chapter 3).

The song "Blue Boy" (LC) enacts a similar drama of entrapment, but in this case the outcome is wholly pessimistic.

> Lady called the blue boy, love,
> She took him home
> Made himself an idol, yes,
> So he turned to stone

Like a pilgrim she traveled
To place her flowers
Before his granite grace
And she prayed aloud for love
To waken in his face

The title character's assumed name wraps him in mystery; part of his allure derives from his arrogance and insistence on remaining free of emotional involvement. Another figure of perverted artistry, the blue boy sets himself up as a statue to which the poem's "lady" must pay homage. The mythic background here is the story of Pygmalion and Galatea (a statue brought to life).[1] But where the ancient tale depicts the consummatory desire of a male artist for his female creation, here the trajectory is reversed: a living woman bears responsibility for her own undoing as an animate subject ("He will come few times more/Till he finds a lady statue/Standing in a door"). The potential symbols of organic nurture ("her flowers," "his seed," "her garden") are negated by the prevailing image of petrification. The place of domestic comfort (portrayed lovingly in "Sisotowbell Lane" [SS] and "Ladies of the Canyon" [LC]) is turned into a confining space out of which the lady is caught gazing at the window or door. Her chance for "travel" is restricted to a pilgrimage of abasement. Her attempts at freedom of personal expression ("boots of leather," "feather fan") never go beneath outer layers and in any case are entirely channeled into her single consuming devotion. Given this scenario, the syntax of the third-person focal character takes on a pointed significance, reflecting the lady's utter surrender of identity to the point that she is unable to take charge of her own lyric utterance. Mitchell's cathartic performance stands in for the lady's voice, groveling without shame and holding back nothing for herself. Another factor adding to the song's overpowering melancholy is its indefinite arrangement of tonal space. The verse begins with a clear sense of "home" in C major (Ex. 4.1). From that bright beginning the harmonies move through a range of darker shades, most phrases coming to rest on G major. But is this recurring cadence point open or closed? Mitchell uses chord successions that lack strong hierarchical function; both C and G exert (fairly weak) gravitational force. Somewhere around the midpoint of the verse (with the swerve to the B♭ chord) the clear sense of a C major home is lost. Harmonies continue to change as if they are going somewhere, but they always return to the same ambivalent place.

"Blue Boy" fearfully imagines a character who never breaks free, indeed who doesn't even fight against her imposed limits. Mitchell's trapped characters are not always women: the man in "Conversation" (LC) is stuck in a bad relationship; the men in "The Arrangement" (LC), "The Last Time I Saw Richard" (B), and "Harry's House" (HSL) are caught in empty cycles of middle-class consumerism.

EXAMPLE 4.1. "BLUE BOY," CHORD CHANGES

Intro:		Dm	C	Am	G	G	
Phrase 1:		C	Am	G	G		
Phrase 2:		C	Am	F	F		
Phrase 3:		Dm	E	Am	G	G	
Phrase 4:		B♭	Dm7	G	G		
Phrase 5:		Dm	C	Am	G	G	

Nor do the pitfalls for women invariably center on relationships: some, like the speaker in "The Last Time I Saw Richard," struggle against "dark cocoons" of inner confusion. But it is notable how in the earliest exemplars of this theme, hindrances to personal growth are manifest in terms of the social phenomenon of restrictive gender roles (housewife, nurturer, submissive partner). In formulating these cautionary tales, Mitchell was not openly advocating a feminist perspective, from which she has consistently distanced herself.[2] Nevertheless, she was articulating in her own medium the anxiety felt by many of her peers over the limitations placed on women's search for fulfillment, as Betty Friedan had begun to document in *The Feminine Mystique* a few years earlier. In particular, Friedan pointed to a strong retrenchment in the 1950s: "After 1949 ... the image of the American woman as a changing, growing individual in a changing world was shattered. Her solo flight to find her own identity was forgotten in the rush for the security of togetherness. Her limitless world shrunk to the cozy walls of home."[3] Mitchell herself has stated in reference to her song "Cactus Tree": "I feel that's the song of *modern* woman. Yes, it has to do with my experiences, but I know a lot of girls like that ... who find that the world is full of lovely men but they're driven by something else other than settling down to frau-duties."[4]

By the mid-1970s, however, Mitchell was capable of treating the theme with wry detachment. "The Hissing of Summer Lawns" (*HSL*, music by John Guerin) portrays a wife in a gilded cage.

> He put up a barbed wire fence
> To keep out the unknown
> And on every metal thorn
> Just a little blood of his own
> She patrols that fence of his
> To a Latin drum
> And the hissing of summer lawns

Her home in the hills, though ringed with barbed wire, has wider sightlines than the abject garden of "Blue Boy" ("She could see the valley barbecues/From her window sill"). Her confinement also comes with material consolations of a different order ("a diamond for her throat," "a roomful of Chippendale/That nobody sits in"). This lady is no ingenue but accepts her compromise with a cynical awareness ("Still she stays with a love of some kind/It's the lady's choice"). With its tropical sound world of buzzing flies, drumbeats, and hissing sprinklers, the poem depicts the upscale housewife in her natural setting as an outlandish tribal specimen, to be documented with anthropological composure.

In "Don't Interrupt the Sorrow," from the same album, the theme of female ensnarement prompts an angry stream of free association rather than a scenic vignette. The musical tone is remarkably light and conversational given the difficult and combative language; Mitchell's performance projects relaxed self-assurance as if taking it all in her stride. In this song we overhear an internal monologue composed of disconnected reactions to the peremptory remarks and veiled threats ("In flames our prophet witches/Be polite") of a faceless male speaker. The cubistic surface renders the sense obscure, but the man appears to be ordering the woman's compliance in a nurturing role ("Bring that bottle kindly") while forbidding dissent (be polite; don't interrupt the status quo; don't disturb the peace of "patriarchs/Snug in your bible belt dreams"). The female speaker, however, is up for a fight; the "room full of glasses" mentioned at the beginning sets the scene for a contest of wills. She lays bare the trap hidden in his words and beliefs ("he chains me with that serpent/To that Ethiopian wall"). She exposes his presumptuous idea of the natural order as nothing but a cycle of "sorrow" for women ("Death and birth and death and birth"). She decries the use of religion as a tool for brainwashing ("The good slaves love the good book"). In fact, the argument rages on an intensely intellectual plane, between competing theological fictions and their consequences for women's lives. In her view, he is playing dirty by using the old propaganda of the "serpent" and Eve's guilt to immobilize her. As an alternative, she upholds icons of matriarchal power: witch, goddess, and Madonna. (In this, Mitchell is atypically explicit in her appeal to imagery of collective female affirmation and resistance.) At first, the archetypes are taken from pagan traditions; in tune with this, background imagery in the first four verses cycles through the primal elements of flames, water, wind, and rock. The Virgin Mary, the last to appear, is a "clandestine" figure of matriarchal worship carried into the established Christian church; she appears as a secret symbol encoded in the bottles of "Rhine wine" (*Liebfraumilch* or "Milk of the Madonna") the man is drinking. The seventeen spent glasses also echo the woman's statement of defiance ("Since I was seventeen/I've had no one over me"), as if the years of her life might be distilled or poured out in service. The final verse when it arrives feels like something of a letdown. Instead of the anger she has been voicing, the woman seems to give ground by expressing compassion ("It takes a heart like

Mary's these days/When your man gets weak"), and it isn't clear whether she will follow through on her earlier promise to "leave on the 1:15." From another angle, however, the last verse supplies a final diminution in the stature of the male speaker. In his first entrance he appears as the mouthpiece for a terrifying oracle ("He says, 'Your notches liberation doll'"), incoherently fusing the idea of freedom with images of objectification and subjugation (as in being taken down a notch, or the "notch" as a mark of sexual conquest). His second speech is still obscure ("Anima rising—/So what—/Petrified wood process/Tall timber down to rock!"), but recognizable as a threat to subdue the woman's soul (using the images familiar from "Blue Boy" of animation vs. petrification). As the poem goes on, his statements become needy and even petulant ("We walked on the moon/You be polite"). Gradually he is humanized and belittled (and subdued by the wine's/ Madonna's influence) until his threat shrinks to nothing.

Later treatments of this theme can be briefly mentioned. "The Tea Leaf Prophecy" (*CMRS*), its central character caught in the routine of house and garden, was the focus of discussion in chapter 3. In her fourth period Mitchell returns several times ("Two Grey Rooms" [*NRH*], "Sunny Sunday," "The Magdalene Laundries" [both *TI*]) to melancholy portraits of characters who never leave, now no longer centered in the scenario of the heterosexual couple. A footnote: it is during this period that Mitchell begins to repeat a pertinent story about her ancestors. "My paternal grandmother came from Norway, and ... the last time she cried in her life she was 14, ... because she knew she would never have a piano. ... My maternal grandmother ... was a classical musician who came east when the Prairies opened up by train. She was Scottish-French, and they brought an organ in for her and a gramophone. She was a poet and musician, but she still kicked the kitchen door off its hinges out of her frustration at being trapped in the role of a housewife."[5] The story ends with Mitchell's assertion that having inherited "the creative gene" from her grandmothers, it was entrusted to her to pursue an artistic career for the sake of those women who never had the opportunity.

QUESTS

Mitchell's earliest period as a musician and songwriter coincided with a surge in popularity of the (medieval) genre of the quest romance, as retold for modern readers. Her familiarity with the great writers of fantasy, J. R. R. Tolkien and C. S. Lewis, is evident from scattered references in interviews. She named her first publishing company after Gandalf, the grey wizard of *The Lord of the Rings*.[6] Tolkien's saga had many things to recommend it to the idealistic youth of the 1960s, among them a veneration of nature and rural folkways (as in the pastoral Shire), a latent critique of industrialism (in the hell-realms of Mordor and Isengard, with their subterranean forges, slavery, and pollution), and an archetypal plot of simple folk caught up in grand deeds and epic adventure. The title of Mitchell's song "The Dawntreader" (*SS*) refers to one of the volumes (*The Voyage of the* Dawn Treader) from Lewis's children's series *The Chronicles of Narnia*, about a sea voyage in search of the islands of the "utter East." One of the characters from this book (Reepicheep the gallant mouse), not satisfied when the quest is achieved, is compelled to strike out even further into the unknown, leaving his companions behind.[7] A similar spirit of adventure is present in many of the British Isle ballads from the folksingers' repertory, about travelers who sail the high seas, bid farewell to tender maidens, or return to them after many a day. These evocative tropes are carried over into folk rock and singer-songwriter genres. David Crosby's song "Guinnevere," for instance, is redolent of Arthurian legend, with its golden-haired sorceress in her garden and the male hero making a temporary landing ("the harbor where I lay, anchored for a day") on his ongoing voyage. Crosby's reference to the world of legend is dreamlike and atmospheric, distilling the quest-plot into an unspecified romantic yearning ("We shall be free").[8]

Typically in such tales, it is the woman who is left behind; Mitchell writes her own version of the well-known scene in songs such as "Urge for Going" (*Hits*), "The Pirate of Penance" (*SS*), and "The Gallery" (*C*). In "Cactus Tree," however, she alters the mythology of the ballads to fit her concept of a new kind of heroine. The song begins like one more adventure tale from the man's perspective—a man who has been sailing to far-off places "in a decade full of dreams." He invites a lady onto his schooner and presents her with jewels. But all of a sudden she is no longer to be found on the ship: "He has heard her off to starboard/In the breaking and the breathing/Of the water weeds." Not content with secondhand exploits, she has gone off on her own expedition, slipping into the water like a mermaid or selkie. Though the sailor is portrayed in the most glamorous terms, the refrain reveals that the lady is the true figure of glamour and mystery in this song; it is she who leaves men behind. (And the phrase structure [see chapter 6 and Ex. 6.12] confirms the status of the refrain, with its focus on the female subject, as the clinching idea to which the preceding lines inevitably move.) For most of the poem she remains an offstage presence, provoking a wry comment from the narrator ("she's so busy") about the elusiveness of her quest.

In succeeding verses there follows a list of the men she has loved from all walks of life, who profess their constant love for her and wait for her reply. While their accomplishments are spelled out (mountain climbing, financial success, military decoration), the woman's search is left tantalizingly vague, though the array of suitors in their variety and geographical spread does imply a future of equally bountiful possibility. Such a wide-eyed view of life (echoed in the effusive density of the album's cover art) is characteristic of an ingenue, in this case presented in archetypal rather than personalized terms. Correspondingly, Mitchell's vocal delivery is uniformly round and resonant, in line with the tone of bardic romance. A stronger touch of irony begins to emerge, however, in the fourth verse, where we learn that "She has brought them to her senses." Mitchell's twist on the common figure of speech underscores the primacy of the heroine's perspective but in a way that goes too far, suggesting the demands of an immoderate ego. Likewise, the revelation of her amoral code in the fifth verse ("She will love them when she sees them/They will lose her if they follow/And she only means to please them") is scandalous in its divergence from the constant maiden role of the ballad tradition. Instead, she evokes the heartless queen (from troubadour verse) in a particularly forbidding form ("And her heart is full and hollow/Like a cactus tree"). The sweeping melodic design is built around important gestures of elation (in the second [b] and penultimate [e] phrases; see Ex. 6.12) where the contour reaches its high point as the tonic pedal is released (more on pedal points in chapter 5). But it also incorporates wistful valedictory gestures in its repeated subdominant-tonic cadences (especially in the d phrases). That is to say, the song's persona admits to a certain melancholy as she bids her farewells; she "seems to know that she is giving up something important in exchange for this freedom."[9]

As time goes on, Mitchell exchanges this tone of romanticized myth for more realistic representation: the indistinct "schooners" and "galleons" of the first album are traded in for "the thumb and the satchel," "whitewalls and windshields" ("Barangrill" [FR]), "railroad cars," and "crowded waiting rooms" ("Just Like This Train" [C&S]). Nevertheless, vestiges of myth persist in the retelling. "Barangrill" is set in a truck stop where the (second-person) narrator is taking a break for coffee.

> Three waitresses all wearing
> Black diamond earrings
> Talking about zombies
> And Singapore slings
> No trouble in their faces
> Not one anxious voice
> None of the crazy you get
> From too much choice
> The thumb and the satchel
> Or the rented Rolls-Royce
> And you think she knows something
> By the second refill
> You think she's enlightened

As she totals your bill
You say "Show me the way
To Barangrill"

The narrator's internal monologue betrays the unease of an ongoing search for enlightenment. Under this inner pressure, her homely surroundings take on subliminal undertones of romanticized adventure. Chitchat about drink orders ("zombies and Singapore slings") conjures up the atmosphere of exotic outposts. The sparkle of "black diamond earrings" recalls the ocean treasure of the earlier mythology ("amber stones and green"). The trio of waitresses in their relaxed camaraderie begin to appear as numinous figures of wisdom the narrator can appeal to for guidance. In its tone the song skillfully combines seriousness and humor. The speaker's coined word for paradise pokes fun at her own overexcited attempts to find Shangri-la in a cheap restaurant. Furthermore, the rhymes leading up to her imaginary utopia ironically call attention to the mundane activities going on around her ("refill," "bill," "till").

On the other hand, her spiritual distress is taken seriously, as a search for fulfillment or peace of mind made difficult in a secular context with a lack of guideposts. The open-endedness portrayed in earlier songs as romantic possibility is now cause for confusion—a kind of craziness due to "too much choice." (In a similar way, the speaker in "Just Like This Train" complains of the craziness that comes when "you can't find your goodness.") Her constant inner pilgrimage sets the narrator apart from ordinary people. It signifies a special personal striving; but it also keeps her wrapped up in her own head (as underscored by the second-person subject syntax). A provisional answer to her open question comes serendipitously, through her encounter with a charismatic gas station attendant, whose spontaneity enables her to forget her self-consciousness and become "lost in the moment." The serious character of the narrator's "longing" is captured musically through a salient harmonic shading. Each time the IV chord appears (A♭m9 in the key of E♭), it borrows a minor-mode quality. At first the special poignancy of this chord is transitory (less than a full measure, e.g.: "Talking about zombies"), like a brief twinge of the heart. Then, in the second half of the verse, the harmony's strong sequential movement (up by fifths: B♭m7–Fm7–Cm7–Gm7) is suddenly arrested by the same A♭m9 chord ("Show me the *way*"; Ex. 4.2). Mitchell lingers on this piercing moment, sustaining a high dissonant note with a breathy, vulnerable voice. The asymmetry of the closing phrase (half as long as the other three phrases) means that its closure feels fragile. Meanwhile, amid the overall tone of light self-mockery, Mitchell highlights the moment of longing with the song's most salient rhetorical gesture.

By making comparisons between songs, one can discern a cluster of semantic elements that recur in connection with the theme of the quest as Mitchell

EXAMPLE 4.2. "BARANGRILL," SECOND HALF OF VERSE
(HARMONIC REDUCTION)

explores it. These include the iconography of vehicles and way stations, place names and itineraries, and the promise of treasure or loot. The open-endedness of the search is often connoted by key words like "somewhere" ("Treasure somewhere in the sea" ["The Dawntreader" (*SS*)]; "Looking for something, what can it be" ["All I Want" (*B*)]). Emotional states are also important, especially the urge or longing for adventure ("I'm porous with travel fever" ["Hejira" (*H*)]), and the mental distraction arising from intense searching ("They'll say that you're crazy" ["The Dawntreader"]). Finally, the searcher is sometimes marked as a breed apart through a symbolic totem ("a diamond snake around my arm" ["Song for Sharon" (*H*)]) or corporeal transformation (into a mermaid, cactus, or "black crow," for instance). This semantic cluster will be useful when we turn our attention to the album *Hejira* and its unifying theme of travel in chapter 7. For now, I will point out some of the recurring elements as they figure in one song from that album, "Song for Sharon."

This song takes the form of an autobiographical conversation with a childhood friend. Mitchell is writing from New York City, and her wandering train of thought crisscrosses various locales in its dense geography (the Staten Island ferry, Greenwich Village, Central Park), while also opening out to wider points of reference from her travels ("a bridge up in Canada," "a North Dakota junction"—where she left her man behind). Looking back on her small-town childhood ("Walking home on the railroad tracks"), it seems that she was already destined for a life of exploration. The treasure at the end of the search is variously expressed as the "bells and lace" of a fairy-tale wedding; the semi-exotic mandolin (requiring a special harbor excursion); the pot of winnings at Bingo (impulsive small-time gambles echoing the larger ones); the jewelled snake bracelet; and the imagined "green pastures" of a settled homestead. Thus love, art, riches, danger, and security all compete for her attention as she "chases" her dreams. There is no guaranteed source of wisdom to appeal to for help in sorting such things out. She sends up a prayer to "Miss Liberty," consults a gypsy fortune-teller, and listens to friends' advice about having children or pursuing "noble causes." Yet, she concludes, we all live close to the line of despair "and so far from satisfaction." In contrast to the words of the ingenue just setting out on her journey, this song conveys the perspective of a seasoned pilgrim, taking stock of her journey so far.

In several ways this missive can be read as a reflection of its times. In respect to the particular concerns of North American women, given their greater ability to forgo the roles of housewife and mother, it represents an adjustment to alternative identities as well as an attempt at reconciling old and new values. In respect to the hippie generation post-Woodstock and post-Vietnam, it reflects a widespread transition from modes of fulfillment through collective political action (the "wide wide world of noble causes") to individually based, introspective modes of self-realization. (Historian Edward D. Berkowitz speaks of "the rush to join self-help and human-potential movements, such things as psychotherapy, existential philosophy, Scientology, and EST, which asked people to expend energy on themselves rather than on one another.")[10] Finally, however, Mitchell's long letter expresses dissatisfaction with this very trend. In the wake of "the dream's malfunction" (i.e., the failure of idealistic hopes for social change), her personal dreams haven't brought her any closer to satisfaction, remaining compulsive and sporadic ("a repetitious danger"). All her intense self-exploration ("the power of reason/And the flowers of deep feelings") has proven to be a poor antidote against emptiness ("a blank face at the window stares and stares and stares and stares"). Insofar as Mitchell represents the inadequacy of the inner quest and shows how it can easily deteriorate into shallow self-interest ("all I really want to do, right now/Is ... find another lover!"), her writing on *Hejira* carries an implicit critique of her own self-absorption. (Around the same time, some influential social commentators were publishing critiques of what they perceived as a social trend toward self-absorption—labeled "The Me Decade" by journalist Tom Wolfe and "the culture of narcissism" by historian Christopher Lasch.)[11]

At first glance, the song "Night Ride Home," a summer holiday nocturne, may not seem to have strong connections to the present theme. Its narrator is not earnestly striving but romantically settled and relaxing away from work. I include the song here for its retrospective echoes of quest imagery from the viewpoint of someone who has achieved some of her desired goals. The song's characters are living or vacationing on Hawaii—portrayed as modernized though still retaining the quality of a remote destination. At the moment, they are traveling—not setting out but heading home. The beach is peopled with local merrymakers ("hula girls," "the ukulele man"). Power lines throw off a gleam of silver. Suddenly a "big dark horse" looms out of the night, running alongside the car like a wild spirit of nature. These are familiar symbols of adventure, but the mood is not prospective or open-ended. The narrator is focused on the here and now: instead of "somewhere" she speaks of "the man beside me," instead of "by and by" she speaks of "a night like this." Like the pilgrim in "Barangrill," the narrator in "Night Ride Home" is lost in the moment as an elusive longing is fulfilled. Moonbeams and headlight beams combine with fireworks in an intricate light show; hula girls dance whimsically with "caterpillar tractors"; the pert sound of crickets marks time alongside voice and guitar. The temporary paradise in this song is an unlooked-for experience of wonder as the worlds of nature and man are harmonized by an unseen choreographer.

BOHEMIA

On the other side of the spectrum from the men trapped in middle-class circumstance are a series of rebel characters that turn up in Mitchell's work as tempters and charmers. The first one to appear is the carnival drifter in "That Song about the Midway" (C), gambling and playing guitar "like a devil wearing wings." There is the sidewalk busker in "Court and Spark" (C&S), coming to the door "with a sleeping roll/And a madman's soul." There are the rock 'n' roll rebels, like Lead Foot Melvin ("In France They Kiss on Main Street" [HSL]) and Rowdy Yates ("Dancin' Clown" [CMRS]). The title character in "Carey" (B) is a cook Mitchell met on a visit to the village of Matala, a hippie hangout on the isle of Crete. He is a "mean old Daddy" and a "bright red devil" who does the "goat dance" very well (he also appears in the song "California"). His diabolical aura is embellished with fire and brimstone in Mitchell's story of her first glimpse of the man, when his gas stove accidentally exploded. *"Kaboom!* I heard, facing the sunset. I turned around and this guy is blowing out the door of this restaurant.... Burned all the red hair off himself right through his white Indian turban."[12]

Such characters embody the attraction of a lifestyle unencumbered by routine or the pressure to conform. The life on Crete, for instance, is easygoing and out of the way. Caves provide natural shelter. One is thrown together with assorted colorful companions ("freaks" and "soldiers") at the local watering hole. Impulse reigns. The music in "Carey" is full of irrepressible energy, expressed in the continuous bouncing dulcimer pedal and the tune that springs up from its lowest to its highest point in a single leap. In the chorus, Mitchell and her friend dress up like roadside royalty for their night out ("Come on, Carey, get out your cane"). The village community allows for a relaxation of social conventions as well as a pocket of alternative culture where one can freely play with the symbols of status that prevail on the mainland. As in other bohemian enclaves, the values are anti-bourgeois, flying in the face of repressive morals and materialist motives. One's liberation from so-called productive society is expressed in dionysian gestures ("Come on down to the Mermaid Café and I will buy you a bottle of wine/ And we'll laugh and toast to nothing and smash our empty glasses down").[13] Significantly, however, Mitchell is careful to emphasize that she is just passing through ("it's really not my home"). Even in this bunch of nonconformers she is unwilling to say that she belongs, so strong is her need to assert a distinct personal identity. Specifically, she wants to be able to encompass the full range of lifestyle expression, moving freely between vagabond slumming and the luxury comforts her earnings make possible ("I miss my clean white linen and my fancy French cologne").[14] Once again, the mermaid (as in the "Mermaid Café") comes in handy as a symbol of her amphibious nature.

Some comments from a 1994 interview are highly illuminating. To the question, "You were never really a hippy, were you?" Mitchell responds:

> I was the queen of the hippies, but in a way I wasn't really a hippy at all. I was always looking at it for its upsides and downsides, balancing it and thinking, here's the beauty of it and here's the exploitative quality of it and here's the silliness of it. I could never buy into it totally as an orthodoxy.[15]

In a nutshell, this passage captures several crucial aspects of Mitchell's personality that shape her songwriting through and through: the need to exercise critical judgment, the dialectical turn of thought, the reluctance to belong wholeheartedly to any group, and the underlying assumption of an observer role. Her maintenance of a certain perceptual distance from her milieu no doubt relates to her perspective as a Canadian expatriate in the United States and as a female songwriter of formidable intelligence and talent in a male-dominated industry. But autobiographical evidence suggests that as a personality trait it was formed much earlier. In the following passage from a 1979 interview, Mitchell casts back to her school days:

> My identity ... was that I was a good dancer and an artist. And also, I was very well dressed. I made a lot of my own clothes. I worked in ladies' wear and I modeled. I had access to sample clothes that were too fashionable for our community, and I could buy them cheaply. I would go hang out on the streets dressed to the T, even in hat and gloves. I hung out downtown with the Ukrainians and the Indians; they were more emotionally honest, and they were better dancers. When I went back to my own neighborhood, I found that I had a provocative image. They thought I was loose because I always liked rowdies.... I remember a recurring statement on my report card—"Joan does not relate well." I know that I was aloof. Perhaps some people thought that I was a snob. There came a split when I rejected sororities and that whole thing.... But there also came a stage when my friends who were juvenile delinquents suddenly became criminals. They could go into very dull jobs or they could go into *crime*. Crime is very romantic in your youth. I suddenly thought, "Here's where the romance ends. I don't see myself in jail."[16]

Mitchell's youthful assertion of nonconformity took the double form of a sartorial sophistication and an attraction to "rowdies." Her desire to move freely between social groups and milieus, while maintaining a distinct identity within each, entailed a certain aloofness.

The reference to the romance of crime brings up an important point of contrast between Mitchell's bohemia and that of some of her male counterparts. Her dionysian gestures are tame in comparison to the actions of the Beats, whose celebration of spontaneous impulse embraced dangerous and criminal extremes of behavior.[17] A similar mystique surfaces in altered form in Bob Dylan's songs of the mid-1960s, peopled with characters who are either down and out or beyond the law: peddlers, vagabonds, roving gamblers, bandits, lepers, and crooks. These outsiders typically appear as loners rather than in groups of companions. Given Dylan's satiric tone and absurdist scenarios, it is hard to pin down a stable angle of identification. Sometimes the outlaw character embodies a comic suspension of ethical responsibility, as in "Bob Dylan's 115th Dream," in which the narrator has to flip a coin to decide whether to go back to the ship or back to jail. At other times, he comes in for mockery, as in the little boy lost of "Visions of Johanna," who lives dangerously and takes himself so seriously. As Elizabeth

Brake argues, Dylan's cumulative intent is to construct a radical outsider perspective from which to question "whatever society expects or requires. [Dylan's outlaw persona] rejects possessive love, a fixed abode, regular work, social niceties, and authority of law."[18] Dionysian gestures are less evident, except in the wicked black humor impelling the carnival of dream imagery. Even the ragged clown of "Mr. Tambourine Man" is imagining a solitary trip of escape ("ready for to fade/Into my own parade"). His long string of renunciations ("no place," "no one," "let me forget") acts like an emptying of personal identity. In contrast, Mitchell's nonconformist scenarios confirm personal identity and its uninhibited expression. Her attractive rebels and drifters stop short of outlaw glamour. Her acts of resistance are concrete and custom-fit rather than abstract and absolute. They celebrate the freedom to embrace different social milieus and all sides of one's nature without the need to be categorized.

These themes come to the fore in "The Boho Dance" (HSL), a song in which the bohemian ("boho") scene is critically scrutinized. The title concept is taken from Tom Wolfe's book The Painted Word in which he skewers what he calls the "mating ritual" of the modern art world. In his withering view, the "downtown" artist clans may spurn bourgeois values, but their definition of success still depends on acceptance by the wealthy "uptown" arbiters of fashion. The ritual has two phases: the Boho Dance, in which the artist dedicates himself to the "sacred squalor" of bohemia "as if ... he has a knife in his teeth against the fashionable world"; and the Consummation, in which the fashionable culturati scout bohemia for new discoveries "and shower them with all the rewards of celebrity." It requires a special kind of mental "double-tracking" for the artist to let go of his carefully nurtured antibourgeois feelings at the moment of discovery/consummation "and submit gracefully to good fortune." There is always the danger of "getting stuck forever in the Boho Dance," maintaining a pathetic pride in remaining a "virgin," untouched by success.[19]

Mitchell sticks fairly closely to the Wolfe-ish take on things in this song, producing the obverse of the viewpoint evident in "Carey." In the earlier song, Mitchell extols bohemian life while looking forward to the perks of success. In the present song, on the other hand, the speaker takes time out from a glamorous lifestyle for a disappointing visit to the "Boho zone."

> Down in the cellar in the Boho zone
> I was looking for some sweet inspiration, oh well
> Just another hard-time band
> With Negro affectations
> I was a hopeful in rooms like this
> When I was working cheap

It's an old romance—the Boho dance
It has not gone to sleep

The wild rebel figure of earlier songs appears here in muted form as the second-person addressee, the "subterranean" in the parking lot (a reference to the Beat ethos by way of Kerouac's novel *The Subterraneans*). But in this tableau the character on the street is contemptuous of the speaker; in Wolfe's terms, he is one of those artists trapped in the bohemian phase. She in turn is stung into a harangue against his self-righteousness and an elaborate defense of her high living. Such issues had autobiographical relevance at this time: in 1974 Mitchell had moved from the funky semi-rural artist's community of Laurel Canyon to the exclusive neighborhood of Bel Air. In songs such as "People's Parties" and "The Same Situation" (both *C&S*) she had already started to probe the customs and ambience of L.A. society, and the change of milieu became more pronounced in *Hissing*. When asked in 1994 to comment on this change and her concomitant transformation in style ("the chic, jazzy Joni of the '70s"), Mitchell explained: "I can only say that you write about that which you have access to. So if you go from the hippy thing to more of a Gatsby community, so what? . . . Life is short and you have an opportunity to explore as much of it as time and fortune allow. No subject matter ever seemed barred to me, and no class ever seemed barred."[20] Mitchell seems to have internalized the Wolfeism about submitting to good fortune, expressed in "The Boho Dance" and echoed in this interview twenty years later.

In line with the new melodic aesthetic established in her second period (see chapter 6), Mitchell's vocal delivery is flexible, moving fluidly between a full singing voice and heightened speech. This permits her to exploit the dramatic possibilities of the situation (a blend of internal monologue and one-sided conversation) through variations in expression, from quiet, letdown sigh ("oh well") to forceful harangue ("*Jesus* was a beggar"). Mitchell harshly disparages her unnamed addressee, insinuating that his outsider status is a calculated pose ("by your own design") and that he hypocritically longs for the rewards he pretends to despise.

Like a priest with a pornographic watch
Looking and longing on the sly
Sure it's stricken from your uniform
But you can't get it out of your eyes

She goes so far as to portray his pose as a "uniform," that is, another kind of conformism. By the same token she represents her own brand of class mobility—roaming at will from the "cellar" to the "cocktail hour"—as more authentic and freer from conformity. Viewed as an act of one-upmanship, the exchange is unfairly matched: the unreported accusations of the subterranean character have little chance of prevailing against the speaker's hyper-articulate rationalizations and imperious rhetoric. But the song can also be viewed as an internal reflection on the speaker's changing relation to the "old romance" of bohemia as she becomes aware of yet another hidden trap. For a dedication to "hard-time" living is no guarantee of creative inspiration. It may just as easily lead to empty affectation, moralistic attitudes (e.g., "noble poverty"), and a dogmatic rejection of middle-class affiliations. Mitchell prefers to override the equation of personal freedom with hippie styles of renunciation.

She does this by exposing the ideological distinction between economic classes (the two "sides of town") as a false dichotomy: both the poor man Jesus and the rich king Solomon were vessels of enlightenment. The categories themselves are psychologically restrictive and insidious: true freedom consists in ignoring or seeking to escape categories ("Nothing is capsulized in me"). Thus even when scrabbling for income, the speaker claims, she never totally abandoned middle-class values ("The cleaner's press was in my jeans"). Even when frequenting fashionable restaurants, signs of hippie negligence show through ("A camera pans the cocktail hour/Behind a blind of potted palms/And finds a lady in a Paris dress/With runs in her nylons"). To convey her metaphorical escape, the speaker actively restructures the poem's symbolic space, so that "the streets" and the parking lot can no longer claim the outsider position: there is an ulterior space of freedom "outside" the Boho dance. This ulterior perspective is embodied in the device of the mobile, omniscient camera, exposing hidden contradictions and mirroring the speaker's role as detached observer.

Significantly, Mitchell portrays nonconformist identity in terms of aesthetic self-presentation (through apparel), thus merging the artistic and the personal. Artistic expression and self-fashioning are indistinguishable, as suggested in the reference to the characters' "style" or their "own design." This means that the poetic argument about self-expression reflects indirectly on Mitchell's newly glamorous musical aesthetic. According to certain well-established codes, authenticity in rock is linked to rough performance styles and overtly rebellious gestures. In her defense of personal glamour, therefore, Mitchell is implicitly defending her music's timbral sheen, slick production, and sense of decorative detail (like "lace along the seams") as an authentic form of expression, in defiance of arbitrary stylistic connotations. She cues this subtext by way of audible dichotomies: the plainness of solo piano and declamatory voice (relating the visit to the Boho zone) versus the polished sound and sparkling highlights of the entire band (entering when the speaker describes her improvised swank). Likewise, the occasional dramatic vocal outburst emerges from an ultra-suave mix of minimal horn riffs and cool emotional control. The central image of "stepping outside" the prescribed dance steps is dramatized in the rhythmic contrast between the verses with their smooth groove and the instrumental interludes with their loss of momentum and triplet figures that resist assimilation to the meter. Conversely, the harmonic progression feels stuck in a limited set of moves that always loop back to the same unresolved dominant chord. Overall, the musical patterns in this song project a highly refined sensibility in line with the intellectual sophistication of its argument and imagery. It is not an easily accessible song but one that requires a bit of effort to follow. Its unique tone derives from Mitchell's unabashed embrace of her quite rarefied perspective (as wealthy celebrity/loner) as well as her willingness to flout preconceptions of genre and individual style.

"A Strange Boy" (*H*), from the following year, is much more accessible: straightforward in language, its bohemian theme is framed within the popular scenario of a romantic affair. The rebel character is a younger man full of an untamable energy (we first see him causing "havoc" by skateboarding through a crowded sidewalk). So far he has managed to evade the disciplinary forces of society: the military system ("the war and the navy/Couldn't bring him to maturity") and behavioral taboos, conveyed by the references to "curfew" and "house-rules," as well as the lifeless stare of the rows of "antique dolls." Not even the speaker herself has succeeded in taming him ("'Grow up!' I cried"). It shows a striking variation on the main theme that she should be associated with the forces of adulthood and discipline in this way. The boy's attraction consists in his wildness, youth, agility, and strong sense of self; the battered ("damaged," "parched") speaker looks to him for rejuvenation, trading her "jewelry" and "power" for his "crazy wisdom." In contrast to "The Boho Dance," this song represents a favorable bohemian episode.

> A thousand glass eyes were staring
> In a cellar full of antique dolls
> I found an old piano
> And sweet chords rose up in waxed New England halls
> While the boarders were snoring
> Under crisp white sheets of curfew
> We were newly lovers then
> We were fire in the stiff-blue-haired-house-rules

However, the thematic elements are arranged differently: the "crisp white sheets" now signify censoriousness rather than comfort; and the "cellar," site of spontaneous music-making, is now inside the very structures of established society ("waxed New England halls"). There is no enclave of free-minded companions here, just two loners coming together. Nor is there an out-of-the-way community; culture and counterculture, "inside" and "outside," are thoroughly entangled. This motif of spatial/temporal paradox is expressed as weaving skillfully through a grid (of intersections, of properly ordered waking hours). The regulated, squared lines of traffic and "stiff-blue-haired" tradition are contrasted with the natural curves of lovemaking and the "rising" forces of surf, fire, and music.

The musical patterns also pick up on the notion of weaving through a grid. The introductory riff with its unhurried, extended chain of syncopations (see Ex. 7.5b) expresses the familiar idea of accents playing "off" the metric pulse (and the voice participates in this too—for instance, in the offbeat stresses of the phrase "midday sidewalk traffic"). The lead guitar enters sporadically in spontaneous solos, a figure of wildness against the steady background rhythm guitar. In fact, the overall aesthetic of melodic flexibility Mitchell is exploring in this album is a sonic symbol of freedom in the midst of established convention: verses that freely breathe within strophic divisions along with the singer's freedom to discover new peaks and valleys within each turn of the melodic cycle. The one consistent melodic peak occurs in the final line of each verse, where it emphasizes the theme of paradox (in verse 1, the strangeness of an immature but wise boy; in verse 2, his blending of selfishness and empathy; in verse 3, her relinquishment of power). Just as the boy's special freedom is portrayed as an illogical balancing act ("holding on to something wild"), the romantic relationship involves a tug of wills or a difficult dance of mutual coordination. The fullness of love ebbs and flows, as does the harmonic color, alternating between the "sweet chord" of full tonic major (lines 1 and 5) and blues inflections (especially the punctuating guitar riff in hollow parallel fifths). A détente of sorts is reached in the final (truncated) verse when the tussling lovers are united in opposition against the representatives of bourgeois conformity. At the same time, in a strange sudden swerve, the last two lines ("We were newly lovers then") place the whole romantic episode in the unrecoverable past.

TALENT

Earlier in this chapter I pointed out how Mitchell occasionally uses the description of a person's artistic talent (as in "I Had a King," "Michael from Mountains," and "The Gallery") as a metaphor for the quality of his or her personality or dealings with other people. In many other songs, she refers in passing to her artistic vocation (whether as painter, writer, or musician) and its related baggage. Certain songs acquire a special status by taking art itself as their theme, pondering the different paths open to the artist given conflicting ideas of success and the elusive nature of creative inspiration. In three early songs, Mitchell dramatizes (or lyricizes) three different accommodations to the muse, in each case enlarging upon the distinct emotional resonance. "Ladies of the Canyon" (*LC*) portrays a bucolic, bohemian haven whose denizens are free to pursue their offbeat lifestyle. This means nurturing their individual gifts without any intrusive influence. Trina, working in paint and fabric, cultivates a unique sense of decoration and "weaves a pattern all her own" (note the important connections to the "weaving" image from "A Strange Boy" and the idea of "your own design" from "The Boho Dance"). Estrella fills the canyon with music, which "pours" out unimpeded. Mitchell's description here employs the precious language of fantasy: "Songs like tiny hammers hurled/At bevelled mirrors in empty halls." The last image is dense in connotation. It evokes a romanticized past ("empty" as in uninhabited and forgotten). In its lack of narrative detail it suggests a sense of stories yet unwritten, appropriate to the ingenue persona. In connection with the image of mirrors, the empty space connotes introspection and the undisturbed solitude necessary for concentrated work. Overall, the song creates an atmosphere of simple pleasures and deep personal fulfillment.

In "For Free" (*LC*), however, there is a split in the path. The lyric speaker is a musician who has already achieved commercial success. At a stop on her tour she comes across a clarinetist playing on the street "so sweet and high." The sight electrifies her; alone, undiscovered, not even asking for change, he embodies a kind of music-making she has left far behind. In explaining her own situation, she never even describes her music; instead, she is preoccupied with the perquisites of fame (wealth, star treatment, bodyguards) which have distanced her from her audience as well as the original source of her inspiration. The "halls" in which she plays represent lucrative business contracts and large audiences (no longer the resonant "empty halls" of solitude). The street musician is not weighed down with such things; his creative gift is free to ramble where it will. He symbolizes a state of grace from which she has fallen.[21] For a moment she stands, undecided as to whether she should cross to his side of the street. But as the signal changes she continues on her way. Mitchell's performance of the song is laden with grief for the path not taken.

"For the Roses" (*FR*) also contains a split between the speaker and an alter ego, but their relative positions are more complicated. This song captures the perspective of a musician seeking temporary refuge from the pressures of the business, conducting an imaginary conversation with a friend and fellow songwriter still in the flush of stardom.

> I heard it in the wind last night
> It sounded like applause
> Did you get a round resounding for you
> Way up here
> It seems like many dim years ago

Since I heard that face to face
Or seen you face to face
Though tonight I can feel you here

Verse 1 turns on the framing sound-image of "applause," which acts like a Proustian sense-memory to unlock thoughts of the life left behind. Employing relaxed, informal language, the opening lines establish the speaker's physical distance from (yet emotional closeness to) her friend. The rustic setting, "way up here" away from civilization, alludes to Mitchell's property in British Columbia to which she had retreated (with the intention of retiring) after undergoing emotional trauma during the recording of the album *Blue*.[22] Obviously, the wounds are still fresh; the conversational flights of fancy are fueled by bitter disappointment. Verse 2 slips into an elliptical narrative mode, suggesting a cinematic montage of a star being born. His breathless rise to fame ("Up the charts/Off to the airport—/Your name's in the news/Everything's first class—") is exhilarating but happens far too fast to absorb. Furthermore, Mitchell's figures of speech project intense dissonance between the musician's sensitive gift and the voracious corporate entity ready to exploit it:

In some office sits a poet
And he trembles as he sings
And he asks some guy
To circulate his soul around

The language of sacralized art and of commodity ventures are in sharp conflict. The poet's "trembling" conveys the excitement and fear of the ingenue, likened to sexual innocence.

As before, entry into the business is experienced as a fall from grace. In verse 3, the speaker acts as a voice of conscience for her friend, recalling the days when his guitar was a direct tool of self-communion: "you used to ... pour your simple sorrow/To the soundhole and your knee." (Significantly, Mitchell recorded the song *au naturel* in its solo guitar version with no additional players.) Once solid and immediate, his music is now converted into media streams for distribution on "giant screens." Once whole, his soul is now cut up into company shares. (Mitchell's voice on the word "slices" has a memorable edge. She also places a great deal of emotional weight on the word "glitter," in pained reaction to the mind-set that corrupts artistic value into purely monetary gain.) The new-fledged star is caught up in the "caressing rev of motors"—that is, the deceptively glamorous machinery of profit and public relations, which has ways of seizing control over one's creative output ("They toss around your latest golden egg"). In short, the industry is an elaborate, well-baited trap. Mitchell caps this motif of the loss of artistic freedom in verse 4, by invoking the heavily freighted image of crucifixion—another story of good intentions spiraling out of control:

> Oh the power and the glory
> Just when you're getting a taste for worship
> They start bringing out the hammers
> And the boards
> And the nails

Her sprawling, offhand tone couches a bitter self-mockery over past delusions. The crucifix image is also apt in that it represents a theatrical form of martyrdom, engineered for the public display of a personal anguish.[23]

Yet, in another burst of candor, the speaker admits that her condemnation of the industry is compromised since she "really can't give up" the material rewards of fame just yet.[24] (With special black humor, this verse begins with a self-portrait as wild dog—"teeth sunk in the hand/That brings me things"—and ends with a self-portrait as the messiah.) Nor is she entirely free of the desire for public recognition, as signified by the ghostly memory of applause. The speaker's conflicted attitude toward her career is captured in the poem's confused sense of place, bouncing back and forth between "up here," "somewhere," "up there," as if deeply unsure of its point of identification. In a similar way, the image of a seated musician as a focus of creative energy is multiplied in a series of locations and ambivalent emotional contexts: the poet sitting and trembling in the office, sitting alone with his guitar; the speaker herself sitting in front of the TV, exiled from the music scene and reduced to watching it secondhand. The poem rigorously adheres to this motif of doubling and displacement: in the parallels between speaker and alter ego (and thus the double signification of the pronoun "you") but also in more abstract perceptual metaphors. Thus the speaker's reflections are set in motion by a sound she imagines as echoing or "resounding" across the distance separating her from her friend. The industrialized media network represents a more insidious kind of displacement, converting organic sounds and performances into images for copying and repeated circulation (until they split up into pixels like "confetti").

The title of the song alludes, on the one hand, to the cut-flower tributes after a performance, passed up in bouquets or thrown singly from afar. On the other hand, and more bitterly, it suggests the wreath placed over the winning horse at the racetrack, thereby reducing the speaker's subjective viewpoint to that of a prize horse in someone else's competition.[25] But the title phrase itself is cut off, and its exact referent is uncertain—say, "the trials we put ourselves through" for the roses, or, "is it all just a race" for the roses, or perhaps, "thank you" for the roses. The latter understanding suggests a farewell note from the speaker to her audience, as if seriously commemorating the end of her career. Thus in the incomplete verse 5, she returns to the echo of applause, recognizing it as an aural illusion formed of the ephemeral sounds of nature. Though on the one hand this represents a return to present reality, on the other she is still lingering over fanciful reflections and wistful recollections of the past:

> It was just the arbutus rustling
> And the bumping of the logs
> And the moon swept down black water
> Like an empty spotlight

Where in verse 1, the ghost-applause evokes her friend's success and acclamation, in the final verse that scene is displaced by the idea of the speaker's own last imaginary bow as she retreats to the "empty halls" of solitude.

On the other end of the spectrum from this earnest head trip is a light anecdotal number from *Mingus*, "The Dry Cleaner from Des Moines."

> I'm down to a roll of dimes
> I'm stalking the slot that's hot
> I keep hearing bells all around me
> Jingling the lucky jackpots
> They keep you tantalized
> They keep you reaching for your wallet
> Here in fool's paradise!

Set on the Las Vegas strip, the song seems an unlikely place to encounter themes pertaining to an artistic calling. But the circumstances of the album as a whole—a collaboration with Charles Mingus, terminally ill at the time—provoked two portraits of the great jazz artist in the songs "God Must Be a Boogie Man" and "A Chair in the Sky," which meditate on his psychological makeup, his achievements, and his place in the "divine plan." Moreover, the poem for "Goodbye Pork Pie Hat" places Mingus within an ongoing generational history of African American music. In the context of its neighboring songs where the figure of the artist is such a strong presence, "Dry Cleaner" serves as a foil, a witty burlesque on a related theme. It is one of those songs in which a lyrical observer expresses fascination with a stranger's skill or charisma—for example, "For Free" and "A Strange Boy," as we have seen in this chapter. In "A Strange Boy," the skill in question is ironically characterized as the childish and fairly trivial art of skateboarding ("He sees the cars as sets of waves"). The dry cleaner's skill is even more trivial—the ability to "clean up" in any game of chance. Mitchell sustains a comic tone by emphasizing the low stakes involved ("a roll of dimes"), the surreal tourist-trap setting ("the cowgirls fill the room/With their big balloons"), and the tackiness of the prizes ("He had Dinos and Pooh Bears/And lions pink and blue there").

Nevertheless, the dry cleaner is amazingly gifted—and maddening to watch. This poem can be seen as a humorous take on the "artist envy" scenario of "For Free": like the street musician from that song, the dry cleaner "plays real good" while the speaker misses every time. The subliminal analogy between gambling and playing music is carried out in a string of noisy action words: "clanking," "pitching," "I blew it," and especially the persistent sound of winning bells ("He kept ringing bells/Nothing to it!"). There is also a suggestion of manual dexterity (or "chops") in his nimble action at the tables as well as his Midas touch ("the cleaner from Des Moines/Could put a coin/In the door of a john/And get twenty for one").[26] On the other hand, unlike Mitchell's usual treatment of the artist and in keeping with her comic purpose, the gambler's skill is absolutely devoid of any ulterior ethical value (such as authenticity or aesthetic ambition)—another meaning behind the phrase "nothing to it." This breezy vignette reflects wryly on the haphazard allotment of worldly success and the inexplicable origin of innate talents ("he must have had a genie in a lamp"). The speaker's rueful refrain ("It's just luck!") is at the same time a shrug of cosmic resignation and a case of sour grapes, belittling the skill she wishes she had ("You get a little lucky and you make a little money!").

What makes the song witty at the level of its *perspective* is that even as Mitchell-the-speaker is putting on the air of a sad sack, Mitchell-the-poet is ringing bells with a virtuosic display of verbal skill. This tune is one of several written by Mingus for Mitchell to set to words. It moves along at a good clip and has a two-octave range (low E♭ to high F). The tune follows no set phrase structure. Instead it originally consisted of improvisation over a standard twelve-bar blues progression, where the aim is unfolding rhythmic variation and contrapuntal interplay with the underlying four-bar units. (In its final form the song consists of three vocal choruses, an intervening instrumental chorus, another vocal chorus, instrumental chorus with scat vocal, a final vocal chorus, four more instrumental choruses with vocal riffs, and a coda on the tonic.) Mitchell was faced with a preexisting melody that was elastic and mercurial, weaving between the grid of a repetitive formal pattern. In response she came up with a rap that is chatty, colorful, and fluid (nonmetric)—yet projecting a strophic form (five verses) with a clear rhyme scheme. (In verse 1, for instance, the first two four-bar units are paired—"slot that's hot/jackpots"—and the third unit contains its own rhyming pair—"tantalized/paradise." This basic scheme persists with variation until verse 5, which contains four rhyming pairs spread asymmetrically.) Her poetic lines have a great rhythmic freedom in order to accommodate melodic fragmentation on the one hand (as in verse 3: "He got three oranges/Three lemons/Three cherries/Three plums/I'm losing my taste for fruit!") and extended enjambment on the other (as in the following lines from verse 4, set to one melodic gesture that bridges two four-bar units: "He picked out a booth at Circus Circus/Where the cowgirls fill the room/With their big balloons"). The resulting dance of interlocking patterns (rhyme scheme, blues progression, variable phrase structure—not to mention Jaco Pastorius's tight horn arrangements and hyperactive bass) is a feat of amazing coordination, carried off with insouciant flair.

FLIGHT

The five thematic strands I am untangling in this chapter are closely related— naturally, in an intense search for personal freedom, one's relationships, career, lifestyle, and creative choices will feel like overlapping aspects of a single goal. Likewise, the desire for personal liberation may be experienced as a spiritual desire, and this is often the case in Mitchell's poetry. In "The Dawntreader" (SS), for instance, her yearning for adventure on the sea (with the accompanying imagery of treasure, mermaids, dolphins, etc.) is expressed in vague and mythical terms so that it can metaphorically encompass a range of personal yearnings. These include the specified desires for love and social change ("A dream that the wars are done") but also desires that remain unspecified ("questions there's no answer for," "A dream that you tell no one but the grey sea"). In the context of wide-open horizons and fabulous creatures, these unspoken desires take on a metaphysical resonance. The refrain, "Like a promise to be free," suggests a utopian longing that is not confined to the earthly realm. We can understand this tentative mysticism as religious expression under the influence of countercultural values (in particular, the rejection of established institutions and doctrines, the emphasis on expanded consciousness, and the sacrosanct value placed on personal expression). Under these conditions, the religious impulse may take the form of a highly personalized reinterpretation of traditional symbols, such as the garden in "Woodstock" (set against cosmic stardust and psychedelic warplane/butterflies); the figures of god and devil, reworked in a Manichean register in "Shadows and Light" (HSL); or the notion of the Trinity, applied to Charles Mingus's own psychology in "God Must Be a Boogie Man" (M). It may look to alternative spiritual traditions, such as the borrowed Native American shamanism found in Carlos Castaneda's books (an inspiration for "Don Juan's Reckless Daughter" [DJRD]) or the Hindu belief in reincarnation alluded to in "A Chair in the Sky" (M).[27] Finally, the impulse for countercultural religious expression may elicit new symbols, tailored for personal use. In "The Dawntreader," the seabird from verse 3 is a prototype for such an idiomatic spiritual symbol. Creature of the sky ("Seabird I have seen you fly above the pilings"), it descends to earth to commune with the speaker about vision-ary ideals ("Fold your fleet wings/I have brought some dreams to share"), thus embodying a bridge between human and metaphysical realms. Avian personas such as this come to assume an important role in Mitchell's work as a means of evoking transcendent perspectives and visionary flights to a better world. As we will see, her expression of utopian longing is rarely free from ambivalence and is usually tempered with an awareness of human frailty and imperfection.

In "Song to a Seagull" (*SS*), the guitar's emphasis on quartal harmony lends a spacious but stark atmosphere (Ex. 4.3). Chords are grounded on a low, toll-ing drone that never abates. Around this primal frame the voice circles in a free, chanting rhythm. The sentiments distilled are pure and naive, one solitary soul calling to another.

> Fly silly seabird
> No dreams can possess you
> No voices can blame you
> For sun on your wings

As the song opens, the speaker hails the seagull as her surrogate, partaking of an unknowing, natural freedom. In the refrain she envisions herself joining the gulls in their flight from the sphere of human contempt and misunderstanding ("My dreams with the seagulls fly/Out of reach out of cry"). In Mitchell's cre-ation of a transcendent poetic perspective, three symbolic elements are crucial: the projection of the speaker's identity outward to a vicariously imagined sub-ject; the defiance of gravity, with the associated experience of physical exhilara-tion and widened spatial focus; and the act of disappearing, flying out of reach of sight or sound. The last element signifies the ultimate freedom to rise above the limits of one's earthbound life and leave it behind. Nevertheless in this instance it produces an uncanny and melancholy ghost-effect. That is, though the speaker's visionary desire is winging away out of sight, such a conceptual image depends on a residual awareness of her actual, gravity-bound position on shore (out of sight of whom?). Furthermore, in contrast to "The Dawntreader," here there is almost no content or shape to her dreams, the goal of which belongs to another realm of knowledge. This ineffability is exhilarating in its suggestion of an escape from mundane thought; at the same time, it implies a conceptual divide that may very well be unbridgeable. (There are plenty of songs in which Mitchell spells out specific social or philosophical ideals; but these often do not coincide with the use of visionary rhetoric. For example, in "Sisotowbell Lane" (*SS*), the utopian geniality of the earthy-crunchy com-munity she portrays consists precisely in its being realizable at this moment in the world.)

EXAMPLE 4.3. "SONG TO A SEAGULL," INTRO

Mitchell goes on to place two other metaphorical sites in counterpoint with the visionary horizon. In verse 2, the speaker cries out against the urban wasteland and its disfigured effigy of nature ("On an island of noise/In a cobblestone sea")—no spiritual nurture here. In verse 3, she escapes to an earthly haven where the seagulls are in view.[28] But even here, the sad facts of mortality soon intrude into consciousness ("But sandcastles crumble/And hunger is human"). This vein continues into the last verse, where a question forms for the seagull, as if it could tell us of those who came before ("where are the footprints/That danced on these beaches/And the hands that cast wishes/That sunk like a stone"). Here the perspective widens once again, this time over a temporal horizon. Once again Mitchell summons images of disappearance: castles that crumble, footprints washed away, dreams that come to nothing.

Thus the powerful visionary urge, which always returns with the refrain, is held in tension with the knowledge of frailty and transience. The rising wing is countered by the sinking stone. At the climactic point in each verse just before the refrain, the melody rises repeatedly to B♭, the seventh degree of the scale (see Ex. 6.8). In the modal language of the song (Mixolydian; see chapter 5), this builds a questioning as well as a directional force (creating expectations for an upward arrival on the tonic). The verse articulations are thus poised on an updraft that is carried through only in the guitar. During the aspirations of the refrain, the vocal melody is in fact sinking on its way back to the tonic. Mitchell's persona in this song may be filled with idealistic longing, but she is well aware of how little effect such longing might have. The longed-for world is incommensurable, a "world we can't share." Where are the signs of the other dreamers that have been here? Her final call to the gull goes unanswered; it seems that her wishes must also fall back to earth, leaving no sign. The final phrase "out of cry" takes on an extra resonance. Not only does it suggest the crying bird moving out of our range of hearing, but it also suggests the imperviousness of the gull to the human cry. Mitchell portrays her visionary flight with an image that evokes both exhilaration and melancholy, transcendence and separation.

In its title and central image, "Sweet Bird" (*HSL*) refers glancingly to the Tennessee Williams play *Sweet Bird of Youth;* the song spins out a meditation on the transience of youth without ever once speaking the word. Where "Song to a

Seagull" moved among three symbolic poles, "Sweet Bird" is absorbed in a single dense image, suspended in time and space.

> Out on some borderline
> Some mark of in-between
> I lay down golden—in time
> And woke up vanishing

The high-flown language of the first four lines works on two levels: its most concrete subject is the passing from one's prime into middle age. Somewhere out there, it says, was a line I crossed, a moment that marked, however subtly, the onset of decline. This concrete meaning is continued with the reference to age-defying makeup in the seventh line. Surrounded as it is by highly abstract utterances, the latter image ("beauty jars") is itself rather jarring, with its assumption that an ideal can be packaged or even contained. The image of facial care also has an oblique retrospective effect on line 4, evoking associations of "vanishing" cream—one vain remedy against the erosions of time.

But the concrete level of meaning is initially quite difficult to pick out, being ironically embedded within a transcendent level. The opening poetic figures are powerfully vague and abstract, placing us on some unspecified horizon, which could be in space or time. If space, it's an airless sort of limbo; if time, it's a gyroscopic balance-point. The speaker is projected or abstracted "out," away from any worldly anchor; her states of sleeping and waking assume a metaphysical connotation. Metaphysical as well, it would seem, is her turn from golden fullness to a state of vanishing, as if her identity, with its inevitable limitations, has just dissolved in the rarefied air. With the invocation of the bird in line 5 ("Sweet bird you are/Briefer than a falling star"), we have all the signs of transcendence: outward projection, flight, and disappearance. One further element contributing to the transcendent perspective in this song is the poetic diction itself. Abstractions and suggestive imprecisions—"out," "up," "somewhere," "horizon," "time and change"—continue throughout. Keeping the language consistently removed from a mundane setting reinforces the effect of elevation and widened focus. That is why the mundane "beauty jars" are so intrusive and why the whole topic of aging stands in an ironic relation to the transcendent. The figurative language (and the music, as we shall see) gives us a taste of an expanded perspective, from which human concerns seem a small matter. This state of privileged vision is embodied in the strange bird, who laughs at our vain anxieties ("Sweet bird of time and change/You must be laughing/Up on your feathers laughing"). The message of the song will turn out to be our inability to grasp firmly the ideals of youth and beauty; but the musical experience extends the seductive illusion that we can inhabit a world of ideals.

The song begins with a very gradual fade-in, as if we are approaching or tuning in to something that's already there. The alternation between two chords (Bm7(6) and Em7) creates a circular rather than a forward motion. Strumming acoustic guitar is set off against a warm glow of background vocals and wailing electric guitars. The voices cluster and shift like a spatial mass; the electric guitars unfurl in a high, haunting stratum; an intermittent, rocking piano is also added to the texture. Each instrument group occupies a distinct registral layer, the rhythmic activity of which is independent of the others; voices and high guitars are especially free floating. A very special sound-world is created: rather static in time, with no beginning; spatially layered, with strata that hover and float; tone colors that combine a "golden" glow with eerily distant reverberations.

The vocal melody maintains a low range and low expressive profile. In fact, the larger section of each verse (all but the first four lines) hovers closely around the single note D. The relative stasis of the melody is offset by the complex harmonic progression (Ex. 4.4). When the melody enters, the harmony breaks out of its alternation between minor chords into a G-major area. The G center is held largely in suspension, however, only rarely touching down as a stable tonic. At certain points in the harmonic circuit, the chords break out dramatically from the G center. The first point occurs at line 3. After "I lay down golden," the chord slips from E minor to an E♭maj9 (or B♭/E♭ "slash") chord (Ex. 4.5). The underlying voice-leading is chromatic, but the arrival on E♭ is far down the flat side of G—the result is something like the bottom dropping out of the key. This effect is heightened by the pungent but open stacked-fifth spacing of the E♭ chord (built into the guitar tuning: C G D G B D). The tonal rupture occurs at

EXAMPLE 4.4. "SWEET BIRD," CHORD CHANGES, VERSE 1

Guitar tuning: C G D G B D

| Intro: | ‖: Bm7(6) | Em7 :‖ Bm7(6) | Em7 G/C | |

Lines:

```
               1                    2
        | C(9) | Em9 | F/G | C(9) |

               3                              4
        | C(9) | Em9 | B♭/E♭ | B♭/E♭ | C(9) | G |

            5/10              6/11
        ‖: A/D | C/F G/C | C(9) | G |

          7/12      8/13    9/14
        | C(9) | G | F/G | C(9)/G | C(9)/G :‖

           15
        | F/G | C(9)/G | C(9)/G |
```

EXAMPLE 4.5. "SWEET BIRD," CHORD CHANGES, LINES 3–5

C(9)   Em9   Bb/Eb   C(9)

G   A/D   C/F   G/C   C(9)   G

the turning moment in the opening poetic gambit—the balance-point between fullness and decline. Mitchell extends the duration of this line of text to linger over the effect.

At "Sweet bird" (line 5) there is another rupture, this time on the sharp side of G (an A/D slash chord). Both ruptures are momentary, quickly folding back into G. They complicate the tonal space of the song in uncanny ways; at the same time, their arrangement on either side of G in the circle of fifths reflects the thematic idea of balance. Balance is evident as well between the introductory material (also used as interlude and coda) on the dominant, or sharp side, and the verse, which tends to the subdominant, or flat side, of G. The flavor of flat and sharp combines with that of major and minor to further distinguish the verses from the interludes. The circling minor harmonies of the instrumental sections imbue them with melancholy; in contrast, the mostly major subdominant shading in the verses gives them a certain serenity. This polarizes the tension maintained in the lyrics between an imagined sphere of Platonic perfection ("golden in time") and our real exclusion from such a sphere ("cities under the sand"). The instrumental sections thus concentrate in themselves the ache of longing or perhaps grief over our shortcomings. This symbolic connotation intensifies in the central interlude, in which the regular meter is audibly truncated, confused by cross-rhythms, and arrested by awkward accents in the guitar figuration. After the contrast of this limping, imperfect world, verse 2 truly soars. At the end of that verse, the song falls into a loop ("Guesses based on what each set of time and change is touching") of alternating subdominant chords (F/G–C(9)/G). The loop repeats so many times that it seems the song will end on this serene plateau. But at the final vocal phrase the balance tips, and we return to the melancholy instrumental loop for the fade-out.

"Sweet Bird" begins from an awareness of lost youth, but this awareness is only evoked through allusion and circuitous expression. Mitchell exploits indirect language in favor of a meaning cloaked in indeterminacy. When the bird first appears it is "briefer than a falling star": it must represent youth itself. At the next invocation, it is now "sweet bird of time and change"; apparently its meaning has shifted to encompass the process of loss and transience. And youth is not all that is lost; we see "power, ideals and beauty fading." When we come to the final moral, it has drifted farther away from the initial concern.

No one knows
They can never get that close
Guesses at most
Guesses based on what each set of time and change is touching

That close to what? Once again the song has moved powerfully toward the abstract, pushing concrete circumstances to the point of disappearance. We are left with "guesses," a rushing sky, and shifting patterns of time and change.

In "Amelia" (H), the autobiographical speaker is a woman on the road, wrapped up in episodic contemplation; each verse teases out a different view of travel as a metaphor for life or love. The various strands of the quest for "paradise"—personal, romantic, artistic, and spiritual fulfillment—are inextricably linked. Mitchell alludes to her rambling persona from the early seafaring period (in the reference to the "Cactus Tree Motel"), but the landscape is now more desolate—dusty and dry, as if the cactus metaphor has taken root. The ethereal bird character of earlier songs has been translated into an airplane and by extension into the romantic figure of Amelia Earhart. A world-weary apostrophe to the aviator rounds off each verse. The visionary aspect of this poem is not as pervasive; from the mundane realm we catch intermittent glimpses of another, "higher" perspective. Significantly, the speaker is behind the wheel of a car while all her meditations are about air travel. Yet her skyward yearnings never quite coalesce into a sustained stratum of privileged vision.

I was driving across the burning desert
When I spotted six jet planes
Leaving six white vapor trails across the bleak terrain
It was the hexagram of the heavens
It was the strings of my guitar
Amelia, it was just a false alarm

In verse 1, the sight of jet planes provides the occasion for the speaker to project her identity outward. The image of her guitar strings (i.e., her creative/expressive persona) spreads to fill the heavens in the wake of the planes and their seductive engine drone. The effect of this metaphoric substitution is one of brief release from a "bleak" physical setting into a cosmic state. But the original image that triggered the vision—the "vapor trails"—is insubstantial and already in the process of disappearing. The refrain brings the point home with its reference to a "false alarm." These words signal a deflation of the transcendent perspective and an inability to sustain it for long. More devastatingly, they reflect upon the speaker's artistic confidence, which has been implicated in the insubstantiality of the vision. (The point is underlined by the rhyming of "guitar" and "false alarm"—and through an imperfect, failed rhyme, at that.) What if her musical achievement itself is nothing more than a vapor trail? The refrain is indeterminate enough to serve for every verse, but at each occurrence the message is one of disappointment at the deceptiveness of appearances, or the failure of hopes and dreams.

A gestural rhythm of elation and deflation is also conveyed in the song's harmonic progression (Ex. 4.6). The beginning of each verse is marked by a series of harmonic upturns. After the intro/interlude in F, line 1 is introduced by an unprepared shift to a G tonic. Line 2 consists of similar material, now shifted up in a momentary tonicization of B♭. Both shifts are accomplished by the left hand sliding on the strings. This upward voice-leading strand reaches its high point at the C chord at the beginning of line 4, after which the bass line turns back down through B, A, and G. The entire verse (except for the B♭ chords) sits within G major; but at the end of line 5 the descending bass overshoots and falls down into F for the refrain and interlude. Verse and refrain thus exist in a false tonal relation with each other, and the slump into F corresponds to the disappointment embodied in the refrain.

A ghost of aviation
She was swallowed by the sky
Or by the sea, like me she had a dream to fly
Like Icarus ascending
On beautiful foolish arms
Amelia, it was just a false alarm

The climactic emergence of the visionary occurs in verse 5, where Mitchell portrays Earhart's historical fate in mythical terms. The pilot disappears over the horizon, following her dream; the speaker identifies her own sense of vision with that of the pilot. But Amelia is an Icarus figure, reckless and flawed. The speaker is admitting to ambivalence about her own "beautiful foolish" aspirations—namely, her relationships and artistic goals, and the precarious balance between the two. As verse 6 bears out, the special vision integral to her artistic personality entails a risk of losing perspective, of being swallowed by the dream ("I've spent my whole

EXAMPLE 4.6. "AMELIA," CHORD CHANGES

Guitar tuning: C G C E G C

Intro/Interlude: circles around an F chord (6 measures)

Lines:
                  1   2
                | G | G | B♭ | B♭ |

                  3
                | Am7 | Bm | G C(9)/G | C(9)/G |

                  4   5
                | C | Em7 | Bm | Am7 | Am7 G |

                  6 (Refrain)
                | F | B♭(9)/F | F | F | (back to Interlude)

For clarity, the transcription omits some ornamental and passing chords.

life in clouds at icy altitudes"). The harmonic overshooting at the refrain has a pointed metaphoric correspondence here to the threefold crash of Icarus, Amelia, and Mitchell herself.

The signs of ambivalence about spiritual matters are sharpened in this song. Take the idea of disappearance. In "Song to a Seagull" and "Sweet Bird," this idea was used complexly to convey the knowledge of mortality ("where are the footprints?"; "vanishing") and the dream of escape from mortality ("out of reach"; "vanishing"). In "Amelia," two things vanish: the vapor trails and Amelia herself. Both are instances of the failure of the visionary, and Amelia's fate offers no escape from mortality. Likewise, in verse 6, being airborne is presented in a seriously negative light ("icy altitudes") as a hindrance to living fully on earth. The song doesn't go so far as to repudiate the visionary impulse, but it does seek to redirect it in search of a healthier, more sustainable relation between the transcendent and the mundane.

"The Beat of Black Wings" (*CMRS*) is largely cast as a dramatic monologue, spoken by a young Vietnam veteran ("Killer Kyle") whose experience in the maw of the war machine has left him morally and psychologically damaged ("There's a war zone inside me—/I can feel things exploding"). The insidiousness of the damage is captured succinctly in the story of his girlfriend's abortion in verse 3.

He said, "I never had nothin'—
Nothin' I could believe in
My girl killed our unborn child
Without even grievin'!
I put my hand on her belly
To feel the kid kickin'—damn!

She'd been to some clinic
Oh—the beat of black wings"

This account ruthlessly recapitulates and externalizes elements of the original trauma: death meted out in a moral void, the obviation of grief, a preemption of his powers of decision, a future scraped hollow. The soldier's words are left offensively raw, in harsh contrast with the highly crafted music. Meanwhile, Mitchell delivers one of the most mannered vocal performances of her career, changing expression with every line and veering from one timbral extreme to another as if barely in control of her characterization. Given the context of despair, one might wonder how the visionary enters into this song. The refrain does invoke bird imagery, but the black wings that squawk, flap, and beat belong to bats or carrion birds. Superimposed on this is the image of a military helicopter; the sound of whirring rotors provides the fundamental rhythmic track for the song. None of these winged things is associated with soaring flight. Instead, they suggest a predatory hovering—a mockery of any wish for transcendence.

The surprise lies in the music, for this is where the vision is to be found. There is still an awareness of pain and outrage in the stumbling piano figures, the jabbing percussive highlights, the plosive keyboard bursts with their reedy edge, and indecipherable background vocal mumbles. But all these elements are extremely stylized and fused into a tone of chilly ecstasy. The basic chord progression is an elated affirmation of D major while the harmonic surface is iridescent and tinted with extended sonorities and oblique shiftings. There are also several metaphorical techniques of suspension at work. In the interludes, for instance, the surface harmonic phenomena change every measure, while at a deeper structural level a much slower rate of harmonic change is projected (a new chord every four bars, as follows: I–V–I–vi; Ex. 4.7). Surface motion is thus suspended over a slowly turning background. The electric bass during these same passages heavily emphasizes the dominant; even during the tonic harmonies, the bass gives the strongest metric position to the dominant, thus suspending the tonal ground. Furthermore, the first and third phrases of every verse extend the regular four-bar scansion by inserting a two-bar half-cadential figure. The suspense just before these cadences is heightened by the sudden emptiness of texture and the momentary disappearance of the harmony (e.g., in verse 1 at "name was Killer Kyle" and "tough one for me to sing"). The prolongation of such up-in-the-air qualities gives a joyous inevitability to the full cadence at each refrain. Mitchell caps this cadence with a high, poignant keyboard descant whose prominent, shimmering overtones resemble an unearthly organum (Ex. 4.8).[29]

EXAMPLE 4.7. "THE BEAT OF BLACK WINGS," INTRO (INSTRUMENTAL PARTS)

One can think of the music as achieving outward projection in an emotional sense. The soldier's vortex of rage and despair hardly affects the musical environment—so polished, so transfixed. Mitchell's setting places a breathtaking emotional distance between her raw subject and her expressive artifice. There is also a defiance of gravity in the multiple musical suspensions, which are not hard to hear as gestures of buoyancy and release. The third element of transcendence—the horizon or vanishing point—is more difficult to conceive in musical terms, but one can interpret the moments of textural dissipation along such lines. At these moments, it seems as if the orchestral body fades to transparency. Through the aperture, we briefly hear the most basic stratum of sound—the rotor wings—unaccompanied before the orchestral substance rushes back in. This basic stratum is ongoing throughout the song but usually not directly perceptible. The aperture effect approaches a privileged perspective through points of musical vanishing.

How do the visions square? I have just interpreted the rotor oscillation almost in spiritual terms as an intimation of fundamental reality. Yet to the poor soldier, the wing-beats that won't go away represent the ongoing nightmare that finally subsumes his identity. The musical figure of disappearance offers an exhilarating

EXAMPLE 4.8. "THE BEAT OF BLACK WINGS," END OF VERSE

sense of weightlessness; but the soldier's experience of disappearance (in the last verse) means the appalling loss of personal solidity:

> There's a man drawing pictures
> On the sidewalk with chalk
> Just as fast as he draws 'em
> Rain come down and wash 'em off
> "Keep the drinks comin' girl

'Til I can't feel anything
I'm just a chalk mark in a rain storm
I'm just the beat of—
The beat of black wings"

The centrifugal forces threatening to rip the young man apart (the internal "war zone") are countered by the music's sublime self-possession: even the (sinister?) helicopter track sounds like an image of perfect balance and control. What is the point of this ironic contradiction? In my view, the affective dissociation between words and music carries no cynical, neutralizing force; it doesn't deaden the pain. By surrounding the young man's harsh outpouring with a visionary joy, Mitchell reminds us of what he has lost. Her indictment of social ill is made all the more piercing by the distance between corrupt reality and the possibility of grace trembling in the music.

One final touch remains to be mentioned. During the interludes, Mitchell adds a brief vocal tag—"Johnny Angel"—from the 1960 hit sung by Shelley Fabares. The dissonance of the importation strikes multiple sparks. The quoted song invokes the (now-distant) time of its release, probably the young man's teen years, before going off to war. Moreover, it is a song about innocence, a simple expression of unrequited love; it refers in its naive way to flights of celestial happiness, in stark counterpoint to the infernal apparitions tormenting the soldier. (Lines from the quoted song include: "Every time he says hello my heart begins to fly" and "Together we will see how lovely heaven can be.") Once again, music (here, a musical recollection) is the bearer of a whole pattern of lost possibility. By now we should realize the pathos behind the soldier's complaint that he "can't even hear the fuckin' music playin'" for the sound of the black wings. He has suffered a spiritual impairment, cutting him off from the innocence, hope, and wholeness which, from our favored perspective, we can hear shimmering all around him.

The pull of freedom in its multiple guises forms a grand theme running through Mitchell's songwriting. Right from the beginning, however, we feel the tug of a counterweight. Imagery of weaving, dancing, dreaming, and flying is tangled up with imagery of entrapment, stone (hardening, sinking), hollowness, and illusion. Musical gestures play with contrapuntal possibilities of constraint and release, elation and deflation. Following a dialectical way of thinking that remains characteristic, Mitchell expresses the urge to be free as a tension between love and solitude, idealism and worldliness, abstract yearnings and concrete realities. It is this skeptical turn of mind, her attraction to polarity and contradiction, that enables Mitchell to explore such rich sources of significance in her chosen thematic domains.

In referring to these themes as "musicopoetic," I stress the fusion of media at the heart of song, a correspondence having special immediacy when music and lyrics spring from a single author. In the preceding discussion of visionary imagery in particular, I have been at pains to emphasize the mutual interaction of musical gesture and poetic imagery in the creation of a conceptual whole. Both here and in chapter 2, my analyses touch upon a number of distinctive musical effects, many conveyed by harmonic means: modal complexity, unorthodox chord progressions, over- or underexposure of tonal center, and dualities of key. In the following chapter, I take a global perspective on Mitchell's approach to harmony, laying the groundwork for an appreciation of her harmonic technique as it informs her expressive sensibility and thematic vision.

5

HARMONIC PALETTE

Joni Mitchell learned and refined her performing and songwriting skills without literacy in music notation—the various writing systems she once flippantly described as "the numerical language, the alphabetical language, and the fly-shit."[1] This circumstance entailed certain practical disadvantages. She had to trust to memory to preserve details of how to play her songs, most of them in custom tunings with unique fingerings.[2] She had to depend on others for the transcription of written records of her music, and she was unable to oversee sheet music publication.[3] When she was playing with a band, someone else had to convert her music into charts for band members to play from, and she had to get by without technical vocabulary in communicating her ideas to them. (JM: "There were moments when I felt handicapped that I couldn't express myself within the number and letter system of musical talk. I would be forced to deal in metaphors that would bewilder the players or that they would think were precious. That put me in the position of having a 'what-she-means-is' guy on the session, and generally he wasn't equipped to speak for me. It would come out safer than I had intended.")[4] On the other hand, notational conventions necessarily encode certain preconceptions as to proper musical syntax (such as chord structure and harmonic movement), and her lack of training in notation may have contributed to a relative freedom from such preconceptions.[5]

   In the absence of a technical vocabulary, Mitchell developed a rich metaphorical language to describe musical qualities and perceptions. She once asked saxophonist Wayne Shorter to play "the sound of high heels clicking on stones."[6] Before discovering a compatible bassist in Jaco Pastorius, she had to find a way to suggest the exact sound she wanted from bass players: "I wanted them to stop putting dark polka dots all over the bottom and instead to treat it like a symphony. When you listen to a symphony, the bass is not always in, it gets light and airy for a while and then boom, it anchors again."[7] When discussing the densely layered textures of her work in the 1980s, she resorts to graphic perceptions: "Wherever there was a hollow I'd put a musical figure in it that had two hollows in it like a W and in those two hollows I'd plant another figure with a hollow in it and then put the cherry on the pudding."[8] In describing her flexible rhythmic aesthetic from the late 1970s, the abundance of her metaphorical imagination is evident: "I wanted everything floating around.... I was trying to become the Jackson Pollock of music. I just wanted all the notes, everybody's part, to tangle. I wanted all the desks pushed out of rows, I wanted the military abolished, anything linear had to go."[9]

The lack of a technical vocabulary places no limits on one's ear; nor does illiteracy in itself imply a lack of subtlety or precision. Like many musicians Mitchell learned by ear and sharpened her gift through hands-on experimentation and curiosity. Particularly noteworthy in this regard is her complex, innovative sense of harmony. Mitchell grew up conversant with the modal harmonies of folk music and jazz and the sophisticated language of standard American songwriters like George Gershwin and Cole Porter. She was also drawn to certain Romantic and modern classical composers known for melodic and harmonic invention. (JM: "[As a child] I loved Debussy, Stravinsky, Chopin, Tchaikovsky, anything with romantic melodies, especially the nocturnes.")[10] In fact, one of her earliest musical infatuations was with a melody by Rachmaninov, whose late-Romantic style is celebrated for its harmonic color and fluidity.[11] In Mitchell's outlook, harmonies have strong emotional qualities; each chord has an "emotional meaning."[12] Since harmony was such a primary medium of what she wanted to express, she sought to explore a highly diversified field of harmonic resources. This is what led to her extended experimentation with alternate tunings:

> It wasn't until I began to write my own songs that I began to crave chords that I didn't have the dexterity with my left hand to make. The voicings that I heard, the music that I wanted to make, I simply couldn't get out. And it was a frustration because, you know, I could learn your F chord and your G chord, and your minor, and a couple of things like that, but after a while there was no—it seemed like every variation or combination of chords had already been a well-traveled course.[13]

In a number of interviews, Mitchell has been even more specific about the central importance of harmony in her approach to songwriting and her intentions in working with complex chords. She was not merely seeking to strike out from the beaten path but was actively investing her music with a critical perspective through harmonic detail:

Chaka Khan once told me my chords were like questions, and in fact, I've always thought of them as chords of inquiry. My emotional life is quite complex, and I try to reflect that in my music. For instance, a minor chord is pure tragedy; in order to infuse it with a thread of optimism you add an odd string to the chord to carry the voice of hope. Then perhaps you add a dissonant because in the stressful society we live in dissonance is aggressing against us at every moment. So, there's an inquiry to the chords comparable to the unresolved quality of much poetry.[14]

This statement reveals a view of harmonic expression as multilayered, sensitive to personal as well as cultural significance, and precise enough to project a questioning force.

In this chapter I will examine Mitchell's complex harmonic language and her exploration of unconventional possibilities of tonal progression. I begin with some general comments about harmonic material. Mitchell has composed some songs in the traditional major mode.[15] However, she is just as likely to use Aeolian, Dorian, or Mixolydian modes, with their special quality due to the lowered seventh scale-degree ($\hat{7}$), and their different arrangement of harmonies around the tonal center (Ex. 5.1).[16] (For a classification of all 152 songs released between 1968 and 1998 according to different harmonic categories, see Table 5.1.) Modal harmony was already a common alternative for popular music in the late twentieth century; folk-derived styles in particular grew out of a venerable tradition of modal usage. Some well-known examples of older tunes in Aeolian mode (with its characteristic lowered $\hat{3}$, $\hat{6}$, and $\hat{7}$) are "O Come, O Come, Emmanuel" (from medieval plainchant) and the carol "God Rest Ye, Merry Gentlemen"; a contemporary example would be Paul Simon's "The Sound of Silence." Older tunes in Dorian mode (lowered $\hat{3}$, raised $\hat{6}$, lowered $\hat{7}$) include the sea shanty "Drunken Sailor," the hymn tune "What Wondrous Love" (derived from the ballad "Captain Kidd"), and "Scarborough Fair"; a contemporary example is Jefferson Airplane's "Somebody to Love." Older tunes in Mixolydian (raised $\hat{3}$ and $\hat{6}$, lowered $\hat{7}$) include the lullaby "All My Trials" (though contemporary arrangements often mix in major harmonies), and some versions of the folk ballad "The Cruel Mother" ("Down by the Greenwood Sidey"); contemporary examples include the Beatles' "Norwegian Wood" and Gordon Lightfoot's "The Wreck of the Edmund Fitzgerald."[17]

Both the major and minor scales include a leading tone, that is, a seventh degree only a semitone below the tonic with a strong tendency to resolve upward (see Ex. 5.1). Both also contain a major dominant (V) triad, traditionally associated with a strong tendency for tonic resolution. In contrast, Aeolian, Dorian, and Mixolydian each have a seventh degree one whole tone below the tonic, thus

TABLE 5.1. Songs Classified by Harmonic Category

ALBUM	1. Modal	2. Polymodal	3. Chromatic	4. Polytonal	5. Pedal Point
Hits (1996)	Urge for Going (A Mixo) (1966)				
Song to a Seagull (1968)	Night in the City (G Mixo) Sisotowbell Lane (D Mixo*) Song to a Seagull (C Mixo) Cactus Tree (F♯M*)	I Had a King (A) Michael from Mountains (F) Nathan La Franeer (G) The Dawntreader (D)	[Michael from Mountains] Marcie (G) The Pirate of Penance (D)		I Had a King (A) The Dawntreader (D) Song to a Seagull (C Mixo) Cactus Tree (F♯M*)
Clouds (1969)	Tin Angel (E Aeol) Chelsea Morning (E Mixo) That Song about the Midway (E Mixo) The Gallery (F♯ Mixo) I Think I Understand (E Mixo) Both Sides, Now (F♯M)	The Fiddle and the Drum (B♭)	Roses Blue (G) Songs to Aging Children Come (B)	I Don't Know Where I Stand (D-F)	Both Sides, Now (F♯M)
Ladies of the Canyon (1970)	Morning Morgantown (AM) Conversation (F♯M) Ladies of the Canyon (D Mixo) Willy (CM*) The Priest (G Dor)	For Free (C) The Arrangement (A) Rainy Night House (D)	[Morning Morgantown]	Blue Boy (C-G) [not strongly centric]	Conversation (F♯M) The Priest (G Dor)

	Big Yellow Taxi (EM) Woodstock (Eb Dor*) The Circle Game (BM*)				
Blue (1971)	Little Green (BM) Carey (DbM*) California (EM) River (CM*) A Case of You (DbM*)	All I Want (Db) My Old Man (A) Blue (B) This Flight Tonight (Ab)	[My Old Man]	The Last Time I Saw Richard (G-A)	All I Want (Db) Carey (DbM*) A Case of You (DbM*)
For the Roses (1972)	Barangrill (Eb Mixo) Electricity (B Mixo) You Turn Me On, I'm a Radio (EbM*)	Banquet (E) Lesson in Survival (A) For the Roses (Bb) Blonde in the Bleachers (A) Woman of Heart and Mind (B)		Cold Blue Steel and Sweet Fire (C-G) Let the Wind Carry Me (F#-A) See You Sometime (F-C) Judgement of the Moon and Stars (D-A-B)	For the Roses (Bb)
Court and Spark (1974)		Court and Spark (E) Free Man in Paris (A) People's Parties (D) The Same Situation (A) Just Like This Train (C) Raised on Robbery (C blues)		Help Me (A-D) Car on a Hill (F#-A) Down to You (D-E) Trouble Child (C-G)	

(continued)

TABLE 5.1. (Continued)

ALBUM	1. Modal	2. Polymodal	3. Chromatic	4. Polytonal	5. Pedal Point
Miles of Aisles (1974)		Love or Money (A)			
The Hissing of Summer Lawns (1975)	Edith and the Kingpin (C Aeol) Shades of Scarlett Conquering (A Dor) The Boho Dance (DM/Bm)	In France They Kiss on Main Street (E) Don't Interrupt the Sorrow (G) Harry's House (C) Sweet Bird (G/Em) Shadows and Light (D)	The Jungle Line (G♯)	The Hissing of Summer Lawns (B-D) (music by John Guerin)	
Hejira (1976)	Coyote (CM) Hejira (BM)	A Strange Boy (D) Song for Sharon (E♭) Blue Motel Room (C) Refuge of the Roads (C)		Amelia (F-G) Furry Sings the Blues (A-D) Black Crow (E♭-G♭)	
Don Juan's Reckless Daughter (1977)	Dreamland (C Aeol*)	Cotton Avenue (C) Jericho (D) Don Juan's Reckless Daughter (C) Off Night Backstreet (C) The Silky Veils of Ardor (C)	[Jericho] Paprika Plains (C)	Talk to Me (B♭-D) Otis and Marlena (E♭-B♭)	Paprika Plains (C)

Album				
Mingus (1979)			God Must Be a Boogie Man (G)	The Wolf That Lives in Lindsey (C-E♭)
Wild Things Run Fast (1982)	Chinese Café (D Mixo) You Dream Flat Tires (D Aeol) Man to Man (D Aeol)	Wild Things Run Fast (C) Ladies' Man (D) Moon at the Window (D) Be Cool (D blues) Underneath the Streetlight (A) Love (E)	Chinese Café/ Unchained Melody (D-C) Solid Love (D♭-A♭-F)	
Dog Eat Dog (1985)	The Three Great Stimulants (CM/Am*) Smokin' (B Aeol*) Shiny Toys (GM) Lucky Girl (CM*)	Good Friends (A-D) Dog Eat Dog (C-G) Ethiopia (G♯-E) Impossible Dreamer (D-A-E)	Fiction (C) (music by Larry Klein) Tax Free (A) (music by Larry Klein)	The Three Great Stimulants (CM/Am*) Smokin' (B Aeol*) Lucky Girl (CM*)
Chalk Mark in a Rain Storm (1988)	My Secret Place (D♭M) Number One (B♭ Aeol*) The Tea Leaf Prophecy (CM/Am*) (co-written with Larry Klein) Dancin' Clown (FM)		The Reoccurring Dream (A♭)	Lakota (A-F) (co-written with Larry Klein)

(continued)

TABLE 5.1. (Continued)

ALBUM	1. Modal	2. Polymodal	3. Chromatic	4. Polytonal	5. Pedal Point
	The Beat of Black Wings (DM*)				Night Ride Home (CM*)
	Snakes and Ladders (CM/Am) (co-written with Larry Klein)				
Night Ride Home (1991)	Night Ride Home (CM*)	Passion Play (D)		Two Grey Rooms (D-G)	
	Cherokee Louise (DM/Bm*)	The Windfall (A)			
	Slouching towards Bethlehem (DM/Bm)	The Only Joy in Town (D)			
	Come In from the Cold (D♭M/B♭m*)				
	Nothing Can Be Done (AM/F♯m*) (music by Larry Klein)				
	Ray's Dad's Cadillac (DM)				
Turbulent Indigo (1994)	Sex Kills (C Aeol)	Sunny Sunday (C♯)		Borderline (E-B)	
	Turbulent Indigo (B Mixo)	Last Chance Lost (B♭)			
	Magdalene Laundries (AM/F♯m*)				
	Not to Blame (EM)				

124

Yvette in English (CM)
(co-written with David Crosby)

The Sire of Sorrow (DM/Bm)

Taming the Tiger (1998)	Man from Mars (B Aeol)	Harlem in Havana (E)
	Love Puts On a New Face (CM)	Lead Balloon (Eb)
	The Crazy Cries of Love (CM)	No Apologies (A)
	Stay in Touch (CM*)	Taming the Tiger (C)
	Face Lift (CM)	

In this table, the abbreviation Aeol refers to the Aeolian mode; Dor is Dorian; Mixo is Mixolydian. In the first column, single modes predominate (though occasional modal mixture is common); the major mode is one of the modes used. An asterisk indicates a pure mode (no modal mixture). A designation of "M/m" refers to a strong polarity between major and relative "minor" (actually Aeolian). "Polymodal" refers to multiple modes based on a single tonal center, where no single mode predominates; the blues scale is one such type. "Polytonal" refers to multiple tonal centers; for simplicity's sake, the modal character of these songs is not listed. (Polytonal songs with centers a minor third apart do not conform to a simple major/relative minor relation: e.g., "Let the Wind Carry Me" {FR} moves between F♯ Aeolian and A Aeolian; "Car on a Hill" {C&S} between F♯ Aeolian and A Major/Aeolian; "Black Crow" {H} between Eb Dorian and Gb Aeolian.) Some songs are listed under more than one category. The albums Hits and Miles of Aisles each contain a single original song unreleased elsewhere. For the Mingus album, only songs with music by Joni Mitchell are included.

125

EXAMPLE 5.1. MODES

Major   Minor

I   ii   iii   IV   V   vi   vii°   I   i   ii°   III   iv   V   VI   vii°   i

Mixolydian   Aeolian

I   ii   iii°   IV   v   vi   VII   I   i   ii°   III   iv   v   VI   VII   i

Lydian   Dorian

I   II   iii   iv°   V   vi   vii   I   i   ii   III   IV   v   vi°   VII   i

The modes on the left begin with a major triad, those on the right with a minor triad.

with no leading-tone tendency. In addition, all three modes share a minor dominant (v) and a major subtonic (VII) triad. The lack of a leading tone and strong dominant function creates a very different sense of hierarchy among the chords of these modes. The latter can be seen by comparing the triads built on successive degrees of each scale. Each mode offers a unique disposition of major, minor, and diminished triads within its scalar hierarchy. The increased use of modal harmony in popular music goes hand in hand with certain widespread stylistic tendencies identified by Ken Stephenson: a relaxation of syntactic rules for harmonic movement in comparison with traditional tonality, a relaxed sense of forward progression and increased interest in cyclic harmonic successions, and an exploration of alternative cadential approaches, including deemphasis of cadential function altogether.[18]

Thus the modal spectrum offers an expanded field of harmonic movement. But beyond this, whatever mode Mitchell may choose as the basis for a song, she rarely adheres to one mode throughout; instead she breaks up the integrity of its scale in a variety of ways, often flickering between two or more modes within a single song. Again, the mixing of modes was not a new practice. The traditional tune "Greensleeves" as commonly performed alternates between a lowered and raised $\hat{7}$, thus alternating between Aeolian and minor mode (Ex. 5.2). In the Beatles

EXAMPLE 5.2. MODAL MIXTURE IN "GREENSLEEVES"

tune "Eleanor Rigby," each of the first two phrases begins in Dorian (with raised 6̂), only to switch to Aeolian (lowered 6̂) in the fourth bar ("Lives in a dream"). Similarly, Gordon Lightfoot's song "If You Could Read My Mind" plays with an alternation between major and Mixolydian modes (switching between raised and lowered 7̂).[19] But though modal mixture does occur in popular music around the beginning of Mitchell's career, she makes use of it to an unprecedented degree. Out of 152 songs written or co-written by Joni Mitchell, only twenty-two are in one pure mode with no modal mixture (these songs are starred in Table 5.1).

MODALITY

My first examples are songs based on single modes. Mixolydian is a favorite mode in the early period, counting for a dozen songs and appearing as a shading in others. It is used in the song "Ladies of the Canyon" (LC), conceived as a triple self-portrait of Mitchell's creative and domestic life in the Laurel Canyon neighborhood of Los Angeles (Ex. 5.3; for an explanation of the chord symbols used in the examples, see the Appendix).[20] The particular Mixolydian flavor that Mitchell paints with here is the juxtaposition of major I and minor v (D and Am, as in phrase 1), an atmospheric pairing made all the more poignant by the ornamental extension of the Am chord (Ex. 5.4). The top two tones (punctuating the guitar figuration) retain the lingering aura of the tonic, but in this chordal context, struck as they are off the beat and directly clashing with a melodic G, they add a delicious sting. Thus already in the first two bars of the verse, Mitchell has fashioned an evocative harmonic resonance in accord with the poem's bardic romanticization of a latterday bohemia.

But the song's intro includes major dominant chords that do not fit into the prevailing mode. This is an instance of modal mixture, switching between Mixolydian and major. The very opening progression (Am–AM, or v–V) plays on what one might call a diatonic loophole in place at the seventh scale degree, which slips between the options of C and C♯. The sunny A9 chord in the intro (also used as a coda) by its contrast enhances the atmospheric flavor of Am13. Most striking,

EXAMPLE 5.3. "LADIES OF THE CANYON," CHORD CHANGES

Guitar tuning: C G D F C E (capo 2)
Intro: | Am(4) A | A9 | D(4) | D(4) |
Phrase 1, 2: ||: D | Am13/C | Gmaj7/B | D(4) :||
Phrase 3: | Am13/C | Em7/B | Am13/C (+ AM) | B13sus |
Phrase 4, 5: ||: D | Am13/C | Gmaj7/B | D(4) :||

EXAMPLE 5.4. THE EXTENDED DOMINANT IN
"LADIES OF THE CANYON" (HARMONIC REDUCTION)

The guitar plays A and "hammers on" to C;
though C is the sustained bass note,
A remains an implied part of the harmony.

however, is how, at the peak of her melodic arch (phrase 3), Mitchell weaves the two options together. At the words, "And her coat's *a* secondhand one," over a sustained C in the low guitar register, the voice briefly reaches to C♯. This simultaneous cross-relation is so artfully spaced that it sounds quite natural—though it is certainly climactic, triggering as it does a move in a chromatic direction. The move is to an extended B chord whose pungent G♯ introduces a Lydian shading (Ex. 5.5).[21] In the densely layered vocalizations that round off the verse (phrase 5), the cross-relation at $\hat{7}$ is once again in evidence, the guitar cleaving to C and the vocal layers (harmonized in sevenths!) to C♯.

EXAMPLE 5.5. "LADIES OF THE CANYON," END
OF PHRASE 3 (HARMONIC REDUCTION)

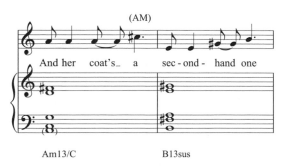

The Mixolydian mode, in other words, is like a base coat, over which Mitchell applies a shifting array of other modal highlights. This painterly conception of harmony is reflected in the poem's conflation of music with color (verse 4), just as the image of filigree reflects the precisely etched guitar figuration. At all levels, in fact, this signature song is expressive of a refined aesthetic sensibility—the poetic structure is classically engineered, with an ingenious set of rhymes for the key words of the refrain (canyon/secondhand one/banyans/companion), and a unique device whereby the word order in the fourth line of each verse is inverted in the fifth. In harmonic subtlety as in other qualities, Mitchell "weaves a pattern all her own."

"Sisotowbell Lane" (*SS*) is the portrait of a place—a rustic retreat whose amenities are detailed with a quirky lack of precision (Ex. 5.6). Mitchell does not use mixed modes here. The harmonic progression, at root, is simplicity itself—D, G, and A chords (I, IV, and V). But Mitchell builds some eccentric structures on those chord roots. The Mixolydian flavor in this song takes the form of an extended chord built on the tonic (D13sus), suggesting a secondary dominant of G (Ex. 5.7).

EXAMPLE 5.6. "SISOTOWBELL LANE," CHORD CHANGES

Guitar tuning: C G D F C E (capo 2)

Interlude:	‖: Dsus(2) D Dsus(2) | D13sus/G :‖
Phrase 1/3:	‖: D | D13sus | D13sus | Gmaj7/B | D |
Phrase 2/4:	| A7sus | A7sus | $\frac{2}{4}$ A7sus |
	| $\frac{4}{4}$ Dsus(2) D Dsus(2) | Dsus(2) D Dsus(2) :‖
Phrase 5:	| D13sus | D13sus |
Phrase 6:	| D7 | D7 |
Phrase 7:	| G/B | D/A |
Phrase 8:	| A7sus | A7sus | $\frac{2}{4}$ A7sus | $\frac{4}{4}$ (to interlude)
Coda:	‖: Dsus(2) D Dsus(2) | D13sus/G :‖ Dsus(2) D |
	| Gmaj7/B | A13sus/D |

EXAMPLE 5.7. THE SECONDARY DOMINANT IN "SISOTOWBELL LANE"
(HARMONIC REDUCTION)

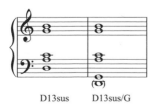

D13sus   D13sus/G

In the instrumental interlude this chord is complicated by a move in the bass register from D to G in the same bar. The sound of the initial D is prominent, but it competes with G for the fundamental harmonic position (D13sus/G). The D chord and its implied resolution are oddly tangled up. In the verse, the D13sus chords are resolved traditionally (to a clear G), but only after lingering to savor their irresistible dissonance. As a result, the first four phrases have unusual proportions. Phrases 1 and 3 (I–V/IV–IV–I) are slightly expanded to five bars; phrases 2 and 4 (V–I) to four and a half bars. This rhythmic dilation, especially the casual addition of half-bars, perfectly suits the poem's blend of indolence and eccentricity.

Those half-bars extend the effect of the song's unusual dominant. Mitchell chooses neither minor v (using C) nor major V (using C♯), but a suspended A7 chord with its own in-between quality. She then embellishes this chord's characteristic D with chromatic neighbors (Ex. 5.8). This extraordinary cadential moment is complemented by a slight dislocation of the tonic; after every dominant, the tonic has to take a moment to hitch up its suspenders, as it were. That is to say, the upper two notes of the triad are approached quickly from below (by "hammering on"). But after a few beats $\hat{3}$ and $\hat{5}$ are already sagging again, so on the whole the impression at cadences is not so much of a straight D triad as of a Dsus(2). The song's final cadence manages to tie up these various loose ends without losing the sense of open-endedness so appealingly maintained throughout. The last chord (produced by strumming open strings) is spelled as in Ex. 5.9. It fuses elements of A7sus, Dsus(2), and DM (i.e., simultaneous dominant, suspension, and resolution), as it rings with the dissonance and promise of a 13th chord.

Mitchell's harmonic scheme in this song uses a series of suspensions, delays, and implications that together create a pleasing relaxation of directedness. The constant impression of hovering in some out-of-the-way, neither-here-nor-there zone chimes with the spaciness of the poem, which creates its own temporal eddies ("we always do, yes sometimes we do"). The diatonic field is intact (pure Mixolydian), but its syntactic elements are mildly askew—a dislocation meant to capture the essence of this spot off the beaten path.

EXAMPLE 5.8. THE SUSPENDED DOMINANT IN
"SISOTOWBELL LANE"

A7sus

EXAMPLE 5.9. "SISOTOWBELL LANE," FINAL CADENCE

Dsus(2) D   D(4)   Gmaj7/B

cadential chord:

A7sus   D

A13sus/D   Dsus(2)   A13sus/D

POLYMODALITY

With the next example, we move beyond the use of single prevailing modes. In "The Dawntreader" (SS), a lyrical seafaring fantasy, D Mixolydian and D Dorian are so entwined that it is impossible to declare either one prevalent (Ex. 5.10). Many of the phrases trace a movement from Dorian to Mixolydian. The guitar interlude (which also serves to accompany phrases 2, 4, and 11) begins by picking out a Dm9 chord (Ex. 5.11). The F♮ places this first chord in Dorian. The third bar arrives at a D major triad, which in the context of the surrounding C♮s is placed in Mixolydian. The intervening G chord belongs to both modes. This recurrent gesture launches in one mode and settles in another. It settles in register as well, filtering from limpid high notes gradually down to a bottom-heavy cadence. Such a gesture of submergence befits the journey imagined here, an internalized, symbolic journey, whose initial vision is of the fabled treasure strewn across the ocean floor.

After the cadence, Mitchell trades D major for an open D (D5), a pivot to the Dorian at the beginning of phrases 1 and 3. This open chord at the portal of each verse encapsulates the tonal equipoise she has constructed between two modes, one given initiatory, the other cadential importance. The harmonic base of this song is thus truly polymodal. Mitchell applies further highlights to this dual base in the long, climactic middle section (phrases 5–9). It begins with an oracular string of quintal structures—open 5ths moving in parallel around a pedal D (Ex. 5.12). This is the most extended passage of Mixolydian in the song (note the melodic F♯s; see Ex. 6.10). But as the voice begins to rise from its murkiest

EXAMPLE 5.10. "THE DAWNTREADER," CHORD CHANGES

Guitar tuning: D G D D A D

| Interlude: | \| Dm9 \| G(4)/D \| D Dsus \| Dsus D \| |
| | Dorian   Mixo |

Interlude: | Dm9 | G(4)/D | D Dsus | Dsus D |
       Dorian   Mixo

Phrase 1/3:   ‖: D5 | Dm7 | Csus2(6) | Csus2(6) |
       Pivot Dorian

Phrase 2/4: | Dm9 | G(4)/D | D Dsus | Dsus D :‖
            Mixo

Phrase 5, 6:   ‖: Csus2 Bm | Csus2 Asus G5 :‖

Phrase 7: | Csus2 Bm | Csus2 Asus | Gsus2 |
              Major

Phrase 8: | Gsus2 | Asus |

Phrase 9: | Asus | B♭maj7 | B♭maj7 |
         Aeolian

Phrase 10: | G7sus | G | G7sus | G |
       Dorian

Phrase 11: | Dm9 | G(4)/D | D Dsus | Dsus D |
            Mixo

EXAMPLE 5.11. "THE DAWNTREADER," INTRO
(AND INSTRUMENTAL REFRAIN)

Dm9   G(4)/D

D   Dsus   D

depths, there is a dramatic shift to the major mode, with melodic accentuation of C♯. At the moment of greatest tension (phrase 9: "he stakes all his *silver*"), as the voice reaches an unexpected high point (dissonant with the chordal root), there is yet another exotic intrusion—B♭maj7, a chord borrowed from the Aeolian. All this tension is magically sprung at phrase 10 ("on a promise to be free") with a

EXAMPLE 5.12. "THE DAWNTREADER,"
PHRASES 5 AND 6 (HARMONIC REDUCTION)

Csus2   Bm   Csus2   Asus   G5

new lilting rhythm, a return to the home Dorian, and a clearing of the thick, low chordal textures that dominated the middle section. Altogether, then, Mitchell exploits three diatonic loopholes in "Dawntreader," not only the central switch at $\hat{3}$ between F and F♯, but two others at $\hat{6}$ (B-B♭) and $\hat{7}$ (C-C♯). This pushes the scalar resources in use toward the full chromatic (only E♭ and A♭ are not used). But Mitchell has carefully apportioned her use of chromatic intrusions to create an arc of modal transformation. This arcing path embodies a siren call of longing, underpinning the song's combined dreams of personal enrichment, social redemption, and mythicized romance.

The previous three examples give an idea of the range of harmonic effects Mitchell can unfold within one key, D Mixolydian, by her use of complex chordal structures, harmonic suspension, and mixed modes. In "Dawntreader," the modal mixture becomes an alloy of two basic modes within a single key. Similarly complex alloys can be found in two other songs from the first album. "Nathan La Franeer," a lament for an inhuman cityscape, has a triple modal base. Like "Dawntreader," it uses suspended chords as pivots between modes. The first two phrases, for instance, begin with a suspended pivot and move through Dorian to tonic major. The blending of G Dorian, major, and minor creates an eerily unwholesome tone. "I Had a King," a requiem for a failed romance, in ironic-medieval garb, is also a triple alloy on A. Here major and Aeolian elements are starkly juxtaposed in the opening bars. Dorian elements are prominent in the second half of the verse. (The song is also notable for its portentous extended quartal structures; see Ex. 2.1.) Such polymodal bases as these in fact represent the most common harmonic scheme found throughout Mitchell's career. Their prismatic effect is tangible in many of her most beloved songs: "All I Want" (B) in D♭ major/Mixolydian (see Ex. 6.11), "My Old Man" (B) in A major/Dorian, "Woman of Heart and Mind" (FR) in B major/Mixolydian/Lydian, and "Court and Spark" (C&S) in E Dorian/Aeolian/Mixolydian. I would say that the forked harmonic paths and expressive polarities made possible by Mitchell's polymodal usage form one of the most characteristic attributes of her musical style. To illustrate further, I will discuss two well-known examples from her third and fourth albums: "Rainy Night House" and "Blue."

Mitchell uses piano rather than guitar to accompany "Rainy Night House" (*LC*) (Ex. 5.13). There is nothing here like the inlaid busywork of layered and suspended voice-leading found in the accompaniment to the first three examples. Instead the harmony takes the form of forthright triads, for the most part, moving in loose-jointed progression. In comparison to the finely strung artifice of the other songs discussed, this song adheres to a rhetoric of natural, direct expression. The nocturnal scenario as it is pressed into lyric form is fragmentary and blurred around the edges: an intense but tenuous assignation, whose circumstances, lightly sketched in, do not come close to anchoring the melancholy that threatens to overwhelm the performer.

The song begins with a long instrumental prelude, Schumannesque in its expansiveness. The tonic Am chord is cramped and depressed by elements of a G triad in the right hand (thus sounding as A7sus). Subsequent moves to a clear G (VII in A Aeolian) provide a sense of alleviation. The next harmonic pass takes us through B♭, whose Phrygian influence imparts another depressive shading. The third pass expands on these dualities: G issues into a breath of C major elation, while B♭ harshly runs up against its tritone relation (E) on the way to cadence. The outcome of all this preparation is a shock of dislocation as the curtain opens with an abrupt move to the key of Dm.

The entire vocal body of the song thus exists in an uncanny relation to its soulful prelude. The polymodal expressive duality is carried over but in inverted configuration, as if pulled through the die of memory. The B♭, originally a foreign intrusion threatening the solace of the Aeolian mode, is now integral to the fabric of D Aeolian. The A7sus chord reappears, now bluffly on the beat, with its effect of emotional truncation like a catch in the throat. We have to wait for the consoling G. When it appears it is now the "foreign" (Dorian) intrusion, in a cycle-of-fifths passage holding out the hope of elation. This whole passage (phrases 3 and

EXAMPLE 5.13. "RAINY NIGHT HOUSE," CHORD CHANGES

Intro (in A): ‖: A7sus Am7 | A7sus Am7 | G | G :‖ C | B♭ | Am | G | G |
                   Aeolian   (Phryg)

                | C G | F | B♭ | B♭ | Em | Em | Am | Am |
                       (Phryg)

Verse (in D)

Phrase 1, 2: ‖: Dm | B♭ | A7sus Am7 | A :‖
               Aeolian   minor

Phrase 3: | Dm | G | C | F |
            Dorian

Phrase 4: | B♭ | Dm | C | Am | Am | G | G | Dm | Dm | Dm | Dm |
            Aeolian   Dorian

4) recalls distinct segments of the prelude, now interpreted in the new key. The Bb and G chords have exchanged priority, and it is the earthbound modal elements that now hold sway. The prelude and the verses consist of much the same events, yet they tell different stories. But which version—the instrumental or the vocal—is to be taken as present experience, and which the transformation of poetic reflection? Which is reinterpreting the other? Neither musical statement establishes more than a dreamy unreality. Unanchored with respect to its modal character, emotional tone, and formal framing, "Rainy Night House" steeps us in its intense search for identity ("who in the world I might be"), a search whose inconclusiveness is scarcely to be distinguished from outright loss.

"Blue" (B) is a devastating love song. The principals are once again imagined as seafarers but here navigating the treacherous waters of drugs and depression (Ex. 5.14). In an image of masterful ambivalence, Mitchell lets the sailor's tattoo stand for the indelible lacerations of love, the needle-tracks of addiction, and the

EXAMPLE 5.14. "BLUE," CHORD CHANGES

Intro: | no chord (D) | G | Bm | G |
            Aeolian

Phr. 1 (a): | Bm A/B | Bm A/B |Gmaj7 D/E | E | D/E | E | A/B D/G | E/A | E/A |
                                     Dorian   mixed

Phr. 2 (a'): | Bm A/B | Bm A/B | D/E | E | D/E | E | A/B D/G | E/A | E/A |
            (Aeol?/Dor?)   Dorian   mixed

Phr. 3 (b): | Bm A/B | Gmaj7 D/G | D/E | E5 |
            Aeolian   (Dor?)

Phr. 4 (b'): | ³⁄₄ Bm A/B | Gmaj7 D/G | ⁴⁄₄ D/E Em7(4) | Asus | Bm | Bm | F♯m |
                Aeolian

Phr. 5 (b''): | D/E A/E D/E | D/E A/E D/E | D/E A/E D/E | D/E A/E |
            Pivot

Phr. 6 (a''): | Bm A/B | Bm A/B | F♯m | F♯m | D/E A/E | D/E | D/A | A |
            (Aeol?/Dor?)   [A major?]   ]

Phr. 7 (a): | Bm A/B | Bm A/B | D/E | E | D/E | Em7(4) | Em7(4) | Em7(4) |
                                   Dorian Aeolian

            | Bm | F♯m | D/E | D/E |
                 Pivot

Coda: | A/B E/B | Bm7 | B7 |
            Dorian   blues

Note: In keeping with Mitchell's left hand piano style, slash chords in this song include a 5th above the bass. Thus an A/B chord includes the pitches B F♯ C♯ E A.

ink of her own pen, filling in the empty spaces. Mitchell's use of the piano creates a more multifaceted harmonic surface than in the previous example. Triadic shapes in the right hand often conflict with the bass, creating extended structures of various kinds. Thus in the characteristic gesture opening phrase 1, the right hand moves down from Bm to A over a constant bass (Ex. 5.15). The pure tonic triad moves to a multiply dissonant, internally conflicted chord (interpretable as B9sus)—as if emotionally sullied, depressed, ambivalent. The weight of this one gestural scrap is enough to send the singer into a weary tailspin before she even starts. As her leaden arabesques give way to a more animated impulse ("I've been to sea before"), the sense of rhythmic release is accompanied by a mode switch from Aeolian to Dorian. The passage rides the uplift of the new mode's major subdominant, only to stall once again at the end of the phrase, in a progression that hopelessly tangles the focal loophole of G and G♯ (Ex. 5.16). These chords form another kind of extended structure (D/G–E/A, or Gmaj9–Amaj9), whose strange parallel dissonance arrests the flow, pulsing in stunned aftershocks.

The Aeolian element in the song (using G) appears in VI (G) and iv (Em), the Dorian element (using G♯) in IV (E), and the emotional polarities between them are set up economically but to maximum effect. Dorian emerges concretely only three times in the body of the song, but its hopeful quality is held in potential through much of phrases 3–6 by the use of a pivot chord, D/E, which could resolve in either mode. Those moments when it does resolve unequivocally to an Aeolian

EXAMPLE 5.15. "BLUE," OPENING OF VERSE

Bm   A/B (B9sus)

EXAMPLE 5.16. "BLUE," END OF PHRASE 1 (HARMONIC REDUCTION)

A/B   D/G   E/A

Em are traumatic, knocking the wind out of the sails (see the fermatas in the diagram, phrases 4 and 7, representing a dramatic loss in rhythmic momentum). From a palette of such deflationary gestures, Mitchell creates a design of poignant emotional irony. The inevitable letdowns are made more powerful because she never abandons her passionate yearning.

The central relationship of the poem is apparently unresolved, poised between anchored commitment and undone moorings. On a formal level, the song is correspondingly torn between rhapsodic flight and broken structure. Atypically, "Blue" is through-composed rather than strophic. The musical phrases, uneven in length and prone to wandering, are anchored by two recurrent melodic segments. The first segment (**a**) is characterized by its initial address to "Blue," Mitchell's totemic name for her beloved; its melodic contour begins on a middle F♯, dips low, and ends by rising toward B ("let me sail away"). The **a** segment is stated freely in the first phrase, then repeated more succinctly and with a new rhythmic vigor in phrase 2 (both 9 bars long). Phrases 3 and 4 state the **b** segment (a repeated descending figure: "there's so many sinking"), again with variations in its rhythmic integrity. Phrase 5 is built from transposed repetitions of **b** and leads directly into phrase 6, a climactic condensation and heightening of **a** ("Blue, I love you"). The final phrase returns to the original **a** (though with a new close). The underlying symmetry can be schematized as: **aa' bb' b'' a'' a**. But this structural clarity is brilliantly unbalanced by the unexpected, extraneous elements introduced in the form of rhapsodic digressions. The first of these comes at the end of phrase 4. The rhythmic flow, halted at the Aeolian iv, struggles to regain composure. When it does, the moment is made remarkable by the introduction of a new harmony, F♯m (v)—the first dominant to appear, which will have a cadential role from this point on in the song. Another digression occurs at the end of phrase 6, when the harmonies seem to spin off into a new key altogether, by cadencing strongly on A. This momentary sidetrack is patently wishful, its gestures somehow not fully integrated into the song's fabric. And in fact the piano cadences in these four measures do represent a kind of intrusion, constituting as they do an almost exact quotation of a passage from another love song on the album—the introduction to "My Old Man." They thus (subconsciously?) capture and import the brief memory of a happier time and a different outcome.

The final phrase makes a strong move toward formal closure, on the one hand, by melding the beginning of phrase 1 with the closing harmonies of phrase 4 and thus recapitulating the song's expository gestures while foreclosing their hopeful turn to Dorian. Yet as the piano postlude winds down, not only does it return to Dorian but it comes to rest on a *major* tonic sonority— yet another unexpected, extraneous flight of fancy, a symbol of hope not quite deferred. Like the previous points of departure, the song's final moments make a bid for freedom and open-endedness, with a wry nod to the classic musical vehicle of ambivalent emotion, the blues.

CHROMATICISM

A third harmonic strategy in Mitchell's songwriting, much less common than modal and polymodal usage, is directly chromatic progression. Chromatic passages spice up the relative innocence of songs such as "Michael from Mountains" (*SS*) (see Ex. 6.15) and "Morning Morgantown" (*LC*). A more thorough chromaticism lies behind some of Mitchell's spacier tunes. A good example of this is "Songs to Aging Children Come" (Ex. 5.17). The hallucinatory lyrics and helium-infused vocal warbling are matched by the far-out chord progressions, which experiment with tritone and third relations. The chorus is notable for shifting upward first through two minor thirds (B–D–F), then again through two major thirds (B–E♭–G). A no less thorough chromaticism can be found in "Marcie," but here careful stepwise voice-leading mitigates the unsettling effect of the far-flung harmonic path (Ex. 5.18). Perhaps it should also be mentioned that this example can be heard in terms of polymodality. In its melancholy cycling down through the chromatic scale (mirroring the cycle of the seasons in the poem's urban backdrop), the song presents a shifting kaleidoscope of Aeolian, Lydian, and major qualities on G (Ex. 5.19).

EXAMPLE 5.17. "SONGS TO AGING CHILDREN COME," CHORD CHANGES

Guitar tuning: B F♯ B F♯ B D♯
Intro: | B Lydian | ...
Phrase 1: | G | F♯ | F | B |
Phrase 2: | A | G | F♯ | B | B |
Chorus: | D | F | F Lydian | F Lydian | B | E♭ | E♭ Lydian | E♭ Lydian | G | G |

EXAMPLE 5.18. "MARCIE," CHORD CHANGES (VERSE)

Guitar tuning: D G D G B D
Phrase 1: | B♭6 | A | Am7 | G Gsus(2) G |
Phrase 2: | B♭6 | A | Am7 | G Gsus(2) | G Gsus(2) G |
Phrase 3: | E♭maj7 | D | C | B |
Phrase 4: | B♭6 | A | Am7 | G Gsus(2) | G Gsus(2) G |

EXAMPLE 5.19. "MARCIE," PHRASES 3 AND 4
(HARMONIC REDUCTION)

Ebmaj7   D   C   B   Bb6

A   Am7   G   Gsus(2)

POLYTONALITY

All the songs discussed so far in this chapter, whether modal, polymodal, or chromatic, are defined by a single key center (save "Rainy Night House," which modulates once, to remain in the new key). But one of the most original paths of exploration in Mitchell's work has to do with the fission or doubling of tonal center.[22]

> JM: People started telling me that I was playing in two keys at the same time. "Oh, really?" I said (laughs) ... see, a lot of this is intuitive so it's up to other people really to analyze it. A song like "Amelia," for instance, modulates. It goes along for a while in one key and then suddenly it drops down to the low chord. It's crossed over into a whole other key reference. And then it crosses back with complete disregard to the fact that it stepped outside of its family of colors. So I'm told (laughs).[23]

While the self-assured essays into dual tonalities really only begin with the fifth album (*FR*), we find an isolated example from 1967 at the beginning of her output (Ex. 5.20). Each verse of "I Don't Know Where I Stand" (*C*) begins in D Mixolydian and modulates by a single dramatic swerve at the end of phrase 2 to F major (by way of a secondary dominant, V/IV [F9]). Seams between verses (i.e., between the F chord at the end of one verse and the D chord at the beginning of the next) remain exposed. Furthermore, the song ultimately cadences, by a Phrygian progression, on yet a third tonal center, as follows: D–Ab–G. Assigning a key requires a double (D-F) or perhaps even triple label (D-F-G). The title (also

EXAMPLE 5.20. "I DON'T KNOW WHERE I STAND,"
CHORD CHANGES

Guitar tuning: F F C G A C

Phrase 1:		D(9)	D(9)	C(9)	C(9)	
Phrase 2:		D(9)	D(9)	F9	F9	
Phrase 3:		B♭(9)	B♭(9)	Am7	Am7	
Phrase 4:		B♭m6	Gm	F	F	

the refrain) of this engaging song thus acquires an added pertinence to its uncertain harmonic structure—although the effect is by no means confused or uneasy but consists rather of refreshing changes of perspective.

Five years later, in *For the Roses*, Mitchell begins to explore multiple tonalities in earnest. I will discuss two songs from that album, one whose tonal poles are harmonically distant from one another, the other whose poles are closely interrelated. The first example, "Let the Wind Carry Me," takes personal dualities as its theme (Ex. 5.21). From the day-to-day disagreements between her mother and father during her formative years, Mitchell extrapolates a dichotomy between two belief systems: the work ethic and the pleasure principle, the domestic urge and the urge for rootlessness. She finds both urges in contradiction within her own soul. A similar contradiction is played out in the song's tonal structure, which is split between F♯m and Am, triads with only one pitch in common (though due to the prevalent 7th structures, there are two common pitches, A and E, between the two tonic chords, F♯m7 and Am7). Mitchell makes the most out of this harmonic distance by leaving the modulations very exposed—a bald exchange of one tonic for another. Each verse modulates once; in fact, little of harmonic interest occurs in the verses save for the focal modulation.

EXAMPLE 5.21. "LET THE WIND CARRY ME," CHORD CHANGES

Intro: | F♯m E | Dmaj7 | F♯m7 E | D | F♯m7 | E | D | A/D | F♯m7...

VERSE 1— Phrase 1: | F♯m7 | E | F♯m7 | F♯m7 |
         Phrase 2: | Am7 | Am7 | Am7 | Am7 |
         Phrase 3: | G | F | Am7 | Am7 |

VERSE 2— Phrase 1: | Am7 | F | Am7 | Am7 |
         Phrase 2: | F♯m7 | F♯m7 | F♯m7 | F♯m7 |
         Phrase 3: | E | D | F♯m7 | F♯m7 |

Interlude: | Am7 | Am7 | Am7 | Am7 | F♯m7 | Em7 | Em7 | Am7 | Am7 |
           | F♯m7 | Em7 | Em7 | Em7 | F♯ Em | C♯sus | C♯sus |
           | F♯m7 | E | F♯m7 | E | G | Asus | Bsus | Bsus | Bsus | Bsus |
           | Am7 D | G | G | Bm7 Asus | B♭(♮4) | B♭(♮4) | Esus | Esus | Am7 | Am7 |

These building blocks, though simple, are set into a formal plan of stunning design. Key to the overall plan is the remarkable use of commutative modulation; that is, the verses, instead of always beginning from the same tonal pole, go both back and forth between F♯m and Am. Verse 1 begins in F♯m, modulates, then cadences in Am. Verse 2 begins in Am, modulates, then cadences in F♯m. After an extended orchestral interlude (beginning and ending in Am), Mitchell reverses this tonal arrangement: verse 3 moves from Am to F♯m, verse 4 from F♯m to Am. Given that the introduction and coda are both in F♯m, the whole song thus works as a set of interlocking palindromes:

[F♯m] 1. F♯m–Am 2. Am–F♯m [Am–unstable–Am] 3. Am–F♯m 4. F♯m–Am [F♯m]

In fact, another duality is evident here—between a tonal orientation of constant volatility and its arrangement in a design of mathematical symmetry.

The volatile, rootless quality comes to the fore in the lengthy interlude. It is difficult to ascertain any progression of keys here, since tonal allegiances are so thoroughly adrift. Clearly this instrumental passage conveys the alluring vagrancy captured in the poetic image of the wild seed on the wind. Yet at the same time, it is within this passage that Mitchell explores a liaison between her two tonal poles. In contrast to the body of the song, which preserves and exposes the distance between F♯m and Am as a leap between unrelated worlds, the interlude intertwines the two triads as if in pursuit of a higher synthesis. In line with the romantic impulse of the song, however, such a synthesis never does materialize.[24]

My second example from *For the Roses* is "Cold Blue Steel and Sweet Fire," a fiendishly cool portrayal of heroin addiction (Ex. 5.22). Where "Let the Wind Carry Me" used a distant third relation between tonal poles, this song uses C and G, a much closer fifth relation. Since these two keys share so much harmonic territory, Mitchell is able to set up a more muddled, irresolute sense of duality. To compound the experience of vacillation, the passages centered on C are cast

EXAMPLE 5.22. "COLD BLUE STEEL AND SWEET FIRE," CHORD CHANGES

Guitar tuning: C G D G B D

Intro:	G5 F5 G5 B♭5	G5 F5 G5	G5 F5 G5 B♭5	G5 F5 D5 G
Phrase 1:	C (Lydian)	C(9)	C(9)	C(9)
Phrase 2:	G5 F5 G5 B♭5	G5 F5 G5	G5 F5 G5 B♭5	G5 F5 D5 G
Phrase 3:	C (Lydian)	C(9)	C(9)	C(9)
Phrase 4:	G5 F5 G5	D	C	C
Chorus:	C B♭ C G	C B♭ C	D/G F/B♭	C/F	C/F G
	C (Lydian)	C(9)	C(9)	C(9)
	G5 F5 G5 B♭5	G5 F5 G5	G5 F5 G5 B♭5	G5 F5 D5 G

in the Lydian mode, whose F♯ carries a leading-tone momentum toward G. The passages on G are cast in a mixed mode (similar to a blues scale) which favors F♮. Another way to put this is that the C passages are infused with elements of G major, and vice versa. Arrival on one or the other tonal pole thus usually provides only a momentary stability, since an impetus toward the other pole is immediately set up. The first phrase is in C but already pushes toward G; phrase 2, on G, is immediately ready to fall back down to C. Neither pole is clearly differentiated from the other.

The only moment of clarity occurs at the end of each verse, where the poetic lens focuses on the images of "Sweet Fire" and "Lady Release." At this point (phrase 4) the appearance of a D chord allows the tonality to resolve to a G center. The D chord is clearly a dominant, and the C chords that follow are clearly subdominants of G. The way seems clear for a moment. But where does it lead?—"down, down the dark ladder." At these words the bottom drops out of the clear dominant. From C we are thrown, by way of exquisite harmonic sensations (extended triadic structures: D/G–F/B♭–C/F), back into the familiar muddle and vacillation. The reigning tonal gesture thus creates an inextricable, vicious cycle, a perfect foil for the hollow, elusive release that taunts the junkie. Tonal centers and words blur together indistinctly for the "hollow-grey-fire-escape-thief" who can find no escape from the concrete urban jungle or the fever burning in her veins. Yet the tone of this song remains cool and unruffled, ironically detached from the human pathos it portrays. The authorial voice enjoys a modernist control over the symbolic language, gelid and obscure, and a modernist distance from its disintegrating subject. The suave, bluesy cadences are closer to the taunting, disembodied perspective of Lady Release than to the addict's private descent into hell.

STRICT PEDAL POINTS

My final category has to do with the use of pedal points. In diametric contrast to her forays into multiple tonalities, Mitchell has written songs that explore a strong, almost unceasing rootedness to a single pitch center. Harmonically, such songs do overlap with the single or mixed modes of my first two categories, but their use of insistent tonal anchors constitutes a distinct organizing principle. For this reason I have placed them in their own category. The pedals are typically on the tonic, but in three dulcimer songs (from *Blue*) Mitchell experiments with a dominant pedal.

Mitchell uses pedal points not as a tried-and-true, folk-derived, naive expression of affirmation but as a special technique with a striking range of effects. The textural and rhythmic profiles of the pedals vary from song to song. In "Song to a Seagull" (*SS*) the pedal occupies its own registral plane, tolling at regular intervals deep beneath the melodic surface (see Ex. 4.3). This pattern establishes a symbol of open, multilayered space and a solemnity suitable to the poem's oracular delivery. In "Cactus Tree" (*SS*), a nostalgic catalogue of past loves, the tonic throbs in a constant pulse amid a closely knit texture as if the listener were pressed intimately to a warm musical body. The pedal in "I Had a King" (*SS*) is further in the background and more subtly crafted, merely an accompanimental fabric that always retains the same lower limit (A). (In a further intricacy, the guitar establishes a persistent emphasis on E near its upper limit as well, which is in fact a secondary pedal on the dominant; see Ex. 2.1.) The harmonic effects Mitchell achieves are just as varied. In "Song to a Seagull" the tonic C bass supports two competing harmonic layers: the voice remains almost wholly in Mixolydian while the guitar's upper reaches stray onto darker modal paths. In "For the Roses" (*FR*) the unchanging B♭ pedal is set in a fluid polymodal context (Lydian, Aeolian, and Mixolydian), as if caught in an ever-shifting play of light. "Cactus Tree" works with a limited range of colors (only four basic chord-forms in the entire song: I, Imaj7, IV, Vsus), deriving a great deal of sentiment from simple plagal cadences (IV–I) on F♯ (see Ex. 6.12).

Beyond their expressive leverage, Mitchell uses such limitations of harmony and voice-leading to engage with the song's thematics, by fashioning gestures of confinement and freedom. In "Cactus Tree," the rhythmic pedal's gravitational field—periodically released—is used to enact the dilemma of the song's heroine, caught between the pull of romantic attachments and her yearning for independence and self-fulfillment. The pedal in "Song to a Seagull" likewise has thematic impact, as an ironic anchor tugging against the impulse toward visionary flight. In the faux-medieval "I Had a King," the narrator cast as "queen" is confined (presumably for childbirth) till the end of the year. The song's progressions creep by stepwise motion from one chord to the next, with dominants pressed into unwonted positions to accommodate the tonic bass. In contrast, the dulcimer songs from *Blue*, strung on dominant pedals, enjoy a much more unencumbered harmonic activity. The poet in "All I Want" is traveling on a personal quest, looking for the key to set her free. The song's harmonies are restless and polymodal, dancing around a joyously jangling internal pedal. The more laid-back love song "A Case of You," in straight D♭ major, has cadences that unwind with a Baroque precision and inevitability.

I would like to consider one example in greater detail. "Both Sides, Now" (*C*) is one of Mitchell's most celebrated songs, though her own dejected performance bears little resemblance to the Judy Collins cover version from 1967 which first made it a hit (Ex. 5.23). The harmonies are almost pure major and tend toward the monochrome (I, IV, and V).[25] By now we can appreciate how incredibly limited

EXAMPLE 5.23. "BOTH SIDES, NOW," CHORD CHANGES

Guitar tuning: E B E G♯ B E (capo 2)

Phrase 1/3: ‖: F♯/E♯ B(9)/D♯ | C♯7sus F♯ B(9)/F♯ | F♯ C♯7 | C♯7 F♯ C♯7sus |

Phrase 2/4: | F♯/E♯ B(9)/D♯ | C♯7sus | F♯/E♯ B(9)/D♯ | C♯7sus (blues) :‖

Chorus: | F♯ C♯5(7) | F♯ C♯5(7) F♯ | F♯ C♯5(7) F♯ | F♯ C♯5(7) F♯ |
            | F♯/E♯ B(9)/D♯ | F♯ B(9)/D♯ F♯ | F♯/E♯ B(9)/D♯ | C♯7sus | C♯7sus |

Interlude: | F♯ B(9)/F♯ | F♯ F♯maj7 B(9)/D♯ | F♯ B(9)/F♯ | F♯ B(9)/F♯ |

such a palette is in the context of Mitchell's style. She exploits the redundancy for expressive purpose: the repetitive treading of the same harmonic paths captures an appropriately world-weary tone. Yet, within this monochromatic spectrum, Mitchell is careful to create textural variety and sculpt a precise lyrical shape with its own highs and lows.

The tonic pedal (F♯) is rarely relinquished. The I and IV chords are able to swivel freely around this axis, but many of the dominants are more constrained, appearing as they do in a suspended form which retains the F♯. The pedal is not restricted to a single plane, however, but traverses a two-octave spread. In the guitar interludes, the pedal is present at all three pitch-levels, in a series of plagal cadences whose full chords are bounded at top and bottom by F♯ (Ex. 5.24). During the verses, the pedal bounces between octaves. At the beginning of phrase 1 (as well as in many of the F♯maj7 chords throughout), the texture contracts around the central F♯. The C♯7sus chords drop the central F♯ in favor of high F♯ (Ex. 5.25). The sovereignty of the pedal, while harmonically constant, is texturally mobile and variegated, allowing for a moving bass. But the resulting bass

EXAMPLE 5.24. "BOTH SIDES, NOW,"
INTERLUDE PATTERN

F♯   B(9)/F♯ F♯

EXAMPLE 5.25. "BOTH SIDES, NOW," BEGINNING
OF PHRASE 1 (HARMONIC REDUCTION)

F♯/E♯   B(9)/D♯   C♯7sus   F♯

line uses tonal homing as a repetitive, despondent gesture. Again and again, the bass E♯ moves down to C♯ and thence to the low F♯. E♯, having lost its upward-leading function, is now "acting strange" and serves as the departure point for a dispirited course downward.

Only twice does E♯ lead directly up to the tonic, in the vocal line at the end of phrases 1 and 3 (e.g., "ice cream castles *in the air*"). These parallel moments stand out for several reasons. The voice, within a verse of generally drooping contours, rises a full octave span. At the same time, the guitar bursts past the F♯ which has capped its range until now. Not least, the vocal cadence with its leading-tone and clear unconstrained dominant momentarily revokes the tyranny of the pedal. This elated gesture first corresponds with the high spirits at the outset of each verse of the poem. But then something goes awry: the second half of each verse repeats the gesture of elation, but the words are no longer joyous. The poet now views her former joy with a jaded eye. The same music is used for both takes, the buoyant and the disillusioned. Not only that, but the emphatically rising gesture is followed every time by downcast gestures. First the voice peaks on A♯ only to fall dramatically by a major seventh ("and fea*ther can*yons"; note Mitchell's poignant glissando over this interval in verse 2 on "and if *you care*"). Next, at the end of phrases 2 and 4, the bass line breaks out into a bluesy riff in the Dorian mode, whose E♮ and A♮ tug dissonantly and depressively at the otherwise uniformly major key.

The beginning of the chorus provides a spell of relief from all this tonal gravity. For four measures, the guitar interpolates dominants (C♯5(7)) released from the sway of the F♯ pedal. The voice, leaping and hovering in its highest range, mostly avoids the tonic. In the chorus's second half, though, the singer sinks back to her low alto, and the sovereign pedal returns. The end of the chorus is made up of two cadential phrases, in both of which the vocal line moves down to the tonic. The first phrase (2 bars long) is a straightforward plagal cadence, but the second is pungently displaced. In fact, the voice arrives at the tonic too early ("don't know *clouds*"), while the guitar has only reached the dominant. The voice's cadential note is thus dissonant for two full measures as the guitar picks out a humble cadenza (Ex. 5.26). The emphasis in this final cadence is on the harmonic element (C♯7sus) of the greatest tension and constraint within the song's bland scheme. To further the sense of constraint, Mitchell arranges for the guitar cadenza to peak in a chord bounded by F♯ on both sides. The voice is planted in the middle of this chord, on a third F♯. When the harmony finally resolves to I, the voice has only enough energy to turn over in a spent, anticlimactic roulade. Mitchell is treating tonality perversely in this song, using cadential movement as a downer and using a surfeit of tonal center as a symbol of tedium and disenchantment. To get the full effect of this virtuosic achievement, one need only compare Mitchell's version

EXAMPLE 5.26. "BOTH SIDES, NOW," END OF CHORUS

C♯7sus   F♯sus(2)

to the Judy Collins cover, in which the astringent, landlocked tonal nuances are swept away in a sugary barrage of primary colors.[26]

In closing, I want to offer some general comments on the harmonic categories I have identified and their use throughout Mitchell's career. I have tabulated the five categories in her complete work (1966–1998) in Table 5.1.

Songs with a single predominant mode form one of the two largest categories in Mitchell's career, numbering over sixty songs. There are three in Dorian and nine in Aeolian. Mixolydian becomes rarer as a base after the early period; she revisits it in "Turbulent Indigo" (*TI*) and "Chinese Café" (*WTRF*) (in this D Mixolydian song the VII is gradually transformed into a second key center, CM, for her nostalgic quotation of "Unchained Melody"). The major mode makes strong appearances in *Ladies of the Canyon* and *Blue*, then becomes scarce for awhile, to return as a favored choice in the 1980s and '90s. (Note that all these modes are well represented in the polymodal category. Also, given the prevalence of modal mixture in the first category, the boundaries between the first and second categories are not completely cut-and-dried.) An interesting subgroup of major-mode songs consists of those in which Mitchell sets up a forceful polarity between the tonic major and the relative "minor" (actually Aeolian). She explores this extensively in the late 1980s and early '90s.[27]

Polymodality is an equally common and fertile harmonic scheme in Mitchell's work. Counting for nearly sixty songs, it never loses its fascination. Beginning with *For the Roses*, polytonality grows in importance, eventually appearing in a remarkable twenty-seven songs.

In contrast, chromaticism and pedal points have nearly exhausted their interest after the early period. In two experimental songs from the second period, Mitchell brings each technique to a climax. "The Jungle Line" (*HSL*), noted for its importation of Burundi drumming as a rhythm track before such borrowing was the fashion, works with a basic two-part contrapuntal texture. The synthesized bass is extremely restless, moving mostly by tritone and half-step, and traversing the chromatic aggregate save for one pitch (F). Though each verse returns three times to a G♯ bass vamp (by way of a Locrian scale in the vocal line), the song's harmonic fabric is best described as atonal. Both chromaticism and pedal points figure in "Paprika Plains" (*DJRD*), which runs to sixteen minutes, an entire side of an LP on the original release. The song's three-verse structure is interrupted by a vast orchestral interlude, whose far-flung harmonic wanderings are characterized by a strikingly liberal use of dissonance.[28] Equally striking is the fact that Mitchell prints parenthetical, unperformed lyrics to correspond with the instrumental passage. This quite extensive interpolation (72 poetic lines, in a metric scheme unrelated to the rest of the song) gives voice, like some Yeats of the desert, to a protean collage of oracular imagery. All such formal and tonal expansiveness is counterbalanced in the verses by the use of marked (but intermittent) pedal textures. The pedal is threefold—a chord made up of C, D, and G—appearing in many harmonic contexts and symbolizing, among other things, an indigenous American drumbeat. Once again the tonal techniques are expressive of thematic dichotomies between the centered and the unbounded. Just as the chromatic orchestral rhapsody is signaled by a visionary, expansive movement in the text ("I'm floating into dreams"), the long jazzy postlude, with its apotheosis of the pedal chord, follows a contraction back to earth, the present, and the bonds of human company ("I'm floating back to you").[29]

As we have seen, Joni Mitchell's harmonic palette is multivalent, subtly shaded, and highly distinctive, with effects that are always integrated into memorable, well-reasoned poetic conceptions. She creates novel structures from the most commonplace resources and incorporates bold experimentation into engaging, exuberant grooves. As she has explained, she views such alternatives to traditional harmony in metaphorical terms, as exploring different ways of looking at the world:

> There's one chord [in "Moon at the Window"] that changes the interval as it goes into the C section that's a bit shocking. It comes in a little bit odd, but it's a good odd. It's no odder than any change in life. It's kind of like a "but." The thing is drifting off ..."but." That's how I think that chord works. It sets up an alternative viewpoint.[30]

> The arts at their best ... make people look at things they wouldn't ordinarily look at and maybe plant the seeds of difference, like a different way of looking at things.... That's my optimism, ... that art could change somebody's course, change the way they look at things.[31]

On occasion in this chapter (notable cases being "Blue" and "Both Sides, Now") my harmonic analyses have touched on aspects of song form, phrase structure, and melodic contour. I now turn to a more thorough exposition of these topics.

6

MELODIC TURNS

SONG FORMS

With few exceptions, Joni Mitchell worked within the standard song forms in use in North American popular music by the 1960s: strophic, verse-chorus, and verse-bridge forms. *Strophic* form refers to a succession of verses, each with the same musical pattern but different lyrics.[1] Songs from the album *Blue* using strophic form include "All I Want," "River," and "The Last Time I Saw Richard." In *verse-chorus* form, the verses alternate with a chorus, a self-contained section with unchanging music and lyrics. Songs from *Blue* using verse-chorus form include "Little Green," "Carey," "This Flight Tonight," and "A Case of You." In *verse-bridge* form, verses alternate with a so-called bridge section, containing music that contrasts (melodically, harmonically, and so on) with the verse while eventually preparing for the verse's return. Commonly, the bridge first enters after two statements of the verse.[2] The bridge may be stated only once (as in "Court and Spark" and "Help Me" [both *C&S*]) but is usually stated twice. Songs from *Blue* using verse-bridge form include "My Old Man" and "California." Notice that in this album Mitchell doesn't favor any particular form over another. Her first album (*SS*) likewise contains a balanced mix: five strophic songs ("Nathan La Franeer," "Sisotowbell Lane," "The Dawntreader," "Song to a Seagull," "Cactus Tree"), three verse-chorus songs ("I Had a King," "Michael from Mountains," "Night in the City"), and two verse-bridge songs ("Marcie," "The Pirate of Penance"). In some albums, however, strophic forms predominate (*C, LC, H*).

Instrumental introductions are common; songs may also be embellished with significant instrumental interludes or codas. Any of the three main forms may also contain a refrain. A *refrain* occurs when a portion of each verse always has the same lyrics. In contrast to a chorus, a refrain is not musically self-contained; it begins or ends incompletely. Thus the chorus in "The Circle Game" (*LC*) (seven poetic lines: "And the seasons . . .") begins and ends in the tonic and could be sung out of context without detracting from its sense of sectional closure. In contrast, the refrain line concluding each verse in "California" (*B*) ("California I'm coming home") begins in the middle of a cadential progression and is completely dependent on its context for formal coherence. Mitchell uses refrain elements with great inventiveness, as one way to create variations on the standard forms.

In popular song in general around the beginning of Mitchell's career, refrains commonly appear at the ends of verses (often stating the title of the song). Typically they consist of a single line with a culminating function ("Will You Love Me Tomorrow?" [Goffin-King], "And I Love Her" [Lennon-McCartney], "The Sound of Silence" [Simon], "It's All Over Now, Baby Blue" [Dylan]). Sometimes these end refrains are more extended (often through repetition of poetic lines): examples include the Beatles' "I Want to Hold Your Hand" (three lines), Dylan's "It Ain't Me Babe" (three lines), and Paul Simon's "Bridge over Troubled Water" (four lines). Mitchell uses the typical single-line end refrain in many strophic songs such as "Cactus Tree" (*SS*) ("And she's so busy being free"), "Raised on Robbery" (*C&S*) (title line), and "Black Crow" (*H*) ("a black crow flying in a blue sky"). She also uses such a refrain at the end of the verse in some verse-chorus songs ("Free Man in Paris" [*C&S*], "The Only Joy in Town" [*NRH*]) and verse-bridge songs ("See You Sometime" [*FR*], "Wild Things Run Fast" [*WTRF*]). Her interest in more extended end refrains is well illustrated by the song "My Old Man" (*B*). Here the refrain (five poetic lines: "We don't need no piece of paper ...") is equal in length (eight bars of music) to the opening half of the verse. The refrain would be substantial enough to constitute a chorus if the verse opening were not so clearly initiatory in quality, requiring the refrain for completion. (Note that the length of this refrain is not due to any verbal repetition.) Other long end refrains can be found in "Just Like This Train" (*C&S*) (three lines), "The Wolf That Lives in Lindsey" (*M*) (five lines), and "Man to Man" (*WTRF*) (four lines).

Refrain devices are not limited to the end of the verse, however; they can also occupy initial or internal positions. Bob Dylan's "Subterranean Homesick Blues" has an internal refrain: at the midpoint of every verse, the phrase "Look out kid" marks a sectional division. The verses in Paul Simon's "Scarborough Fair" have an internal refrain ("Parsley, sage, rosemary and thyme") as well as an end refrain. I will be referring to such patterns, where multiple refrain lines occur in nonadjacent positions, as *split refrains*. Another kind of split refrain places the recurring text lines at the beginning and end of the verse, as in Paul Simon's "Old Friends," the Beatles' "Yesterday," and Laura Nyro's "Wedding Bell Blues" (which begins, "Bill/I love you so/I always will"). Mitchell's "Both Sides, Now" (*C*) contains an internal refrain marking the transition between the first and second halves of each verse: "I've looked at [clouds/love/life] that way/But now ..." Internal refrains also occur in "Furry Sings the Blues" and "A Strange Boy" (both *H*). The song "Chelsea

Morning" (*C*) has a substantial initial refrain ("Woke up, it was a Chelsea morning, and the first thing that I [heard/saw/knew]"). "Morning Morgantown" (*LC*) has a simple split refrain with the same recurring line ("In morning, Morgantown") at the midpoint and end of each verse. In "California" (*B*), a split refrain frames the final section of the verse: "California/California I'm coming home/[. . .]/California I'm coming home." Other examples of split refrains are more complex. In fact, one of Mitchell's earliest examples, "Sisotowbell Lane" (*SS*), has refrain elements scattered throughout the verse in numerous poetic lines (but not the final one):

sec. 1   Sisotowbell Lane
          [. . .]
          . . . always [every] . . .
          . . . always [every] . . .
sec. 2   [. . .]
          Sometimes [always] . . .
          Yes sometimes [always] . . .
sec. 3   We have a rocking chair
          [. . .]
          Sometimes we do
          [. . .]

(Sections notated here are poetic subsections articulated by metric, rhyme, and refrain structure.) The most stable of these refrain elements occur at important structural points: the initial line, the beginning of the final section, and the penultimate line. In "River" (*B*), refrain lines mark the end of the first two sections of the verse, as well as occupying the entire final section:

sec. 1   [. . .]
          Oh I wish I had a river
          I could skate away on
sec. 2   [. . .]
          Oh I wish I had a river
          I could skate away on
sec. 3   I wish I had a river so long
          I would teach my feet to fly
          Oh I wish I had a river
          I could skate away on
          I made my baby cry

This is another song where the combined refrain is equal in proportion to the rest of the verse.

By factoring in the occurrence of refrains, we can see how the three standard formal types are further differentiated. In *Song to a Seagull*, for instance, the five strophic songs divide into those with end refrain ("Nathan La Franeer," "Song to a Seagull," "Cactus Tree"), and those with split refrain ("Sisotowbell Lane," "The Dawntreader"); two of the verse-chorus songs have no refrain, while one has an initial refrain element ("I Had a King"). The songs on *Court and Spark* use the following range of forms: strophic ("People's Parties," "The Same Situation"), strophic with end refrain ("Raised on Robbery" [plus vocal introduction], "Trouble Child"), strophic with split refrain ("Car on a Hill"), verse-chorus with end refrain ("Free Man in Paris"), verse-bridge ("Down to You"), verse-bridge with end refrain ("Court and Spark," "Just Like This Train"), and verse-bridge with split refrain ("Help Me").

It should be mentioned in passing that the difference between refrain and chorus is not always cut-and-dried; both refer to passages of unchanging music and text providing a periodic sense of return. As I use the terms, the distinction between the two is based on notions of structural coherence: a clear-cut chorus will consist of a complete, closed musical section, markedly distinct from the verse that is itself a complete section. But in practice, of course, songwriters may wish to explore ambiguity or interdependence rather than clarity of formal division. For instance, it is not uncommon for verses to end with a phrase that is melodically or harmonically open, in the interests of continuity between verses or verse and chorus. Open-ended verses leading into a chorus can be found in Dylan's "Mr. Tambourine Man" and "Like a Rolling Stone." The lack of cadence at the end of the verse is used to build anticipation for the chorus. In these examples, the verses are sufficiently substantial and formally balanced to feel like a coherent musical section, even if they are not technically closed. But in other examples, sectional divisions may be less clear. Take Mitchell's "Chelsea Morning" (*C*), for instance (Ex. 6.1). Is the recurring section beginning with the lines "Oh, won't you stay/We'll put on the day" a refrain at the end of the verse, or a separate brief chorus? On the one hand, Mitchell sets this section apart with a lengthy and dramatic pause just beforehand (at the end of line 3) on an open sonority, and a marked change in vocal expression on "Oh."[3] On the other hand, the text in this section is not completely uniform or self-contained; the final line changes with each verse, linking through a rhyme to the previous section's line 3 (e.g., verse 1: "drums/comes"). Thus in some ways Mitchell emphasizes the division between lines 1–3 and 4–6 (as if they constitute distinct verse and chorus). In other ways she emphasizes their interdependence (as if lines 4–6 constitute a refrain, necessary to complete the poetic and harmonic structure of the verse). Songs with similar formal ambiguity include "Tin Angel," "Songs to Aging Children Come" (both *C*) and "Harlem in Havana" (*TT*).[4] Given the sometimes subjective nature of the criteria for perceiving musical closure and formal hierarchy, I acknowledge that in some cases other listeners may well interpret sectional divisions and functions differently than I do.

EXAMPLE 6.1. "CHELSEA MORNING," VERSE 1

The problem presented by ambiguous cases highlights a general aesthetic issue. As Richard Middleton has recently argued, form in pop/rock music of this period involves a reconciliation between two general principles: sectionalism and continuity. Various balances can be struck between the two. Sectional boundaries and relationships can be projected with absolute clarity, or sectional definition can be deemphasized in favor of a continuous musical flow. "In the Beatles' 'She Said, She Said' (1966), for example, the sectionality [verse-bridge] is cloaked by the irregular lengths of sections and phrases, the changes of meter and the similarities of melodic and harmonic material across sections."[5] The point here is not analytical precision (the differences between verse and bridge in the Beatles example are not in question) but the different emphases available to musicians in their execution of musical form.

The existing conventions of sectional form provide the basic vocabulary for formal organization in Mitchell's work. But in many songs, she finds various ways to emphasize continuity over sectionalism. One way to do this is to string together short open-ended verses, with no contrasting sections and no instrumental breaks, thus creating an ongoing cyclic pattern with relatively weak punctuation. (Bob Dylan's "Positively 4th Street" is a model for such an effect.) An excellent example is "People's Parties" (*C&S*). Verses are only eight measures long but rather wordy, giving the impression of a character whose overtalkativeness covers her social anxiety. Several examples of this formal type (with slightly longer verses) are found on *For the Roses*, including the title song, "You Turn Me On I'm a Radio," and "Woman of Heart and Mind." All three songs are cast as one-sided conversations (second-person address), and the formal continuity supports the effect of conversational flow. Another technique Mitchell uses to deemphasize sections is to create long rambling verses, thus deferring punctuation. Several examples are found on *Hejira*, including "Coyote" and the title song. Verses in "Coyote" are around seventeen lines long, in "Hejira" sixteen. These dilatory formal divisions are in keeping with the album's guiding motif of wanderlust. (Remarkably, every song on *Hejira* uses strophic form, avoiding sectional contrast and contributing to the effect of constant motion.)

Other strategies favoring continuity include the use of bridges that sound similar to the verse, as in "Electricity" (*FR*) and "The Wolf that Lives in Lindsey" (*M*). (In the latter song, the bridge begins and ends similarly to the verse, deviating in the middle. In "Electricity," the bridge begins differently but incorporates the end of the verse wholesale—if the three melodic phrases of the verse are diagrammed **abc**, the bridge would be **dbc**.) Numerous songs employ vocal riffs that overlap and link sections. This is true in several songs from *Chalk Mark in a Rain Storm*, such as "Lakota" and "The Tea Leaf Prophecy." Finally, in a handful of songs, Mitchell experiments with long passages that avoid sectional repetition (verses, etc.) altogether. In art song, such unpredictable form is described as "through-composed." The song "Blonde in the Bleachers" (*FR*) contains several distinct sections, only one of which recurs. A piano intro leads to section 1 (introducing the main characters and their relationship), whose melodic phrases (**abcdee**) resist patterning into any kind of verse. A modified version of the piano intro (the only sectional repetition) then leads into section 2 (where the groupie "tapes her regrets to the microphone stand"), consisting of one musical phrase repeating over and over. When this phrase finally comes to a cadence, the music moves to a final section, an extended instrumental jam evoking the rock concert setting of the song. In this song, the through-composition creates a forward-directed form, each section introducing a new idea with minimal large-scale gestures of return. In other through-composed songs, though there are no large sectional repetitions, Mitchell includes partial or heavily modified gestures of return. This is true of "The Arrangement" (*LC*), discussed in chapter 2, and "Blue" (*B*), discussed in chapter 5. The formally ambiguous "Sunny Sunday" (*TI*), which may be heard as through-composed, will be discussed later in this chapter. While the song "Paprika Plains" (*DJRD*) is basically strophic in structure, it encloses a through-composed instrumental interlude of huge proportions. In this case, the unpredictable progress of piano and orchestra evokes the strange exploratory visions of the lyric speaker as she gazes out into the rain.

One the other end of the spectrum, there are songs in which Mitchell emphasizes sectional divisions. This can take place through strong punctuation, as in "Refuge of the Roads" (*H*), where the end refrain is emphasized by a sustained high note in the voice and rhythmic accents in the instruments. Likewise, the refrain in "God Must Be a Boogie Man" (*M*) is reinforced by rowdy backup singers and aggressively marked guitar chords. (Backing vocals also provide punctuation in "Ladies of the Canyon," "Big Yellow Taxi," and "Woodstock" [all *LC*]). A similar emphasis can be achieved through strong contrasts between sections. Musical contrast is expressed in myriad ways; one common approach is a change in timbre or texture, such as the entrance of backing vocals in the choruses to "The Gallery" (*C*), "The Circle Game" (*LC*), and "Free Man in Paris" (*C&S*). The bridge in "Down to You" (*C&S*), depicting an unsatisfying one-night stand, is set off by a change of key and meter (9-beat measures), thicker instrumentation, slower harmonic change, lower vocal range, and more repetitive melody. All these musical contrasts articulate the formal division between verse and bridge, a division underlined by thematic and expressive contrasts between sections. The verse is philosophical and temporally expansive; the bridge narrative and temporally specific. The verse mentions "days"; the bridge "shadows," "night," and "blackness." Thus the musical and poetic features of the bridge create a passage with a distinct tone and focus, interrupting the cylical verse structure with a present-tense depiction of a sexual encounter and replacing the generalized resignation of the verse ("the days *come down* to you") with a personalized, dramatic descent ("you *go down* to the pick up station"). The return of the verse brings an immediate reemergence into the daylight world ("In the morning there are lovers in the street").

One obvious way to create strong divisions is by interpolating instrumental passages (hence the term "breaks"). Extended, vivid or complex interludes can create a special effect of interruption or digression from the formal scheme, as in "Let the Wind Carry Me" (*FR*), "Car on a Hill" (*C&S*), "Sweet Bird" (*HSL*), and

"Paprika Plains" (*DJRD*). More commonly, Mitchell will use a short recurring passage as a way to punctuate formal sections, often stating it first as an introduction that is recalled after each verse or chorus, thus using it as a kind of instrumental refrain. If such a passage is highly distinct from the music of the vocal sections, the punctuating effect is made stronger. The album *Court and Spark* contains a number of examples, featuring members of the band in colorful instrumental refrains with distinct rhythmic hooks. "Court and Spark" has piano chords in a triplet cross-rhythm, "Help Me" has a catchy syncopated riff (see Ex. 2.3), and "Raised on Robbery" features solo sax over a distinct harmonic pattern.[6] "Free Man in Paris" has a striking fanfare-like refrain for the whole band, while "Just Like This Train" features a chromatic chain of woodwind licks, doubling the guitar figuration (Ex. 6.2). Notable examples from other albums include the lyrical piano melody in "Willy" (*LC*), the florid guitar and drumbeat in "The Priest" (*LC*), the guitar chimes and violent fingerwork in "The Wolf That Lives in Lindsey" (*M*) (Ex. 6.3), and "The Beat of Black Wings" (*CMRS*) with its rocking bass, distinct harmonic pattern, and strange wordless vocals (see Ex. 4.7).

But Mitchell does not always use instrumental refrains (IRs) as a means of strong demarcation. Their punctuating effect can be softened in the interests of continuity. One way to accomplish this is by devising IRs with strong parallels to the music of the verse. By using similar melodic or harmonic material, the punctuating instrumental passage will feel like an outgrowth or anticipation of the verse. In "Marcie" (*SS*), the IR is parallel to the opening phrase of the verse. In this case the parallel is exact: the figuration heard in the guitar introduction is immediately repeated as the accompaniment for the first vocal phrase. (And in fact, since the phrase structure of the verse is **aaba**, the same figuration is repeated for phrases 1, 2, and 4; see Ex. 5.18.)[7] The guitar refrain has enough harmonic and

EXAMPLE 6.2. "JUST LIKE THIS TRAIN," INSTRUMENTAL REFRAIN

EXAMPLE 6.3. "THE WOLF THAT LIVES IN LINDSEY,"
INSTRUMENTAL REFRAIN

The marcato accents are strong enough to bend the pitch.

rhythmic interest to stand as a solo, but its punctuating effect is softened by having the same material woven so thoroughly into the fabric of the verse. Additional songs in which the IR anticipates the opening of the verse include "My Old Man" (*B*), "Black Crow" (*H*), and "The Windfall" (*NRH*). In "Cold Blue Steel and Sweet Fire" (*FR*) the IR anticipates the *second* phrase of the verse (see Ex. 5.22). Other songs use an IR that grows out of the end of the verse. In "The Dawntreader" (*SS*), for instance, the end refrain (phrase 11: "All his seadreams come to me") is sung to a complex accompanimental pattern that immediately repeats, thus emerging as an IR (prefigured in the song's intro; see Exx. 5.10 and 5.11).[8] Likewise, the final line of the verse in "Blue Boy" (*LC*) ends in a melodically drawn-out wail that dovetails with the angular piano tune serving as an IR. In "Ray's Dad's Cadillac" (*NRH*), the intro sets up a harmonic pattern punctuated by vocal riffs on the song's title phrase. When the chorus arrives it features similar vocal riffs, and the cadential phrase of the chorus ("Romance in the back of/*Ray's Dad's Cadillac*") ushers in and elides with the IR familiar from the intro. Besides the types of musical parallels already mentioned, there are several songs in which fragmentary elements from an IR appear as internal punctuation scattered between vocal phrases, as in "Sisotowbell Lane" (*SS*), "For Free," "Big Yellow Taxi" (both *LC*), "Trouble Child" (*C&S*), and "Cotton Avenue" (*DJRD*)—another way to weave an IR into the fabric of the verse.

Finally, there are two songs whose form exploits the novel effect of one (quoted) tune embedded within another. "Chinese Café" (*WTRF*), with its internal quotation of "Unchained Melody" (North-Zaret), has already been mentioned in chapter 5. The song "Harry's House" (*HSL*) is a critical vignette of a man "caught up" in the phony rituals of his corporate profession. (Subliminal metaphors suggest a fish caught in a net.) Peripherally, we glimpse the stultifying effect this has on his wife and family. In the midst of a business meeting, Harry drifts off into a memory of his wife when they were first dating (a poolside setting sustains the aquatic motif). The music becomes dreamy and transitional; specifically, a rhythmically ambiguous loop dissolves the previous meter and leads to a new, deliberate swing tempo. In this daydream insert, Mitchell sings a cover of the Mandel-Hendricks tune "Centerpiece," about the excitement of new love and dreams for the future. The idealized "house and garden" of the embedded tune clashes ironically with the glossy, empty "House and Gardens" lifestyle of the present. The sectional form of the double song reads as follows:

"Harry": V1 V2 V3(part 1) ... [*"Centerpiece": V1 V2(instr.) V3*] ... V3(part 2)

The quoted tune interrupting verse 3 represents the lost optimism and authenticity of younger days. As the framing song resumes, Harry has a rude awakening; while he has been busy climbing the corporate ladder, his wife has decided to leave him. The concluding phrases mock Harry's male initiative (in fishy terms); despite his wife's appearance as the alluring water nymph of his daydreams, it is *she* who "reels him in" to tell him what he can do with his house and his take-home pay.

PHRASE STRUCTURE

Focusing now on the internal structure of formal sections, we can identify some important stylistic features. First, Mitchell characteristically avoids uniform phrase lengths. Four-bar phrase lengths are often proposed as a norm in popular music, but the idea of an inflexible norm is misleading. The use of irregular phrases is not unusual; many pop styles can accommodate variations in phrase rhythm without a sense of anomaly. (Walter Everett mentions a range of examples from the Drifters to David Bowie, implying that many more could be found.)[9] In Mitchell's case, asymmetrical phrases sound at times like extensions of four-bar units; at other times they correspond to irregular poetic lines. A clear example of extension occurs in "Marcie" (*SS*). The first phrase of verse 1 is four bars long; when the same guitar pattern is used for the intro and IR, it is extended to five by repeating the fourth bar. When the same pattern occurs in the fourth phrase of verse 1, it is extended to seven bars. All succeeding verses forgo this extra extension at the end; they consist of phrases of 4 + 5 + 4 + 5. This design is balanced, with the extensions providing articulating pauses, yet it avoids foursquare uniformity.[10] Similar subtle extensions, usually prolonging a harmony for another bar, are found in the verses of many other songs, such as "I Think I Understand" (*C*) (5 + 4 + 5 + 5), "The Gallery" (*C*) (5 + 5 + 5 + 5), "Woodstock" (*LC*) (4 + 5 + 4 + 5), "The Same Situation" (*C&S*) (4 + 4 + 5 + 5 + 5 + 5 + 6 + 5), "Amelia" (*H*) (4 + 4 + 5 + 4), and "Come In from the Cold" (*NRH*) (5 + 5 + 5 + 4ov). (The notation 'ov' refers to a phrase overlap, where the closing bar of one phrase overlaps with the initial bar of the following, often instrumental, phrase.)[11] In special cases, Mitchell introduces longer extensions. For instance, in "The Priest" (*LC*) she sets up a pattern of four-bar units in the intro (taking the drum rhythm as a fast beat of four), then casts the verse as 7 + 7 + 7 + 8ov (Ex. 6.4). The seven-bar phrases result from a vocal line of four bars overlapping with an instrumental response of four bars (prolonging the final harmony). However, Mitchell holds back the arrival of the closing word in each phrase, thus blurring the internal point of articulation and fusing melody and response into integral phrases. The fourth, culminating phrase is different, placing the harmonic extension in the middle (heard as 2 + 4 + 2ov), delaying the cadence even longer and finishing with deliberate vocal movement to the downbeat. "For Free" (*LC*) has wonderfully expansive eleven-bar phrases (11 + 11 + 10 + 9). Each phrase begins with a four-bar segment and ends with varying lengths of harmonic extension as the piano toys with fragments of its refrain: (4 + 7) + (4 + 7) + (4 + 6) + (4 + 5) [+ 5IR]. The generous proportions allow listeners to luxuriate in the song's bittersweet longing for a lost musical innocence.

In some cases, asymmetries accommodate irregular poetic structures.[12] A simple example would be "Electricity" (*FR*), with phrases of 4 + 4 + 3. Here the verse begins with paired poetic lines, following a rhyme scheme of ab + ab; Mitchell casts these lines as balanced four-bar phrases. A shorter phrase of three bars occurs at every appearance of the refrain ("She's not going to fix it up/Too easy"), which stands alone, unpaired with any other line in the verse and thus is freer from expectations of proportional balance. Furthermore, the line as spoken does not fit into the prevalent triple poetic meter, which heightens its uniqueness within the structure (as well as subtly illustrating the image of mechanical breakdown). Another simple example is "Night in the City" (*SS*) whose foursquare verses are altered by the addition of a final unpaired poetic line. The added phrase is shorter than the rest (4 + 4 + 4 + 4 + 2 [+ 2instr]). A more complex example is "Willy"

EXAMPLE 6.4. "THE PRIEST," CHORD CHANGES

Guitar tuning: D A D G A E (capo 5)
Phrase 1, 2 (a): ||: Gm | Gm | G9sus | Gm | Gm | Gm | Gm :||
Phrase 3 (b₀): | Dsus | Bb/F | Am/E | D5 | D5 | D5(7) | D5(7) |
Phrase 4 (a'): | Gm | Gm | G9sus | G9sus | G9sus | G9sus | Gm(4)/D D5(7) | Gsus2 |

(*LC*). The poetic meter changes frequently, beginning with two clear five-beat lines, then two four-beat lines, then an anomalous line of two beats coinciding with the end of a sentence:

Willy is my child, he is my father
I would be his lady all my life
He says he'd love to live with me
But for an ancient injury
That has not healed

The remainder of the verse does not clearly scan into a meter, due to variable feet and syllable counts (the two verses are wildly different in this section), though there is a clear pairing of lines through the rhyme scheme. In support of this odd structure, Mitchell designs a musical verse of eight phrases: 4 + 4 + 6 + 4 + 4 + 3 + 3 + 4 (Ex. 6.5). Note how proportional balance suggests pairing of phrases 1–2, 4–5, 6–7, while the third and final phrases stand alone; this pairing is made audible through parallel musical gestures. The first pair of phrases (4 + 4) sets the two five-beat lines; the following single phrase encompasses the next three poetic lines, through the odd unpaired line that completes a thought. The subsequent untidy lines are fit into regular paired phrases following the rhyme scheme. The final unpaired phrase is devoted to the refrain ("There are still more reasons why/I love him"), which stands outside the rhyme scheme as well as ending with another anomalous, emphatic short line. (Note that the final phrase is the *only* one in the song cadencing on the tonic.) Irregularities in phrase rhythm are thus molded to specific poetic contours, endowing them with compelling musical gestures of continuation and closure.

Other songs with flexible phrase rhythm in support of irregular poetic structures are "Urge for Going" (*Hits*) (V: 4 + 4 + 6 + 5), "Nathan La Franeer" (*SS*) (4 + 5 + 3 + 3 + 4), "Lesson in Survival" (*FR*) (2 + 4 + 3 + 2 + 3 + 4 + 4?),[13] "See You Sometime" (*FR*) (4 + 4 + 2 + 3 + 2 + 2), and "Paprika Plains" (*DJRD*) (8 + 6 + 6ov [+ 4instr] + 8 + 5 + 6ov). Another song, "Love" (*WTRF*), is interesting in that Mitchell has paraphrased her text from I Corinthians 13, creating five verses with a variable poetic structure. Presumably she could have arranged the paraphrased lines to fit a regular musical structure, but instead she chose irregular phrases of 6 + 4 + 6. Also telling are songs like "I Had a King" (*SS*), in which irregular poetic lines cut across foursquare musical units. The first eight bars of this song project regular four-bar segments in their harmonic motion and guitar figuration; but the poetic lines fall into odd lengths (4 beats/5 beats/3 beats), resulting in vocal phrases (2 + 3 + 3) out of synch with the underlying segmentation. Similar effects occur in "Edith and the Kingpin" (*HSL*) ([2 + 3 + 3] + [2 + 3 + 3] + 3 + 5) (Ex. 6.6) and "Two Grey Rooms" (*NRH*) (8 + 8 + 6 + 4 + 6). In

EXAMPLE 6.5. "WILLY," VERSE 1

the latter case, we know that the music was composed first, the poem (and precise melody) written much later (the initial demo, without words, is included in *The Complete Geffen Recordings*). Here is a song in which Mitchell responds freely to a

EXAMPLE 6.6. "EDITH AND THE KINGPIN," VERSE 1

regular set of chord changes, devising an irregular poetic construction in counterpoint with the underlying rhythmic/harmonic motion.

As I mentioned, such flexibility of phrasing is not uncommon in popular music (although the number of songs in which Mitchell avoids uniform phrasing is remarkable). More unusual are her experiments with metric disruption, in which the underlying unit of rhythmic grouping is momentarily disturbed. Her interest in such experiments began with her first album and climaxed in the early 1970s with the albums *For the Roses* and *Court and Spark*. One way she plays with the metric flow is by occasionally slipping in extra half-bars. This happens three times in "Sisotowbell Lane" (*SS*) (see Ex. 5.6). The hiccup in the metric scheme is associated with a recurring cadential figure that defines three subsections of the verse. The phrase lengths fall out as follows: (5 + 4.5) + (5 + 4.5) + (2 + 2 + 2 + 3.5ov). (Note that the 5-bar phrases are due to irregular poetic lines.) The metric quirks are also in line with the quirky tone maintained in the poem ("We always knew that he always knew"). Mitchell has saturated this song with irregular phrases, while arranging them in a clearly articulated, elegantly balanced pattern. Recurrence of melodic material also helps to shape this pattern; the phrases can be diagrammed **ab + ab + cdeb**. Mitchell also introduces half-bars into "All I Want" (*B*) (see Ex. 6.11). The first part of the verse has parallel melodic phrases (**abab**) but irregular phrase rhythm (4 + 2.5 + 4 + 3.5). In this song, the metric quirks match well with the spontaneous outpouring of words as well as the restless emotional tone (e.g., the first added half-bar occurs on "Looking for something, what can it be"). Other songs with occasional half-bars include "A Case of You" (*B*) (Ch: 4 + 3.5 + 4), "Barangrill" (*FR*) (5.5 + 5.5 + 4 + 2.5), "Court and Spark" (*C&S*) (in the IR), and "The Wolf That Lives in Lindsey" (*M*) (V: 5 + 5 + 5 + 4.5 + 3).

Another type of metric disruption occurs when the meter distinctly changes for a few bars or longer. This can take a number of different forms. "Blue" (*B*), for example, is mainly in 4/4. A striking shift occurs during the **b** section: when the poetic lines shift from around seven syllables ("Well there's so many sinking") to five syllables ("Acid, booze and ass"), the meter shrinks to 3/4, grinding to a halt after a few bars before being able to resume (see Ex. 5.14). The verse in "Banquet" (*FR*) shifts back and forth between 6/4 and 4/4. "Cactus Tree" (*SS*) contains a more prolonged shift from 4/4 to 6/4 at midverse when the rhyme scheme changes (see Ex. 6.12). While "Trouble Child" (*C&S*) is in 4/4, its intro/IR shifts to 3/4 every other bar. As already mentioned, the bridge in "Down to You" (*C&S*), depicting a one-night stand, presents a sharp contrast to the verse. Though the harmony here is nearly motionless and the vocal line not strongly metric (contributing to a feeling of suspended momentum), close listening reveals the piano vamp marking off measures of 9 beats, until the culminating phrase when the spell is released ("You hurry/To the blackness"). In "Harry's House" (*HSL*), mentioned in the previous section, the transition to the embedded tune "Centerpiece" involves a metric modulation. The bass line introduces a syncopated riff (♪♩♪♩) cutting across the 4/4 meter, previously heard in the IR but now greatly prolonged. By the time the embedded tune begins, the previous dotted-quarter duration has become the new (slower, shuffle) beat ($\downarrow. = \downarrow$). The same process occurs in reverse at the transition back to the framing song ($\downarrow = \downarrow.$).

In other songs, the meter changes are more irregular. "Lesson in Survival" (*FR*) is in 4/4, with occasional interpolated bars of 5/4 and 2/4 (= half-bar). The end of each verse, however, unexpectedly becomes stalled in repetitive piano arpeggiation suggesting 3/8. In "Jericho" (*DJRD*), the 4/4 verses are punctuated by a few bars of 6/8 (or 3/4). But the song's intro allows any clear sense of meter to peter out into an unregulated rhythmic loop (an effect which returns in the coda) (Ex. 6.7). The instrumental interlude in "Sweet Bird" (*HSL*) is suddenly extremely syncopated and plagued by dropped beats, thus suggesting irregular alternation between 3/4 and 4/4, although in the context it is difficult to distinguish between syncopations and downbeats. Such an absence of metric guideposts is distressing—an effect which seems to illustrate the song's contemplation of human imperfection and "compromise."

We have seen how through a variety of devices—harmonic extension, odd poetic structures, and metric disruption—Mitchell explores a flexible phrase rhythm. Her verses too are variable in proportion, generally ranging from two

EXAMPLE 6.7. "JERICHO," INTRO

musical phrases, as in "Songs to Aging Children Come" (C) (see Ex. 5.17) and "Big Yellow Taxi" (LC), to eight phrases, as in "That Song about the Midway" (C), "Willy" (LC), and "Hejira" (H), with some songs even longer. This leads me to the second important characteristic of phrase structure in Mitchell's work: phrases relate to one another (and cohere into formal sections) through audible patterns of parallelism, contrast, and complementarity. In particular, Mitchell makes use of hierarchic cadences whereby certain phrases are more inconclusive than others (e.g., in harmony or linear motion), setting up the expectation of eventual closure. Phrases can be paired through complementary relations in which the inconclusive aspects of one phrase are answered in a later, conclusive phrase; open phrases are generally treated as structurally subordinate to closed phrases. Melodic structures based on open/closed patterns are common in many popular song repertories, but not all.[14] They seem especially appropriate to the singer-songwriter genre: usually intended for spectatorial or private listening (rather than participatory music-making or dance), the genre valorizes literate verbal texts and individual expressive styles—all of which encourages attention to subtleties of construction (or "internally articulated 'shapeliness,'" as Middleton puts it).[15] Nevertheless, the singer-songwriter genre is not homogeneous in this respect. A few examples from the music of Bob Dylan will introduce the basic concepts.

"Blowin' in the Wind" is strophic in form. Verses are four phrases long, the fourth phrase being the refrain. Phrase lengths are entirely uniform (8 + 8 + 8 + 8). The melodic material in the first three phrases is repetitive, with phrase 2 varied at the end (diagrammed as aa'ab). The refrain is set apart with different music. So far, my description covers relationships of parallelism and contrast. To investigate complementary (open/closed) relationships we need to consider other factors. Harmonically, the phrases end on I, V, I, and I; only the second phrase is open (I will diagram this with a subscript o, as follows: aa'$_o$ab).[16] But this situation is modified by the linear design. In linear terms, closure consists of motion directed toward the tonal center (the first degree of the scale, or $\hat{1}$). The first three phrases end inconclusively on $\hat{5}$, $\hat{2}$, and $\hat{5}$; only the final phrase closes on $\hat{1}$. Thus through the interaction of musical elements, phrases can project differing degrees of conclusiveness. In phrase 2 (the midpoint of the verse), harmony and linear motion work together to create the most open-ended phrase; this is answered (and structurally completed) by the strongest closure in phrase 4. In other words, the second half of the verse complements the first half in harmonic and linear terms. When each member of a complementary pair begins with the same material, as here, the pair is known as a *period*. (In this case, the verse is a single period, each member comprising two phrases: aa'$_o$ + ab.)[17] Note that complementary or period structures are not necessarily complex. "Blowin' in the Wind" has a fairly simple, pleasing symmetrical structure appropriate for communal singing.

"Like a Rolling Stone" presents a contrasting sense of relationships between phrases. The sectional structure is more complex, with a verse of irregular lines and a chorus of uniform lines. Musical phrases fall mostly into repeated pairs: the verse a_o a_o b_o b_o c c d_o the chorus $e_o e_o e_o e_o e_o$ (4 bars each). Each phrase pair is
$$8+8+4+4+4+4+8$$
an exact musical repetition. But though the phrase structure is consistently parallel, it is not complementary; open phrases are not answered by closed phrases. The only phrases that close on a tonic harmony are the c phrases, but the melody is inconclusive here (ending on $\hat{5}$). Even in the chorus, the harmony continually cycles through I-IV-V, without closure (though the melody finally closes on $\hat{1}$ in the concluding phrase). There is a strong sense of arrival in the chorus due to the climactic vocal range and the tonic chord that initiates each phrase. But the structure is not based on complementary relations. Instead, the effect is basically a string of open gestures, some more intense than others.[18] The looser relation between phrases (parallel but not subordinate) is reflected in the way Dylan casually adds an extra line to subsequent choruses without upsetting the formal balance. (Note that noncomplementary structures are not necessarily simple.)

"Like a Rolling Stone" showcases a literate, highly personalized poem by way of a looping, additive melodic design. In contrast, Joni Mitchell's melodic designs persistently feature interlocking relations of symmetry and complementarity. Her melodies work in tandem with the details of poetic structure to create a counterpoint of musical and verbal shapeliness. Individual phrase patterns are exceptionally diverse. "Woodstock" (LC) follows a regularly alternating complementary structure of open/closed pairs: V: a_o ba_o b Ch: c_o d. Harmonically, a and c end on the subdominant (A♭); b and d return to the tonic (E♭m).[19] The linear contour is made up of parallel melodic arches that repeatedly strive and fall. The a phrases initiate an arch by moving up from $\hat{1}$ to $\hat{7}$; the b phrases close the arch by attaining the tonic octave, then falling to $\hat{1}$. (The d phrase falls past $\hat{1}$, the resulting inconclusiveness evoking unfulfilled longing; see Ex. 2.7a.) Note that this song, while complementary in phrase structure, has no period construction; the complementary phrases lack parallel material.[20] The open/closed pairings group phrases into slightly larger formal units. These in turn combine into a comprehensive formal plan that spans the entire verse and chorus. The first two phrases (a_o b) state the basic idea, which is then restated; these parallel statements have an initiatory or presentational function. The c phrase develops the basic idea (by compressing its contour, by moving directly to the subdominant, and by dividing into two-bar subphrases); while d moves to closure (in this case by the most active, complex harmonic progression occurring in the song). The functional sequence of statement/restatement/continuation/closure is a formal model basic to a number of popular song repertories.[21] The model is at work in many of Mitchell's songs; she uses it flexibly, playing with the proportions of individual sections at will. We will encounter a variety of examples in the ensuing discussion. Other songs, similar to "Woodstock" in using a regularly alternating open/closed pattern, may be briefly mentioned. In "The Last Time I Saw Richard" (*B*), the regular complementarity (a$_\circ$ba$_\circ$bc$_\circ$d) is somewhat blurred by the dense poetic lines and breathless delivery.[22] The verse in "Chelsea Morning" (*C*) is also regularly complementary, though the melodic material is asymmetrical: a$_\circ$bb'$_\circ$c (see Ex. 6.1). Here Mitchell extends and punctuates the open b' phrase to build anticipation for the end refrain (c).

Mitchell employs the standard phrase pattern **aaba** in a number of songs. (This is the most succinct expression of the statement/restatement/continuation/closure model. It is related to the **aaba** pattern of the Tin Pan Alley ballad while smaller in scale.) When the pattern is combined with a closed/closed/open/closed structure, the result is a parallel phrase pair followed by a complementary pair in which the **a** phrase returns to answer and complete the **b** phrase (aab$_\circ$a). Such a pattern occurs in the verses of "Marcie" (*SS*) (see Ex. 5.18), "The Gallery" (*C*), "The Priest" (*LC*) (see Ex. 6.4) and "Ladies of the Canyon" (*LC*). In the last song there is an added nonverbal phrase extending the refrain: aab$_\circ$aa' (see Ex. 5.3). In the verse of "My Old Man" (*B*) there is a modal change at the end of phrase 2 (from tonic major to tonic Dorian) which modifies the parallel relation between the initial pair (aa'b$_\circ$a). In other songs, the **aaba** pattern has a different distribution of open and closed. One example is "Yvette in English" (*TI*), with the intriguing pattern of a$_\circ$a'b$_\circ$a''$_\circ$ (the first two phrases form a period; the last phrase has a beautiful deceptive cadence, wavering between ♭VI and vi). In "For Free" (*LC*), though the **a** phrases are closed in linear terms, no phrase attains harmonic closure: a$_\circ$a$_\circ$b$_\circ$a$_\circ$. (Phrases end on IV, IV, V, and IV–vi–V. Mitchell elaborates on the cadential dissociation in the song's coda: the piano's cadence on the tonic C has no connection to the overlaid clarinet solo, which eventually closes on G.) Here, Mitchell's characteristic dialectical irony operates on the level of phrase structure, in the tension between the two systems of melodic completion and the melancholy that results.

Mitchell explores other four-phrase structures as well, combining various patterns of repetition and open/closed relations. The **aabc** pattern is similar to **aaba** (though not as well rounded). She uses it in "I Don't Know Where I Stand" (*C*) (a$_\circ$a'$_\circ$b$_\circ$c) (see Ex. 5.20), "Rainy Night House" (*LC*) (aab$_\circ$c) (see Ex. 5.13),[23] "Blue Boy" (*LC*) (where she adds a final vocal tag: aa$_\circ$bcd; see Ex. 4.1), "Song for Sharon" (*H*) (aa'b$_\circ$c), "The Only Joy in Town" (*NRH*) (V: aa'$_\circ$bc Ch: dd$_\circ$d$_\circ$), and others. No two of the specific variations I have listed are identical. She uses **aaab** (with one contrasting phrase placed at the end) in "The Circle Game" (*LC*) (aa'$_\circ$a''$_\circ$b), "Ladies' Man" (*WTRF*) (aaa'$_\circ$b), and "Last Chance Lost" (*TI*) (aaa'b) (see Ex. 6.23); and the nonrepetitive **abcd** in "The Fiddle and the Drum" (*C*) (a$_\circ$b$_\circ$cd), "The Silky Veils of Ardor" (*DJRD*) (ab$_\circ$c$_\circ$d), and "Be Cool"

(*WTRF*) (V: $\mathbf{abc_o d}$). It is clear from the examples listed so far that Mitchell treats her open/closed structures flexibly; regular alternation is not a norm but one possibility among others. Many four-phrase songs close with a complementary pair while varying the sequence at the beginning of the verse. For instance, a closed/closed/open/closed structure is found in "Be Cool," "Ladies' Man" (as diagrammed above), and "Turbulent Indigo" (*TI*) ($\mathbf{aab_o c}$) (besides those examples already listed under **aaba** and **aabc**). Other songs, like "The Circle Game" (*LC*) (see above), "Little Green" (*B*) (V: $\mathbf{aa^1{}_o b_o c}$), and "You Dream Flat Tires" (*WTRF*) (V: $\mathbf{aa_o b_o c}$) use closed/open/open/closed.[24] Quite a few begin with three open phrases in a row before closing, for instance "Tin Angel" (*C*) (V: $\mathbf{a_o b_o a_o c}$), "Amelia" (*H*) ($\mathbf{a_o b_o c_o d}$) (see Ex. 4.6), "Man to Man" (*WTRF*) ($\mathbf{a_o a_o b_o c}$), "Cherokee Louise" (*NRH*) (V: $\mathbf{a_o a_o b_o c}$), and "Borderline" (*TI*) ($\mathbf{a_o b_o c_o a^1}$).[25] But some four-phrase verses end with an open phrase, as a way of leading into the chorus. This occurs, for example, in "I Think I Understand" (*C*) (V: $\mathbf{abab^1{}_o}$ Ch: $\mathbf{cdd^1}$) and "Both Sides, Now" (*C*) (V: $\mathbf{ab_o ab_o}$ Ch: $\mathbf{cd}$) (see Ex. 5.23). Some verses are entirely closed, as in "Morning Morgantown" (*LC*) (V: $\mathbf{abab}$ Ch: $\mathbf{cd}$). (These last three songs all conform to the overarching four-section [statement/restatement/continuation/closure] model.)

By no means, however, does Mitchell limit herself to the standard length of four phrases. "Big Yellow Taxi" (*LC*) has a verse that's short and sweet, with a chorus that echoes the end of the verse: V: $\mathbf{aa^1}$ Ch: $\mathbf{ba^1}$. "Let the Wind Carry Me" (*FR*) has a short verse of three phrases ($\mathbf{aab}$) set off by a long intro and interlude. "You Turn Me On, I'm a Radio" (*FR*) has a short verse ($\mathbf{a_o bc}$) that cycles continuously without punctuation. Sometimes Mitchell plays with ambiguous phrase boundaries or subdivisions, allowing for more than one way to understand the structure. If one goes by the standard four-bar phrase length, the song "Court and Spark" (*C&S*) has two phrases: $\mathbf{a_o b}$ (with a bridge of $\mathbf{c_o d_o}$). But those four bars cover a lot of text, and the melody emphasizes internal repetition and pauses; it makes just as much sense to subdivide the verse further into three or four shorter phrases. Likewise, "People's Parties" (*C&S*) can be heard as two densely packed four-bar phrases ($\mathbf{a_o b_o}$), or four short phrases ($\mathbf{a_o b_o c_o c^1{}_o}$). (Note that some of these examples are noncomplementary.)

"Song to a Seagull" (*SS*) has a pattern of five phrases in which the final phrase (the refrain) is strongly set off from the rest by guitar punctuation: $\mathbf{a_o b_o a_o b^1{}_o /b^{11}}$ (Ex. 6.8). Note the highly asymmetrical phrase structure here. Most of the verse proceeds in a series of parallel arcs, all remaining open; then one final statement of **b** attains closure, its single arc absorbing the anticipation built up over the previous four phrases. (Interestingly, closure is attained primarily in linear terms, as the harmony remains suspended at verse's end.) In effect, this song truncates the four-section functional model, presenting statement(**ab**)/restatement(**ab**)/closure(**b**), with no medial function. "Car on a Hill" (*C&S*) (Ex. 6.9) has a six-phrase pattern of irregular phrase lengths with split refrain:

$$a_0 \, a_0 \, / b_0 \, b'_0 \, c_0 \, d$$
$$4+5+2+2+2+3.5 \, \text{ov}$$

This verse also audibly divides into subsections. Mitchell punctuates the first phrase pair with a refrain line, a harmonic extension, and backing vocals. The move to the **b** phrases is marked as a departure by a temporary modulation as well as a reduction in phrase lengths—that is, a quickening in phrase rhythm. (While some listeners may prefer to group the two short **b** phrases together into one in order to preserve the four-bar grouping, I base my groupings here on the unit of melodic repetition. With the **a** phrase the melody doesn't start repeating until after a four-bar statement; with the **b** phrases repetition begins after two bars.) These qualities of contrast and fragmentation mark phrases **bbc** as the continu-

EXAMPLE 6.8. "SONG TO A SEAGULL," VERSE 1

EXAMPLE 6.9. "CAR ON A HILL," VERSE 1

ation section in the overall plan; in this case, the continuation section is longer than other sections. Note that this song, like the previous one, has a long string of open phrases before closure at the end refrain.

Through devices such as these (articulation of subsections, changes in phrase rhythm, and deferred closure), Mitchell is able to sustain formal interest and coherence over the span of even longer verses. "The Dawntreader" (*SS*) (Ex. 6.10) has the following phrase pattern:

$$a_o \; b \quad a_o \; b \; / c_o \; c_o \; c'_o \; d_o \; e_o \; f_o \; g$$
$$4+4+4+4+2+2+3+2+3+4+4$$

EXAMPLE 6.10. "THE DAWNTREADER," VERSE 1

(continued)

EXAMPLE 6.10. (CONTINUED)

The statement and restatement of the basic idea (**ab**) form a presentational subsection defined by regular complementarity, with a narrow range of melodic motion. Its **b** phrases also restate the instrumental refrain in the guitar accompaniment, thus reinforcing the cadential function for each pair. The second subsection ("The roll of the harbor wake") is immediately differentiated by quicker phrase rhythm. At the same time, its goal orientation operates over a longer span. The melody climbs gradually in pitch, peaking on phrase **f**. Its short phrases set up a concatenated string of musically rhyming pairs, even more than I have been able to show in my diagram: e.g., the end of **d** echoes the end of **c'**, the beginnings of **d** and **e** are parallel, while **f** contains two similar falling subphrases. Finally, harmonic closure is deferred until **g** (the refrain), where the guitar again states the IR, establishing a cadence parallel to that of section one. "All I Want" (*B*) (Ex. 6.11) exhibits a similar pattern:

$$a_o\ b\quad a_o\ b\ /c_o c_o c_o\ c\quad d_o e_o$$
$$4+2.5+4+3.5+2+2+2+2ov+4+4ov$$

The presentational section is punctuated by a harmonic extension, while the continuation section ("I want to be strong") is marked off by a chain of open phrases and a quickening in phrase rhythm. In this case, however, Mitchell continues and intensifies the phrase acceleration. The final statement of **c** is condensed and elided with the beginning of **d** (hear how the cadence on the tonic arrives a measure earlier than expected [skipping a bar of A♭] according to the established phrase rhythm).[26] This feels like a further acceleration from two bars to one bar. Then the **d** phrase begins with even quicker melodic repetition at the half bar ("Do you want—do you want—do you want"). The phrase rhythm is propelled forward from four bars through two, then one, down to the breathless excitement of half bars. Mitchell maintains the excitement and forward propulsion through the lack of closure at the end of the verse (building expectation for the return of **a**).[27]

The song "Cactus Tree" (*SS*) (Ex. 6.12) has different proportions and a different arrangement of complementary relations. Its phrase pattern is

$$a_o \quad b_o \quad c_o \quad /d \quad d \quad d \quad e_o \quad f$$
$$2+2+3.5+1.5+1.5+1.5+3+2$$

EXAMPLE 6.11. "ALL I WANT," VERSE 1

(*continued*)

EXAMPLE 6.11. (CONTINUED)

to the liv - ing. A - live, a - live, I want to get up and

jive, I want to wreck my stockings in some juke - box dive. Do you want? Do you

want? Do you want to dance with me, ba - by? Do you want to

take a chance on may - be find - ing some

sweet ro - mance with me, ba - by, well come on.

(The odd bar lengths in the diagram connote a metric shift from 4/4 to 6/4, equivalent to the addition of half-bars.) The presentational section **abc** (in this case, not conforming to the statement/restatement model) builds anticipation through a string of open phrases (and a harmonic extension). The continuation section ("He has called her") is differentiated by its prolonged affirmation of closure as well as its initial metric shift (from duple to triple groupings). In this melody, Mitchell creates a satisfying sense of linear arrival on $\hat{3}$ (low in the voice). Section one hovers on $\hat{5}$, ultimately to pause on an unresolved $\hat{4}$. In answer, section two cadences four times on the same low $\hat{3}$. Other songs using accelerated phrase rhythm in the second half of the verse are "Sisotowbell Lane" (*SS*) (abab/c$_o$d$_o$eb), "Just Like This Train" (*C&S*) (a$_o$bcb/d$_o$d$_o$e), and "Trouble Child" (*C&S*) (a$_o$a^{1}b$_o$b$_o$a^1/c$_o$cc$_o$d).

EXAMPLE 6.12. "CACTUS TREE," VERSE 1

Three additional songs with long verses deserve mention for their unique designs. "Willy" (*LC*) (see Ex. 6.5), unlike the other songs I have been discussing, has no strong internal punctuation:

$$a_o \ b_o \ c_o \ d_o \ d_o \ e_o \ f_o \ g$$
$$4+4+6+4+4+3+3+4$$

Instead, the melody feels like one thread, spun into heavenly length through deceptive harmonic motion. Mitchell creates an elegant proportional balance by casting phrases into matching pairs (with two exceptions). No pair is complementary (thus closure is deferred), yet links are created through parallelism and sequence. The **a** and **b** phrases begin the same way, then move in different directions; the end of **b** is marked by a melancholy harmonic gesture, sinking from F down by step to Dm (in the key of C). Phrase **c** rises to a high point, then moves by sequence (note the melodic pitches on each downbeat: D–B, C–A) before breaking the parallel construction to accommodate the odd poetic line. Note that this phrase extension restates the melancholy chords: F, Em, Dm. The next two phrases, closely parallel, are stalled in the low range and in harmonies that evade cadence (G to Am). Phrase **e** returns to the melodic peak, the earlier sequential pitches (now twice as fast), and the melancholy chord progression, knitting these elements together. Phrase **f** has a contour that answers that of **e**, while finally moving the harmony forward to cadential preparation. Phrase **g** stands alone, diving to the melodic depths for the climactic expression of love, while the chords move directly from F to C, thus breaking the melancholy pattern to achieve tonic closure.

"Coyote" (*H*) (Ex. 6.13) has a cyclic phrase pattern, moving twice through the same melodic and harmonic succession:

$$a_o \ b_o \ c_o \ d_o \ a'_o \ b_o \ c_o \ d_o \ a''$$
$$4+4+4+4+2+4+4+4+5ov$$

This would be a straightforward case of internal repetition, were it not for the sleight of hand brought about by a discrepancy between melodic and harmonic cycles. The melodic unit of repetition (phrases **a** to **d**) appears to be sixteen bars long the first time around; it takes this long to complete the rhyme scheme. But the harmonic unit of repetition is only fourteen bars long; the harmonic progression starts to repeat before the melody has finished! The beginning of the progression is audibly highlighted with a special chord: E♭ in the context of C major, an instance of modal mixture. The first **a** phrase begins with the modal shift to E♭, then a dominant chord (G13sus). The **d** phrase *ends* with the shift to E♭, continuing on in the next (**a**) phrase to G13sus and so on. This means that the second **a** phrase ("Just how close to the bone") has to drop half of its material to catch up with the harmonic progression. (The poetic rhymes normally occur every four bars, but the rhyme scheme picks up here with the odd two-bar **a** phrase: "bone/ alone," etc.) Another way to describe the disruption in phrase structure here is in terms of the song's four-bar hypermeter. (Hypermeter refers to the grouping of measures into larger rhythmic units.) In the first **a** phrase, E♭ occurs on a hyper-metrically strong downbeat (bar 1 of a four-bar group), the following G13sus on a weak downbeat (bar 3). In the **d** phrase, however, E♭ occurs on a weak down-beat (bar 3), and the following G13sus now occurs on a strong downbeat. The subsequent tonic arrival is strong as well, restoring the regular hypermeter after a

EXAMPLE 6.13. "COYOTE," VERSE 1

EXAMPLE 6.13. (CONTINUED)

strange two-bar glitch. For the concluding statement of **a** (the refrain), Mitchell prolongs the dominant chord, restoring the regular phrase length, breaking the cyclic pattern, and leading at last to tonic closure.

"Harlem in Havana" (*TT*) (Ex. 6.14), unusually, has not a single open phrase:

a a b b b c d d'
4+4+2+2+2+6+4+4ov

Though every phrase ends on tonic E, Mitchell creates internal variety through changes in modality, phrase rhythm, vocal range, and instrumentation. The tonic goal (E major, except for the final phrase) is approached by way of different chords at different times. Harmonic tension is produced by varying the length of time between E major resolutions (every fourth bar in **a**, every second bar in **b**, not

EXAMPLE 6.14. "HARLEM IN HAVANA," CHORD CHANGES

Standard guitar tuning

Phrase 1, 2 (a): ‖: Em7 | Em7 | D | E(9) :‖
Phrase 3, 4, 5 (b): ‖: D Bm7 | D E(9) :‖ (repeat 2x)
Phrase 6 (c): | A9 | A9 | G13 | G13 | E Emaj13 | Emaj13 |
Phrase 7 (d): | Em6 Em/maj9 | Em7 | E Emaj13 | Emaj13 |
Phrase 8 (d'): | Em6 Em/maj9 | Em7 | D/E | Em |

until the fifth bar in c). But formal extension is created without recourse to complementary relations.

A special case of noncomplementary structure occurs when all phrases are open, creating continuous forward momentum. This is the case in "Roses Blue" (C) ($a_o a_o a_o b_o$), "Electricity" (FR) (V: $a_o b_o c_o$ B: $d_o b_o c_o$), "Woman of Heart and Mind" (FR) ($a_o b_o a_o b_o$), and "People's Parties" (C&S) ($a_o b_o$). In "Woman of Heart and Mind," Mitchell adds a brief tag at the end of the entire song (verse 3) to achieve final closure. "Conversation" (LC) has an open first half and a periodic second half: $a_o b_o a_o b_o / c_o c'$. In essence, this song consists of a continuous chain of open phrases punctuated by one emphasized tonic arrival at the final poetic line ("I want to free him").[28]

In their seemingly endless variety, these examples show Mitchell's careful attention to detail work, her highly individualized treatment of each song, and her nonformulaic, exploratory approach to phrase construction.

CONTOUR

In my discussion of phrase structure, I have made occasional reference to melodic contour, speaking of arcs, high points, hovering, and so on. Now I would like to address this musical aspect directly. In turning to the vocal line as it moves through musical space, we seem to be isolating what many would consider the most memorable aspect, perhaps the core, of Joni Mitchell's songwriting—the tunes. However, I would emphasize that a "tune" is more than just a linear pitch succession; it is a musical whole, foregrounding specific linear gestures but also encompassing distinct rhythmic, harmonic, and formal qualities from which the linear aspect is inseparable. My discussions of contour will necessarily refer to these other qualities in the interests of an integral picture of Mitchell's melodic composition. I would also emphasize that in approaching melodic shape and gesture, it is less meaningful to think in terms of technical labels. While harmony and phrase structure, for instance, deal with specifiable units of perception and syntactic relations for which an analytical vocabulary has been developed, contour is a more elusive aesthetic quality.[29] How does movement through musical space contribute to emotional expression? Why are some shapes more beautiful or memorable than others? In considering a relatively small number of tunes, I aim to illustrate the issues involved rather than provide exhaustive classification.

"Michael from Mountains" (*SS*) (Ex. 6.15) is a modest tune, moving in conjunct motion with occasional triadic descents, mostly remaining within an octave reach (C to C) and mostly sticking to the F major scale. Mitchell sets up all these parameters in the first two phrases; any movement outside the expected bounds later in the song constitutes a salient gesture. Thus the entry of chromatic pitches in phrases 3 and 4 reinforces the sense of departure in that portion of the melody.[30] In the chorus, melodic intervals expand, especially in the upward leaps on "go to" and "know you." On the latter phrase, the voice also scoops below its previous floor. Expanding pitch space is used expressively, to capture the special speech situation in the chorus (second-person address, asserting commitment and devotion). Mitchell creates other salient moments by means of hooks, motives, and special harmonic colors. A hook is an appealing musical figure meant to grab the listener's attention.[31] In this song, the opening phrase is marked by a syncopated accent pattern (332, in both voice and guitar) that serves as a gentle hook, suiting the song's delicate character. A motive is a short figure that recurs as a unifying element. An example in this song is the descending figure B♭–A–F–C, occurring at the end of phrase 1 in the verse and at the end of the chorus ("I may know you"), as well as in varied form in phrase 2 of the verse and in the first part of the chorus. Mitchell adds a special dash of color with the B♭m guitar chord in m. 3: the voice does not leave its limpid diatonic path here, so the chromatic borrowing in the accompaniment imparts an unexpected poignance. A similar moment occurs upon the unusual cadence via A♭ at the end of the chorus. One final characteristic to mention is the consistency of the melody over its several strophic restatements; the changing text does not disturb the original contour in any significant way (this feature will become clearer when we encounter contrasting treatment in other examples).

"Little Green" (*B*) (Ex. 6.16) has a slightly wider vocal range (an octave and a fifth: F♯ to C♯). The opening phrases are enhanced by a guitar hook combining several elements: a 332 rhythmic pattern, a major-seventh sweetening of the tonic, and a iii–ii–I cadential progression.[32] After the low placement of the first two phrases, the sense of departure in phrase 3 is due to its sudden quick rise to the melodic highpoint. In contrast, the chorus returns to the low range; its salient features include the touches of color added through modal mixture (e.g., on the word "color"). This song also has a prominent motive (E–D♯–B–F♯) introduced in phrase 1 and brought back repeatedly to close the chorus, each statement of the motive exploiting a different dissonant relation with the changing cadential

EXAMPLE 6.15. "MICHAEL FROM MOUNTAINS," VERSE 1 AND CHORUS

EXAMPLE 6.16. "LITTLE GREEN," VERSE 1

harmonies (thus expressing the "sorrow" just beneath the surface). In fact, this motive is the *same* descending motive that appeared in "Michael from Mountains" (transposed down). The motive ($\hat{4}$–$\hat{3}$–$\hat{1}$–$\hat{5}$) is a favorite of Mitchell's in her first style period; it is so prevalent as to constitute something of a stylistic signature in the early years. Prominent statements of the motive occur, for example, in "I Had a King" (*SS*) (chorus, guitar part), "Chelsea Morning" (*C*) (see Ex. 6.1), "Both Sides, Now" (*C*) (varied form, chorus), "Ladies of the Canyon" (*LC*) (phrases 1, 2, 4), "The Circle Game" (*LC*) (close of verse), and "The Last Time I Saw Richard" (*B*) (IR, varied form). I will refer to it as motive *j*.

Both of the previous examples are quiet songs and restrained in their gestures; even delicate changes of shading stand out as salient features. In contrast, "The Gallery" (*C*) (Ex. 6.17) is a more showy melody. It begins immediately with an upward octave leap, following with three prominent leaps of a sixth just in phrase 1 (articulating the midpoint and close of the phrase). The voice inhabits its full range of motion right away, evoking an exuberant persona who leaps before she looks. (The vocal opening is also recklessly mismatched with the harmony.) In the chorus Mitchell creates contrast by turning to a more restricted motion by step. This continues for six measures, building expectation for a return to

EXAMPLE 6.17. "THE GALLERY," PHRASE 1

When I first saw_ your gal - ler - y,

I liked the ones of la- dies._____

melodic freedom (just as the speaker chafes against the restrictions of her relationship). The tension is sprung in the final line, which reclaims the entire space in a unique melodic hook ("I can be cruel"—a distorted version of motive *j*) with deliberate grinding emphasis on a dissonant tone. Other songs using dramatic leaps and reckless motion through melodic space are "Conversation" (*LC*), whose opening line establishes a high point, then plunges without a net; "Carey" (*B*), whose **b** phrase springs up irrepressibly by an interval of an eleventh; and "The Arrangement" (*LC*), which sets up a persistent registral divide between the groveling **a** phrase (ending on low B) and the keening **b** phrase (beginning on high D), echoing the protagonist's personal alienation in his anonymous eyrie "on the thirty-third floor."

Some songs segment their space by way of important nodal pitches. Movement between nodes is used to project qualities of expressiveness or directionality. In "Tin Angel" (*C*) (Ex. 6.18), for instance, the verse is placed rather low. There is a modest arching motion between the nodal pitches of B–E–B–G, with an inconclusive ending on G ($\hat{3}$ in the Em context). The chorus projects elation (and closure) by moving to a higher set of nodal pitches (E–G–E). The overall motion here is restrained and classically balanced. "Blue Boy" (*LC*), on the other hand, is less predictable in its movement. Nodal pitches (C,A,G,D,C in various successions) do not conform to any underlying tonal structure as they do in "Tin Angel." The voice's expressive swooping between nodes feels almost random, as if unstructured (or lost).

So far all my examples have been taken from the early period. As Mitchell moved into her second style period, her approach to melody changed. In interviews since the 1980s, she has expressed irritation with reviewers who found fault with her melodic style as it evolved. Her shorthand reference for such critiques is the claim that her songs had "no melody" in comparison with the earlier hits. The following interview excerpt provides some useful context for her compositional perspective.

EXAMPLE 6.18. "TIN ANGEL," VERSE 1 AND CHORUS

Var-nished weeds_____ in win-dow jars, Tar-nished beads_

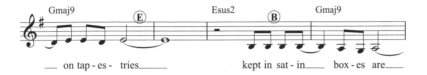

_ on tap-es- tries____ kept in sat-in__ box-es are__

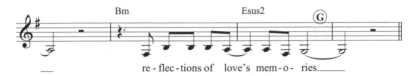

_ re-flec-tions of love's mem-o- ries.___

Guess I'll throw them all_____ a- way.____

I found some-one to love_ to- day.____

MUSICIAN: *Comparing this album* [WTRF] *to* Court and Spark, *it's apparent that you've learned how to bend and stretch the music to complement the lyrics and the emotional tone of each song.* [...]

MITCHELL: [...] I've been trying to do that with the music and lyrics for years, but I don't think it worked as well in the past because I wasn't as anchored to the rhythm. I was pushing it, kind of creating a certain friction against the rhythm. "Coyote," for instance, is a lot of stacking up. When I first started doing that years ago, there was a lot of criticism along the lines of "Hey, there's no melody, and it sounds like she's talking." In other words, the limitation of meter became oppressive, and wouldn't contain the poetry anymore, 'cause it wanted to go in a more blank-verse direction.[33]

Mitchell speaks of her stylistic evolution in terms of a conscious pursuit of changing artistic goals: in the new aesthetic, she identifies a productive tension between the dual demands of a less regulated text declamation and an underlying rhythmic groove. (For the time being, I will set aside her negative judgment regarding past endeavors. This self-critique may have been colored by the circumstance that at the time of these remarks she was embarking on yet another style transition, into period three.)[34] Before examining the music for evidence of the changing aesthetic, I would like to go back to the reviewers and take a close look at the actual nature of their critiques.

Pertinent reviews appeared in major publications in the mid-1970s, as Mitchell followed her greatest commercial success (*C&S*) with increasingly adventurous projects. In a review of *Hissing of Summer Lawns*, Stephen Holden takes Mitchell to task for her musical choices, with a significant focus on melody: "Mitchell's tunes for the first time often lack harmonic focus. They are free-form in the most self-indulgent sense, i.e., they exist only to carry the lyrics.... The only catchy melody is the non-original 'Centerpiece.'" The following year, in a review of *Hejira*, Ariel Swartley makes similar observations but with more allowances for ongoing stylistic exploration:

> It is true that she has all but abandoned melodies anyone can whistle, and her brief fling with the standard bridge seems to be over. But if she has denied her listeners memorable tunes and conventional formats, Mitchell displays other musical charms.... While *Hejira*...represents a retreat from the inviting accessibility of *Court and Spark*, it is a retreat with a self-renewing purpose.... Mitchell has taken advantage of the music's structural freedom to write some of her most incisive and humorous lyrics.... In fact, her voice is often flexible enough to create the continuity and the climaxes that her melodies lack.

Don Juan's Reckless Daughter provoked several telling responses. For Kristine McKenna, the "lyrics are rambling free verse that fight against the structure of the melodies, which are fragmented and oblique." For Michael Watts, the "adoption of a more implied melody has thrust greater emphasis upon her lyrics, [and] has also demanded of her music a great degree of tension and range of careful nuance to ensure that her songs do not become elegant Muzak, best suited to dinner parties." For Janet Maslin (the harshest overall), Mitchell has "let her music become shapeless as she tries to incorporate jazz and calypso rhythms that eventually overpower her." Stephen Holden, meanwhile, has come to a new understanding of Mitchell's artistic aims: since *Blue*, he claims, she has amassed the most impressive body of work of any post-Dylan singer/songwriter, elaborating the free-form narrative ballad form that Dylan thrust into popular song and polishing a melismatic melodic line more flexible than Dylan's and many times more sophisticated. Mitchell's finest verse-music fusions on *Hejira* and *Don Juan's Reckless Daughter* represent an incredible formal achievement. Whole poems scan so freely one would hardly suspect they were song lyrics, and although some melodic accessibility has been sacrificed, "Amelia" [*H*] and "Cotton Avenue" [*DJRD*] stand up as great pop and jazz tunes.[35]

All in all, while the critics are not as appreciative as they could be, their judgments are not without nuance, certainly not as blunt as crying "no melody."[36] The picture that emerges is of intelligent listeners grappling with the strong vision of an artist on a path of dynamic and very rapid change, making unwonted demands on her audience to keep up.[37] Only two years had elapsed, after all, between Holden's two reviews cited here, in which time Mitchell had released three idiosyncratic, challenging albums.

These reviews invoke rules of thumb valuing tunes that are accessible, catchy, and well structured. Accessibility implies appeal for a broad audience ("melodies anyone can whistle"). There is a consensus that Mitchell is moving toward a more specialized appeal by pursuing musical goals that are more "sophisticated," that is, that take more effort to appreciate. (In its hostile form, the term is "self-indulgent.") A catchy tune is one that is easily remembered, probably due to the skillful placement of hooks. These first two aesthetic criteria are fairly subjective. Consideration of melodic structure, however, requires some objective description. The reviewers claim (on the negative side) that Mitchell's tunes lack focus, continuity, and climax; viewed positively, the tunes possess special freedom, flexibility, and complex ("melismatic," "oblique") contour. (Technically, "melismatic" refers to florid text-setting, that is, a flourish of pitches set to one syllable.) The related issue of poetic structure also comes up, with references to rambling or free verse.

"Coyote" (*H*) is a good example of Mitchell's exploration of free verse. The poem is rhymed but nonmetric, each verse with an erratic sequence of syllables per line. Line 1, for instance, is a short six syllables in verse 1 ("No regrets, Coyote"), ten syllables in verse 3 ("I looked a Coyote right in the face"). Line 2 ranges from ten ("He's staring a hole in his scrambled eggs") to fourteen syllables ("In the middle of nowhere, in the middle of the night"). Such poetic variation requires a highly elastic sense of melodic identity. Whereas an early tune like "Little Green" is designed with a stable number of pitches per phrase in a fairly precise, tightly patterned succession, the vocal phrases in "Coyote" stretch and contract according to the verse. Mitchell treats both the rhythm and the pitch succession as variable. The placement of long and short durations changes according to speech inflection; the rhythmic activity and span of each phrase can also shift in relation to the regular underlying groove (what Mitchell describes as "stacking up").[38] Mitchell handles this variation by conceiving of the melody as an imprecise basic contour, strung between nodal pitches and incorporating recurrent internal shapes while allowing for modification in detail. In "Coyote," the melody in mm. 1–2 (when not spoken) hovers around B♭, in mm. 3–6 around E, in mm. 7–8 around G, and so on (see Ex. 6.13). The vocal range is diffuse, that is, fairly wide but without dramatic emphasis on movement through melodic space; a lot of time is spent in the middle range. Mitchell places minor peaks or rhythmic stresses at the end of each **c** phrase (marked by a IV chord in the harmonic progression); but in general the contour is low in relief. In contrast to the melody, the harmonic progression is stable and regular, supplying the music's endoskeleton and forward impulse. The most audible hooks adorn the punctuating passages, namely, the refrain and IR. Otherwise, the free vocal melody moves in a fluid duet with Jaco Pastorius's equally elastic bass playing.

Judged by an earlier aesthetic, this tune *is* weak in focus, climax, and dramatic shape. But Mitchell is after an altogether different effect, where these qualities are secondary to flexibility of motion and greater independence from the rhythmic groove. (JM: "I think that around the time of *Hejira*, I let the writer, the poet, take precedence over the singer. But my feeling is that a lot of those songs were, in fact, superior to the earlier stuff. Yet they were jazz melodies. Conversational improvisation around a given melody. But as such it wasn't always necessary to state the melody. And often I didn't.")[39] Though the negative reactions in the press didn't appear until 1976, she had already been exploring freer melodic construction in songs as far back as *Blue*. Daniel Sonenberg has analyzed the verses of "The Last Time I Saw Richard" in terms similar to those I have just proposed, as variable interpretations of an "underlying melodic scheme" or "blueprint."[40] This song is notorious for its wordy, unruly poetic lines. The verses in "A Case of You" project a melody every bit as elastic as that of "Coyote." "A Case of You" does include some dramatic leaps, however; its chorus also provides contrast through its stable recurring elements as well as its rhythmic hooks ("I could drink"), strong cadential motion, and clearly directed melodic voice-leading (traversing an octave, D♭ down to D♭). These features contribute to the song's accessibility, offsetting the freer form of the verse with more conventional musical salience and structural focus. Likewise, "California" contrasts a rhythmically elastic verse with a chorus of clearer rhythmic shape and direction. In this case, though the verse is rhythmically free, its pitch content is rather consistent: a strong pattern of three-note groups based on a single shape (G♯–B–C♯, C♯–E–F♯, B–C♯–E). (The chorus shares the same motive.) The album *Court and Spark* also intermittently explores melodic flexibility; "Help Me" is a good example. Again, Mitchell adorns the freer melodic structure with accessible features such as dramatic upward sweeps, special harmonic colors (parallel major sevenths), and a catchy refrain.

By the time of *Hissing*, however, the flexible approach to melody is more pervasive. Contours are flatter. Many of the instrumental arrangements are mellower than those on *Court and Spark*; in addition, it sounds as if the band is more thoroughly blended and mixed down in relation to the vocal. Mitchell seems to have muted the showiness and drama of the tunes in order to direct attention more fully toward her delivery of the lyrics. In "Edith and the Kingpin," for instance, the melody starts with a "tumbling" contour, repeatedly falling through the same melodic space (see Ex. 6.6). The range is very narrow, mostly staying within a six-note span (G down to B♭). When in the very last line of the verse the voice reaches up an octave, the gesture has particular salience within the low-key context (though the vocal delivery always remains cool). Musical interest encompasses an overall polished sound in which subtle details are telling: moments of special warmth or gloss in the vocal, momentary shifts in timbre, one-note horn licks like added brushstrokes. Much the same can be said for "Shades of Scarlett Conquering." This is the new aesthetic which gave the critics pause.

In general, then, there are basic aspects to be aware of when considering melodic shape: the precision or flexibility of a tune from verse to verse, the exploitation of tonal space (overall range, register, intervallic motion, directionality, patterning, constrained or dramatic gestures, etc.), in conjunction with other ways of creating moments of musical salience (hooks, motives, harmonic shading). Certain aspects may be more or less significant in specific cases, depending on text expression and overall aesthetic aims. But these categories provide a useful set of tools for analysis. I will end with assorted highlights from a few examples later in Mitchell's career.

The bitingly satirical "Otis and Marlena" (*DJRD*) has the amorphous melodic contour of the later 1970s, though not devoid of hooks. In fact, the song obsessively harps on a single hook—a rhythmic snap from D to E♭. The hook's punchy, relentless repetition in the guitar borders on the maladroit. The voice shadows the guitar's pitch focus while ironically offsetting its manner with an extremely suave and unctuous persona. Also ironic in its exaggeration is the vocal decoration of the melodic line in plentiful miniature curves. It comes as a relief and a prominent feature when the voice sustains a pure undecorated note at the refrain.

"Ladies' Man" (*WTRF*) (Ex. 6.19) exemplifies the move in the 1980s from the imprecise, elastic melodic conception of period two to a melody that is more rhythmically anchored and articulated into more well-defined segments. Melodic phrases are relatively stable in length and rhythmic placement, though Mitchell still allows for a certain amount of adjustment to textual expression in different verses. Most of the phrases of this song begin with an identical hook: a chromatic snippet high in the vocal range, with a sassy anticipation of the downbeat. Many phrases are also punctuated by a refrain-like response low in the voice (on the title phrase), always on the same pitches and in the same rhythmic position (similar to the initial hook). These salient features provide stable structural landmarks. The melody distinguishes itself from first-period style in its dry delivery—many short rhythmic values, few sustained notes, and lots of air between phrases. In "Impossible Dreamer" (*DED*) (Ex. 6.20), Mitchell continues to explore dry vocal delivery, in this case setting up a severe dichotomy between two vocal manners. The opening of the verse alternates between pithy, highly disconnected, bitten-off

EXAMPLE 6.19. "LADIES' MAN," VERSE 1

EXAMPLE 6.20. "IMPOSSIBLE DREAMER," PHRASES 1 AND 2

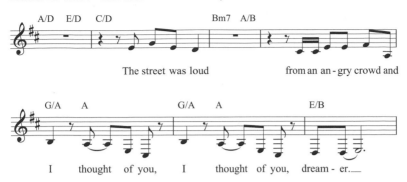

phrases ("The street was loud") and more lyrical triadic curves in Mitchell's unique whiskey baritone range (on the refrain lines, e.g., "And I thought of you").[41] The "impossible" hope for a better world is linked to a performance aesthetic in which the singer only reluctantly drops her defenses and relaxes into generous contours and fuller timbre.

In contrast, "Night Ride Home" (*NRH*) (Ex. 6.21) from period four has a melody of grand sweeping curves. Its beauty does not depend on ornament or rhythmic complexity but on the elegant counterpoise of bold movements through space. Lyricism is sustained through a stately structure that spans the verse and bridge. Likewise, "Sunny Sunday" (*TI*) (Ex. 6.22) is composed of shapely arches. Mitchell separates subphrases with significant pauses, but the secondary curves in

EXAMPLE 6.21. "NIGHT RIDE HOME," VERSE 1

EXAMPLE 6.22. "SUNNY SUNDAY"

(continued)

EXAMPLE 6.22. (CONTINUED)

each subphrase never lose their place in a larger melodic arc. While the verse in "Night Ride Home" is relatively succinct, in "Sunny Sunday" the formal span is much more protracted. Mitchell prolongs the expectation of forward movement through long-range harmonic and linear goals. F♯ (IV) is treated as a pivotal chord. In the first two (a) phrases, vocal statement of the F♯ triad ("She dodges the light") leads to closure through an authentic cadence (IV–V–I). In the next two (b) phrases, the chord initiates a deceptive progression (IV–V–vi) ("Then she points her pistol through the door"). At the same time, the melody sets up a sequence of gradual upward movement, only to plunge dramatically at the end of each b phrase. Finally, in the c phrase, the melody attains its desired high point, A♯ ("That one little victory"). Harmonic movement at this point is still deceptive, however. But with the return of a, the crucial IV chord once again leads to closure. The form of this song is unique, implying two distinct interpretations. With its return to the opening phrase, it implies a truncated strophic structure (aab$_o$b$_o$c$_o$, a ...), as if the music could continue through another cycle (just as the protagonist cycles through a futile daily routine). But in fact, as we have seen, the return of a brings closure to an overarching harmonic gesture. Thus the song's form can be heard as through-composed, with no sectional repetition, but rounded off and complete as it is (aab$_o$b$_o$c$_o$a). In this reading, the arching melodic plan extends not merely over the span of one verse, as is typical, but over the span of the entire song.

"Last Chance Lost" (*TI*) (Ex. 6.23), on the other hand, moves in stops and starts, as if hampered by the hazardous emotional situation surrounding the breakdown of a relationship. Most phrases consist of two opposed elements: a hook on the title phrase, sounding like a stark, stylized wail with minimal contour, and a shapely flourish unscrolling in response ("in the tyranny of a long goodbye"). This pattern is stated three times with little development, as if taking shelter in ritual repetition. The closing phrase disintegrates into two-note fragments, drifting apart. The expressive power of this melody is enhanced by its failure to cohere into a long-range span.

Earlier in this chapter I spoke of tunes as holistic concepts, encompassing qualities of rhythm, harmony, and form as well as melodic contour. For analytic clarity I have chosen to focus on song form, phrase structure, and contour each in its turn, but they are not separate phenomena. The same qualification applies to the overall structure of this book. As befits a preliminary study, I have paid scrupulous attention to basic concepts. A division of the songwriter's art into distinct parameters has allowed me to develop a precise methodology appropriate to the various topics of style, voice, theme, harmony, and melody. But once the method is absorbed, the goal for future analysis is to show how such properties go hand in hand. With that in mind, I have tried to design an approach to Mitchell's work as a whole that is multifaceted, highly adaptable, sensitive to subtle detail, and exacting in descriptive power while respecting the more elusive qualities of music and poetry.

EXAMPLE 6.23. "LAST CHANCE LOST," VERSE 1

From considerations of formal coherence within individual songs I now turn to the succession of songs on specific albums and their arrangement into larger formal spans.

7

COLLECTIONS AND CYCLES

I first started listening avidly to Joni Mitchell's music as a teenager in the 1970s, after being introduced to her albums by a college roommate, who adored *Ladies of the Canyon* and *Blue*. We were attending conservatory in Baltimore, both studying piano performance. Officially, we were there to discover our callings as musicians, to be initiated into music's secrets and gain some control over its brute power. Just as importantly, though not listed on the curriculum, we were learning to sort through our own raw and confusing emotions as we formed our adult selves, and for both of us, the two programs of study were inseparably linked. My roommate was especially drawn to the hyperexpressive style of *Blue*, treating Joni's romantic, vulnerable persona as a key to unlock the impulsive emotional outpourings we were being asked to perform. I remember coming home one evening to find him lying on the living room couch in the dark, listening to *Blue* for the umpteenth time. This time, though, he told me he had had a revelation: Joni intended the album to be heard as a song cycle. As I look back at this moment of insight from thirty years on, it seems to have brought about a much-desired reconciliation of the competing spheres of personal development, professional acumen, and artistic value. By applying high-art concepts to popular music, my friend legitimated his private musical pleasures. At the same time, he proved that our newly acquired technical knowledge was not limited to the world of connoisseurs but had relevance for everyday life. He validated Joni Mitchell's status as a composer by recognizing her creative ambitions in the pursuit of organic unity and large-scale formal planning, even in the case of an album usually understood in terms of immediate, uncalculated expression. Finally, his epiphany touched on a matter of expressly personal significance. It was well known that Mitchell had experienced intense psychological distress during the making of *Blue*: "I was absolutely transparent, like cellophane. If you looked at me, I would weep.... Socially I was an absolute wreck."[1] Yet from such emotional turmoil she had wrested an artistic creation with an enduring structural arch. Her achievement of musical coherence against the odds held out hope for those of us struggling to achieve psychic coherence and maturity.

As my story suggests, the magical shift in perception whereby a casual collection of songs resolves into an ordered, interrelated whole conjures up notions of aesthetic legitimation, interpretive insight, and the ethical formation of the self. But the setting of the darkened living room implies a fundamentally private scene of listening. That is to say, the distinction between collection and cycle may be decided at the point of consumption. The recognition of connections between individual songs arises from repeated listening: the more one listens to an album, the greater one's chances of perceiving connections. Furthermore, the attribution of a special overall coherence is often a question of degree, resting on subjective judgments. After all, in assembling an album, even one without a unifying concept, most artists are careful to arrange songs in a suitable order, considering such matters as effective initial and closing gestures, internal groupings (such as sides of an LP), general emotional progression, and specific relations between adjacent songs (whether rhyming, contrasting, or linked by transitional material). I prefer to understand the possibilities of large-scale form on popular music albums in terms of a continuum stretching from the haphazard through the loosely coherent to the firmly coherent. In the middle of this continuum, there is room for disagreement over whether an album may be considered a collection or a cycle. One's personal perceptions and listening history will be the deciding factors. Ruth Bingham has made a similar claim for art song genres in the nineteenth century:

> The only unqualified characteristics [of a song cycle] are multiplicity—three or more poems—and coherence—achieved through the poetry, the music, or the interaction between them. Inevitably, collections approach cycles, particularly if the collector possesses some skill. The definition dictates only that the songs cohere, not that they cohere to any particular degree, yielding an unbroken continuum where carefully arranged collections neighbor loosely constructed cycles.[2]

In the context of pop music intended for release as recordings, the song cycle genre is commonly represented in the notion of the concept album, in which songs are unified or framed by a ruling idea. Pop music historians usually point to the Beatles album *Sgt. Pepper's Lonely Hearts Club Band* (1968)—with its framing concept of a fictional concert performance, its thematically linked cover art, and its connective passages between tracks—as the album that ignited a widespread interest in such a form.[3] Some would argue that the distinction of the "first" concept album belongs either to the Beach Boys' *Pet Sounds* or Frank Zappa and the Mothers of Invention's *Freak Out!* (both released in 1966).[4] One can identify other artists who were experimenting with the idea of the concept album before the release of *Sgt. Pepper*, including Joni Mitchell in her debut recording (March 1968), as we shall see.[5] It should be pointed out, however, that the possibility of grouping songs by genre, occasion (e.g., the holiday album), theme (e.g., Johnny Cash, *Ride This Train* [1960]), or mood was inherent in the format and marketing of the long-playing record from the time of its development in the 1950s.[6]

In Bingham's description of the cycle, she emphasizes that coherence is not necessarily achieved through musical means, and in fact when Mitchell constructs cycles she works primarily with textual connections, concepts, or frames. Musical connections are supportive of a guiding textual rationale—in some cases perhaps accidentally so. Before turning our attention to specific concept albums in Mitchell's work, it will be helpful to identify a range of techniques used in the construction of cyclic coherence. Poetic techniques include the use of central themes, recurrent motifs, unifying expressive tones, or overarching plans. Examples of Joni Mitchell albums with strong central themes would be *Hejira* (travel), *Hissing* (bourgeois disillusionment), and *Wild Things* (love).[7] Note that the occurrence of one of these techniques in isolation does not necessarily make a concept album: *Wild Things*, for instance, is thematically unified, but by a topic that is so diffuse (and ubiquitous in the pop song genre) that only a loose coherence is created. A good example of a recurrent motif would be the use of color imagery in *Blue*. Six out of the ten songs on that album make striking reference to "the blues" or the color blue; the remaining songs make subsidiary mention of red, black, white, and green. The penultimate song, "A Case of You," consummates the motif with the line "I live in a box of paints." *Blue* is also unified by melancholy and bittersweet tones; *Dog Eat Dog* by tones of righteous indignation. (Note that expressive tones encompass both poetry and music.) An overarching plan may take the form of a framing structure, as in *Mingus*, with its interspersion of verbal "raps," featuring Mingus's recorded voice, providing oblique introductions to every song but one. Alternatively, it may take the form of an emotional or narrative progression, as in the jazz standard album *Both Sides Now*, whose songs were chosen and ordered to "trace the arc of a modern romantic relationship" (as explained in the liner notes).

Musical techniques include motivic relations, continuity between adjacent songs, and overarching plans.[8] A series of motives connect individual songs in *For the Roses*. Most audible are the rising sixteenth-note pickups prominent in both "For the Roses" and "Woman of Heart and Mind" (Ex. 7.1). The adjoining songs "Barangrill" and "Lesson in Survival" begin with similar syncopated figures (Ex. 7.2). The opening and closing songs, "Banquet" and "Judgement of the Moon

EXAMPLE 7.1. PICKUP MOTIVES IN *FOR THE ROSES*

a. "For the Roses"

b. "Woman of Heart and Mind"

EXAMPLE 7.2. OPENING MOTIVES IN *FOR THE ROSES*

a. "Barangrill"

b. "Lesson in Survival"

EXAMPLE 7.3. OPENING MOTIVES IN *FOR THE ROSES*

a. "Banquet"

b. "Judgement of the Moon and Stars"

and Stars," also share similar beginnings (a falling figure followed by offbeat chords; Ex. 7.3). Nevertheless, as this album shows, individual connections between songs do not by themselves necessarily add up to overall tight construction. Adjacent songs can be connected by continuous musical transitions. This occurs twice on *Court and Spark*: "People's Parties" segues into "The Same Situation" by way of a transitional piano solo, and "Trouble Child" segues into "Twisted" by way of a trumpet solo. It also occurs on *Hissing*, where "The Boho Dance" leads into "Harry's House" by way of a Doppler effect in the horns. Even without transitions, continuity between adjacent songs can be effected by close affinities between the final sonority of one song and the initial sonority of the next. On *Clouds*, for instance, the final chord of the gloomy "Tin Angel" (spelled E-B-E-F♯-D) and the opening chord of the upbeat "Chelsea Morning" (E-B-F♯-D) are identical in pitch (though the guitar tunings are very different). On *Ladies of the Canyon*, the song "Willy" ends with the chord G-B-G in the piano; after the pause, the top two notes are carried over, now clothed in the anguished piano harmony that begins "The Arrangement" (A-E-B-D-G; see Ex. 2.2). (Given that "Willy" is in C major, the harmonic move between songs resembles a deceptive cadential progression.)

As for the musical construction of an overarching plan, one way this can be done is through a key scheme. Songs can fall into internal groupings (adjacent or nonadjacent) according to key relations.[9] For instance, the final three songs on side 1 of *Song to a Seagull* are all in G; the first three songs on side 2 are all in D. All the acoustic piano songs on *Ladies of the Canyon* are related to the key of C or its relative minor key, A. ("For Free" and "Willy" are in C; "Blue Boy" is ambiguously centered between C and G. "The Arrangement" is in A Aeolian/Dorian; "Rainy Night House" is in A Aeolian/Phrygian for its long introduction, then moves to D.) In *Court and Spark*, four tonal centers (E, A, D, C) account for all eleven songs (see Table 7.1); songs related by tonal center form interlocking subgroups. Rarely, however, does the tonal structure of an album show a rigorous logical progression accounting for all songs (this is true for classical song cycles as well).[10] Besides tonal planning, there are other possible means of musical patterning. One such possibility is a progression made up of genres or musical idioms, such as Peter Kaminsky finds in Paul Simon's album *Still Crazy after All These Years*.[11] Another is the use of explicit musical return, as in *Sgt. Pepper*, with its reprise of the title song near the end of the album; or as in the variation-rondo forms used by Frank Zappa in the 1960s.[12]

TABLE 7.1.   Tonal Centers in *Court and Spark*

Song	Key	Key + Mode
SIDE 1		
1. "Court and Spark"	E	E Dorian/Aeolian/Mixolydian
2. "Help Me"	A–D	A Mixolydian/Aeolian–D major/Aeolian
3. "Free Man in Paris"	A	A major/Aeolian
4. "People's Parties"	D	D major/Mixolydian
5. "The Same Situation"	A	A Dorian/minor/major
SIDE 2		
6. "Car on a Hill"	F♯–A	F♯ Aeolian–A major/Aeolian
7. "Down to You"	D–E	D major/Dorian–E Mixolydian
8. "Just Like This Train"	C	C major/Lydian/Mixolydian
9. "Raised on Robbery"	C	C blues
10. "Trouble Child"	C–G	C major/Lydian–G Dorian/major
11. "Twisted"	D	D blues

For analytical clarity, I have listed the poetic and musical techniques separately, but in reality they are interdependent. (Recall Bingham's definition of cyclic coherence, "achieved through the poetry, the music, or the interaction between them.") Mitchell emphasizes this fact in her liner note to *Hissing*, which she explicitly identifies as a concept album: "This record is a total work conceived graphically, musically, lyrically and accidentally—as a whole. The performances were guided by the given compositional structures and the audibly inspired beauty of every player. The whole unfolded like a mystery." In this statement, Mitchell calls attention to two further factors not to be forgotten when considering the totality of an album concept: graphic design and the element of chance. From the beginning of her career Mitchell has maintained control over album design, usually creating the cover art herself; we can expect central themes or motifs to be reflected visually in some way. The nod to chance is an acknowledgement that, despite the impossibility of planning every aspect of a recording, some of its unforeseen, "accidental" features (subconscious, intuitive, or collaborative) end up reinforcing its coherence fortuitously.

In my view, ten of Mitchell's records are inarguably concept albums. (Some listeners may wish to present arguments in favor of others as well.) Of the sixteen original albums, six are "conceived as a whole": *Song to a Seagull*, *Blue*, and the four consecutive albums beginning with *Hissing* (*Hissing, Hejira, Don Juan's Reckless Daughter*, and *Mingus*).[13] Of the seven compilations, four are organized around a concept: *Both Sides Now, Travelogue, The Beginning of Survival*, and *Songs of a Prairie Girl*. I plan to examine the nature of the formal coherence—graphic, musical, lyrical and accidental—in three different albums.

SONG TO A SEAGULL

In her first album, Mitchell organizes the ten songs according to an explicit poetic frame. The record's two sides are grouped thematically under headings taken from the lyrics of the title song: "Part One: I came to the city," and "Part Two: Out of the city and down to the seaside."[14] All of the songs on side 1 have an urban setting. Most of the songs on side 2 have a seaside setting, while the final song, "Cactus Tree," bridges city and seaside in its more expansive geographic scope.[15] The strong thematic break between sides is supported by the tonal shift between the G center of songs 3–5 and the D center of songs 6–8 (see Table 7.2). Central themes include heartbreak (especially in "I Had a King," "Marcie," "The Pirate of Penance," and "Cactus Tree"), people's relation to their natural surroundings (alienated or nurturing), and the struggle between personal ideals of domesticity and freedom. In regard to the latter, on the one hand, "I Had a King," "Michael from Mountains,"

TABLE 7.2.   Aspects of Musical Coherence in *Song to a Seagull*

Song	Key	Cadence: a) Harmony	b) Melody	Harmonic/Textural Motive
PART 1: I came to the city				
1. "I Had a King"	A	sus2	$\hat{5}$	M/m, pedal, quartal
2. "Michael from Mountains"	F	triad	$\hat{1}$	
3. "Night in the City"	G	triad	$\hat{1}$	
4. "Marcie"	G	sus(2)	$\hat{5}$	
5. "Nathan La Franeer"	G	triad	$\hat{3}$	M/m
PART 2: Out of the city and down to the seaside				
6. "Sisotowbell Lane"	D	V13sus/I	$\hat{5}$	
7. "The Dawntreader"	D	triad	$\hat{1}$	M/m, pedal, quartal
8. "The Pirate of Penance"	D	+4	$\hat{1}$	
9. "Song to a Seagull"	C	open 5	$\hat{1}$	M/m, pedal, quartal
10. "Cactus Tree"	F♯	triad	$\hat{3}$	Pedal

"Sisotowbell Lane," and "The Pirate of Penance" paint various pictures of home life; on the other, all but two songs ("Night in the City," "Sisotowbell Lane") thematize abandonment, travel, or escape. In support of the polarity between the domestic and the fantasy quest, there are strong subsidiary motifs based on clothing ("gingham," "taffeta," "satins," "Persian lace") and treasure ("silver," "peridots," "amber stones"). Again, "Cactus Tree" has a summational role in bringing together a number of important symbols and motifs from preceding songs, such as the sailing ship (from songs 4, 7, and 8), the queen (song 1), the mountains (song 2), the unanswered letter (song 4), and the dreamer (songs 7 and 9).

The album's cover art elaborates many of the same symbols in graphic form, especially the ship, the queen, clothing, and the natural world. The iconic lady on the front is sumptuously attired in paisley, with a diadem of daisies and leaves and a veil of beads. Her lemon-gold hair streams outward in abundant, unconstrained, lyrical waves. The bipartite structure of the album is echoed in the dissonance between the pastoral watercolor portrait on the front—the lady engulfed by a fantasy bouquet of flowers and birds—and the dystopic photographic portrait on the back, in which Joni picks her way through a sooty, garbage-encrusted canyon in Manhattan, clutching her childlike belongings while huddling beneath a flimsy rose-tinted umbrella. But rather than contrasting these two visual realms through static juxtaposition, Mitchell sets up a dynamic interaction between them. A smaller version of the photographic urban space appears on the front, as a bauble hovering above the lady's head, thus suggesting a thought bubble—a memory internal to the utopian persona and transformed through imagination into a glossy adornment. But if the cover art is viewed in a progression from front to back (following the gaze of the lady, the goose, and the peacock), the urban image becomes intrusive, expanding and crowding out the fantasy images. The wide-angle lens adds to the effect of bulging dimensionality. The circle shape of the photograph, decorative on the front, is transformed on the back into the sink-hole shape of the open garbage can. Another circle, the Gulf sign in the distance above Joni's head, subtly (accidentally) alludes to the chasm or gulf between the urban and pastoral as well as the idea of engulfment implied in the composition, whereby each spatial realm is poised to swallow the other. Yet a third spatial area, the transcendent ocean expanse on the right front cover, is drained of color, rhyming with the lady's strikingly white face and thus perhaps symbolizing her "seadreams." Upon opening the gatefold of the album, one encounters a graphic reconciliation of all three visual realms. The inside image is a photographic self-portrait, now pastoral in tone, capturing the wind in Joni's hair in an echo of the flowing fantasy tresses. The background of the photo is completely featureless, however, as if we have entered the third, infinite, oceanic space.

In a similar fashion, the bipartite structure of the song cycle does not merely express a polar opposition (city/seaside) but involves a dramatic progression. Songs 2 and 3 ("Michael from Mountains" and "Night in the City") express happiness in love and excitement about the colorful urban setting. In song 4 ("Marcie"), the title character is sadly disillusioned with both her absent lover and her life in New York (rooms are collecting dust, the faucet needs fixing, colors are fading, the shipyards are wintry cold). Song 5 ("Nathan La Franeer") dramatizes an escape from an increasingly toxic environment. Side 2 opens with two songs ("Sisotowbell Lane," "The Dawntreader") expressing contentment and emotional fulfillment in the new setting. Song 8 ("The Pirate of Penance"), like song 4, is a tale of heartbreak, translated from New York harbor to a mythical harbor town. Song 9 ("Song to a Seagull") embraces the utopian associations of the seaside, while tinged with regret over human failings and a longing to soar "out of reach." The inner eight songs (2 through 9) thus form a double, parallel emotional arc, from happiness through disillusionment to the wish to escape. The two outer songs project another kind of symmetry, presenting opposing poles in the struggle between settling down and cutting loose: song 1 ("I Had a King") warns against the pitfalls of commitment and domesticity, while song 10 ("Cactus Tree") warns against the dangers of restless self-exploration. But the framing songs also carry a dynamic temporal charge. In relation to the emotional arc of side 1, the opening song is already leaping ahead to disillusionment and escape from a toxic environment. At the other end, song 9 is backward-looking, recapitulating the emotional and geographic journey traveled so far (recall that the album's headings are taken from this song). In song 10, however, the lady is still "in the city," as if she has yet to make the crucial crossing. Just as in the cover art, the two symbolic realms interpenetrate in the cyclic narrative, but in this case by way of a shifting temporal perspective.

The overarching plan in this album is primarily poetic, but there are motivic connections in the music that strengthen cyclic coherence (see Table 7.2). For example, if one considers the quality of cadential closure in each of the songs, one finds a prevalence of inconclusive or weakly conclusive endings. Mitchell creates this open-endedness both melodically and harmonically. The melodies of songs 1, 4, and 6 end on $\hat{5}$, essentially hovering in linear space. In songs 5 and 10 (that is, at the close of Parts 1 and 2), the melodies end on the weakly conclusive $\hat{3}$. Harmonically, songs 1 and 9 end on open sonorities ("I Had a King" on Asus2, "Song to a Seagull" on C5). "The Pirate of Penance" ends with a dissonant tritone in the backing vocal ("I don't know"). Songs 4 and 6 end with more complex suspended sonorities ("Marcie" on Gsus(2), "Sisotowbell Lane" on A13sus/D). The only songs that end with linear closure on $\hat{1}$ and a cadential triad are songs 2, 3, and 7—three of the songs expressive of personal fulfillment. Such constant open-endedness helps sustain a sense of forward progression; it also underlines the ambivalence and self-questioning associated with the cycle's lyric personae. A similar open-endedness is conveyed through a verbal motif first introduced in the second bridge of "Marcie," where we learn the reason for her emotional suspension: her lover's false words—"wait for me"—ring out, hovering on $\hat{5}$ and fading in a long decay. Song 6 ends with an echo of this phrase: "we wait for you" (also ending on $\hat{5}$). The following song, "The Dawntreader," has a refrain concluding with the words "come to me" in an exaggerated sustain. (The song "Cactus Tree," in another instance of its culminating function, ties these various open-ended relational phrases together in the passage stating "She has brought them to her senses.")

Another cluster of motivic connections is more subtle (accidental?). The opening song foregrounds a stark juxtaposition of major and minor tonic triads; similar struggles over modal identity are to be found in songs 5, 7, and 9. The opening song is texturally constrained by a constant pedal; songs 7, 9, and 10 are also set in pedal point textures. The opening song features passages of bold quartal harmony (especially notable leading into the chorus; see Ex. 2.1); similar passages are featured in songs 7 and 9 (song 7 has both quartal and quintal progressions). This set of connections has two important consequences. First, it suggests a pattern of musical germination, springing from the motivic density contained in the opening song. Second, it creates a subgroup of songs (1, 7, and 9) linked by all three harmonic/textural characteristics. The symbolic effect of this close motivic relationship is not obvious, given that the first song is landlocked while the latter two ("Dawntreader," "Seagull") are littoral. One could understand the quartal harmony as conveying a bardic resonance, ill-fitting in the urban setting and only coming into its own in the later songs; thus the harmony reflects the character's movement through symbolic space. The pedal point texture, at first a symbol of spiritual constraint, is respaced in Part 2 to suggest wider horizons. Yet the modal quandary of the opening song carries over into the pastoral realm, suggestive of many things: the persona's youthful confusion, the questions still unanswered ("where are the footprints"), the fragility of her hopes for a better world, perhaps even the importation of dangerous knowledge into her innocent Eden.

The lyric terrain of this cycle allows the listener to interpret formal relationships in terms of psychic coherence and the formation of identity. Parts 1 and 2 are defined in relation to decisive moments in a personal trajectory (e.g., "I came to the city"). Harmonic complications—"my keys won't fit" (song 1)—correspond with quandaries over one's place in the world. The ordering of song sequences into dynamic temporal spans (projecting defiantly forward or wistfully backward) can be felt as an attempt to gain a better vantage point on one's disparate intellectual and emotional experiences. Nevertheless, just as with individual song structures, large-scale form can be mined for a sense of ambiguity. Coherence and closure, in Mitchell's aesthetic vision, are bound to be compromised and contradictory. Thus while the album's final song, "Cactus Tree," has features that serve a culminating function, as we have seen, it also has elements that complicate closure, keeping the end of the cycle ambiguous both formally and psychologically. The song expresses an encompassing perspective which is ironically detached—a personal stocktaking done in the *third* person. The implicit speaker recapitulates romantic interludes with intense nostalgia, while her alter ego, the hollow-hearted lady of the poem, looks only to the future and her own freedom. The song's final verse ("She will love them when she sees them/They will lose her if they follow") carries a temporal and ethical double edge: is it pronouncing the wry moral of an old story or New Age words to live by? No doubt one reason Mitchell was drawn to cyclic frameworks like this was the greater scope they offer for developing her favored themes of self-education and self-interrogation.

HEJIRA

In both *Song to a Seagull* and *Mingus*, the overarching conceptual framework is explicitly presented as an aspect of the album's packaging (bipartite headings in *SS*, details of collaboration and homage, as well as the interspersed "raps," in *M*). The listener, given the overt framework, is invited to make further connections among individual songs. On the other hand, in the notes to *Hissing*, Mitchell simply tells the listener that the album is conceived as a whole, without revealing any overarching plan ("It is not my intention to unravel that mystery for anyone"). Listeners may well have come to the same conclusion without any prodding, from their own perception of numerous, pervasive connections woven through the album. The albums *Blue, Hejira*, and *Don Juan's Reckless Daughter* are similar to *Hissing*, in that their conceptual coherence is implicit rather than explicit.

Hejira is without question Mitchell's most tightly unified album. Written in late 1975 and early 1976 and inspired by her experiences on the road during that time, every song reflects in some way on the speaker's own feelings of rootlessness and transition.[16] The grand themes of the album are fortune, mortality, and of course, travel—in particular, flight for the purpose of survival. This is the connotation conveyed by the album's title, an Arabic word translated in the published songbook as "a journey esp. when undertaken to seek refuge away from a dangerous or undesirable environment."[17] The poetry is unified by a consistency of style. As a conduit for a subjective sense of time, Mitchell treats poetic meter as extremely elastic, allowing for a great deal of variation in line length. In accordance with the album's pervasive cyclic patterns, form is consistently strophic (though verses vary in length from six lines in "Amelia" to eighteen in "Blue Motel Room"). All but two of the songs incorporate refrains (see Table 7.3). The verbal discourse is freely associative, marked by frequent lateral shifts in type of utterance. This is evident right away in the opening verse of "Coyote," which begins by casually breaking off an affair, in direct address ("No regrets, Coyote/ We just come from such different sets of circumstance"), then suddenly shifts to a more generalized observation about relationships ("There's no comprehending/Just how close to the bone ... you can get/And still feel so alone"), before returning just as suddenly to direct address ("You're not a hit and run driver, no, no").[18] Even so, every song without exception is spoken in the first person. Thus we identify closely with Mitchell's lyric persona as she sings her hymns to the open road and relates passing encounters along the way.

The rhythms and emotions of solitary travel (wanderlust, melancholy contemplation, fatigue) set the underlying tone. Verbs of motion—racing, rolling, driving, weaving—provide a constant backdrop. Moments of poetic reflection take place in temporary stops like motels, service stations, and cafés; surroundings are strewn with props such as road maps, postcards, and "highway hand-me-downs." The pervasive leitmotif of the car on the highway shifts by free association into other shapes (a 747, a limo, a ferryboat) and blurs into an indistinct symbol of the transitory: "I'm traveling in some vehicle" ("Hejira"). The coordinates of the journey are never precisely mapped out but flow past with the logic of a dream. Thus the imprecise location of the opening song ("the middle of nowhere") gives way to the "burning desert" of the second song, followed by Beale Street (Memphis),

TABLE 7.3. Aspects of Musical Coherence in *Hejira*

Song	Key	Form	Motive	Instruments (+ JM on gtr)*
		SIDE 1		
1. "Coyote"	C	4v., end refrain (final ref altered)	♭III	JP bass, lead gtr, hand drums
2. "Amelia"	F–G	7v., end refrain (final ref altered)	♭III–iii; wrong-key ending	lead gtr, vibes
3. "Furry Sings the Blues"	A–D	4v., internal refrain (final verse adds end refrain)	♭III; open 5th	MB bass, drums, harmonica
4. "A Strange Boy"	D	3½ v., internal refrain (final verse incomplete)	open 5th	lead gtr, hand drums
5. "Hejira"	B	3v., no refrain (partial return)	♭III; wrong-key ending	JP bass, hand drums, clarinet
		SIDE 2		
6. "Song for Sharon"	E♭	10v., no refrain	♭III	MB bass, drums
7. "Black Crow"	E♭–G♭	4v. + instr., end refrain	♭III	JP bass, lead gtr (noise)
8. "Blue Motel Room"	C	2v., internal refrain (partial return)	♭III; only song with no intro hook, no fade-out	acoustic bass, acoustic gtr, drums
9. "Refuge of the Roads"	C	5v., end refrain (varied interludes, final ref altered)	iii; wrong-key ending; coda quotes song 5	JP bass, drums, horns

JP = Jaco Pastorius; MB = Max Bennett; gtr = guitar; v = verse; ref = refrain then New England, Staten Island, Savannah, and the Gulf of Mexico. Meanwhile, Mitchell's ongoing internal monologue calls up personal landmarks from her earlier life in Canada (Baljennie, the Bay of Fundy, Maidstone)—the present landscape in counterpoint with the geography of memory. Though the itinerary is imprecise, Mitchell does create an overarching gesture of wandering and return. After the single mention of home in the first verse of "Coyote" ("I'll just be getting home"), all the songs on side 1 are outward bound (moving east). At exactly halfway through the album (at the end of the fifth song, "Hejira"), the traveler's thoughts begin to turn toward home ("A defector from the petty wars/Until love sucks me back that way"). The homebound direction becomes more palpable as the songs progress. Thus "Song for Sharon" contains just a peripheral mention ("walking home on the railroad tracks"), but "Black Crow" a more heartfelt cry ("How'm I ever going to know my home/When I see it again"), and "Blue Motel Room" returns repeatedly to the homecoming scenario, incorporating it into the refrain ("When I get back to L.A. town"). The album's concluding line ("Westbound and rolling") signals the last leg of the journey.

The grand theme of travel is supported and fleshed out by a dense network of recurrent motifs. Most of these are introduced right away in the opening song, "Coyote." The first to be noted is the motif of the wild animal. In this case Mitchell evokes the figure of the coyote to characterize her partner in a passing affair: a sexually appetitive loner and attractive scoundrel. She overlays her description of the affair with a memory of the animal in its natural setting:

> And a hawk was playing with him
> Coyote was jumping straight up and making passes
> He had those same eyes—just like yours
> Under your dark glasses

In this scenario, Mitchell occupies the position parallel to the hawk who evades the coyote's predatory attentions. In the remainder of the album, the animals that appear serve to characterize Mitchell herself, as mediums for her restlessness: the ragged black crow scavenging for trinkets; the "white-assed deer" running from danger ("Refuge"). This motif is carried over to the cover art, where Joni is draped in fur: a protection against the wintry landscape but also an expression of affinity with the animal spirits. On the album's inner fold and record sleeve, Joni spreads her arms to stretch the black stole like a set of ersatz wings.[19]

Mitchell portrays her encounter with Coyote in part as a clash of strong wills:

> And the next thing I know
> That Coyote's at my door
> He pins me in a corner and he won't take "No!"

This motif carries over into the other relationships featured throughout the album. For instance, "A Strange Boy" hinges on the quarreling dynamic between Mitchell and her immature skateboarder. "Blue Motel Room" affectionately calls for a truce in an ongoing battle of egos:

You and me are like America and Russia
We're always keeping score
We're always balancing the power
And that can get to be a cold cold war

Such skirmishes have left their mark; the damage inflicted by life and relationships is another pervasive motif. At times the idea is expressed in terms of violent accidents—a hit and run ("Coyote"), an airplane crash ("Amelia"), a suicide ("Sharon"). At other times, the damage is more insidious, figured as poison, fever, or simply a "haggard face in the bathroom light" ("Black Crow"). The flight reaction provoked by these toxic conditions provides the psychological motivation at the root of the entire album. In "Coyote" the flight reaction is represented as a matter of self-preservation: "Either he's going to have to stand and fight/Or take off out of here." In "Hejira" Mitchell casts it in a more ironic light, as a conscientious objection perhaps but also as a failing on her part: "I'm sitting in some café/A defector from the petty wars/That shell shock love away." In "Coyote," furthermore, Mitchell imagines that her hotel is filled with people looking for a similar retreat from their own personal traumas:

And peeking through keyholes in numbered doors
Where the players lick their wounds
And take their temporary lovers
And their pills and powders to get them through this passion play

The image of licked wounds reinforces the analogy to animal behavior. But these like-minded sufferers don't run in packs; each is cooped up in his or her own cell. In effect, Mitchell gives the mystique of solitude and self-reliance precedence over fellow-feeling. In the final song ("Refuge"), she wears her loner attitude as a badge of pride: "And it made most people nervous/They just didn't want to know/What I was seeing in the refuge of the roads."

However, Mitchell does not invariably portray travel as a defensive reaction— a running away from troublesome aspects of life. Some of the travel she chronicles in *Hejira* was undertaken professionally, for the purpose of concert tours, inviting a more positive psychological construction, as in "Black Crow": "In search of love and music/My whole life has been." Here, the roadway metaphor extends to cover a lifelong search for musical self-fulfilment. Given that for a singer-songwriter the pursuit of music virtually coincides with the realization of one's personal and professional identity, we can expect the motif of musical performance to encompass a complex field of associations. In "Amelia," Mitchell rhymes the strings of her guitar (visually and conceptually) with a visionary longing to be swallowed by the sky. In "Song for Sharon," on the other hand, the reference to the mandolin is wholly mundane—something she needs for work. Her shopping trip is nothing but a pretext for a sequence of meditations on the cultural myth of everlasting love, triggered by the sight of a wedding dress display. The whole poem is structured by the notion of the side trip, with Mitchell veering off to pursue compulsions or momentary distractions, just as her thoughts veer off on secondary paths. Meanwhile, the opening image of the musical instrument sets off a subliminal motivic thread of phonetic association ("mandolin … mannequin … Manhattan … malfunction … Maidstone") connecting the self-styled, urbane yearnings of the present with those of the virginal past. Eventually, Mitchell's thoughts come back around to music, as she compares her own life accomplishments and sacrifices to those of her friend, singing for her family at home. In "Coyote," a mention of a portable tape recorder serves to underline the differences in lifestyle between the two principal characters: "You'll be brushing out a brood mare's tail/While the sun is ascending/And I'll just be getting home with my reel to reel." The reel-to-reel recorder is a symbol of her trade; it is also a bulky machine, part of the baggage that sometimes gets in the way of human relationships. Its spools move in circles, in parallel with the automobile tires and other pervasive symbols of circularity. Though at a mechanical remove from the emotional substance animating her music (and causing her to "reel"), the recorder preserves a physical trace of those experiences, much like the tracks Mitchell lays down in her journey along the freeway. Finally, in "Furry Sings the Blues," the musical theme is central, as Mitchell takes another side trip to pay her respects to an elderly blues singer. In response to strong impressions of darktown Memphis's glory days, Mitchell seeks a spiritual connection to that milieu by which she can lay claim to its musical legacy. But the connection fails ("He points a bony finger at you and says,/"I don't like you") in the face of disparities of wealth and history.

In this poem the musical motif is woven together with the larger theme of mutable fortune. The landmarks of Beale Street, redolent of a glamorous past, are being torn down. Old Furry ("Propped up in his bed/With his dentures and his leg removed") has also fallen into ruin due to "hard luck/And time and other thieves." In contrast, Mitchell's material success is broadcast by her ostentatious limousine out on the street as well as other symbols of wealth (like the jewelry alluded to in "Strange Boy," "Sharon," and "Black Crow"). But if success is measured in other ways, Mitchell repeatedly admits to her own shortcomings ("I tried to run away" ["Coyote"], "Maybe I've never really loved" ["Amelia"], "He asked me to be patient/Well I failed" ["Strange Boy"]). The culminating instance of this motif reverts to an ancient metaphor: "Like a wheel of fortune/I heard my fate turn, turn, turn" ("Refuge"). In "Amelia," Mitchell associates the motif of failure ("false alarms") with a meditation on mortality (in Amelia/Icarus's fall to earth). Aging and mortality figure strongly in the portrait of Furry; in the "antique," "blue-haired" setting of "Strange Boy"; and the story in "Sharon" of the woman who drowns herself in a well. In the third verse of "Hejira," Mitchell makes reference to her own age, in the immediate context of thoughts about death, fame, and vanity:

> Well I looked at the granite markers
> Those tributes to finality—to eternity
> And then I looked at myself here
> Chicken scratching for my immortality

In this passage she is depressed and self-deprecating as she takes stock of her songwriting achievement. Yet in the numerous references to her earlier recordings scattered throughout the cycle, one senses a more confident stocktaking. The most overt is the reference to the Cactus Tree Motel in "Amelia," alluding to her early paean to the travel impulse (in *SS*). There is a clear reminiscence of *Blue* in "Blue Motel Room," and of *Clouds* in "Amelia" ("I've spent my whole life in clouds"). More covertly, spread over two adjacent songs, she makes reference to "paradise" ("Amelia") and "parking lots" ("Furry"), thus recalling the opening line of her famous song "Big Yellow Taxi."

The passage of time figures as a "wrecker" ("Furry"), as we have seen, and as the fabric of memory. Mitchell also highlights cyclical, circadian rhythms: sunrise and moonrise, sleeping and waking, "the pull of moon on tides" ("Strange Boy"), the ebb and flow of love ("first you get the kisses/And then you get the tears" ["Sharon"]). In line with the ongoing, episodic rhythm of travel, she includes multiple symbols of seriality: "stations in some relay," "numbered doors" in motels ("Coyote"), "sets of waves" ("Strange Boy"), votive candles ("Hejira"), the sequential legs of a long journey ("I took a ferry to the highway/Then I drove to a pontoon plane/I took a plane to a taxi/And a taxi to a train" ["Black Crow"]). Fickle shifts in weather and the inevitable change of seasons play out both externally and internally. Thus in "Coyote" Mitchell speaks of her emotional dualities in terms of climatic extremes: "wrestle … with this flame/You put here in this Eskimo." In later passages she evokes "parched ribs of sand" ("Strange Boy"), "icy altitudes" ("Amelia"), and "winter chimneys" ("Hejira"). In the last-mentioned song, the image of snow gathering "like bolts of lace" conjures up another recurrent motif: that of the bride in her finery (a central icon in "Sharon").[20] The idea of the winter landscape emerges to form the flat black-and-white expanse behind Joni on the cover photo; the figure of the bride appears in the distance, surreally exposed in the middle of a frozen lake, her demure pose offset by the curves of a male figure skater.

I have already mentioned the recurring pattern of a clash of wills; in "Coyote" Mitchell also admits to an ongoing internal struggle with her own ego. Therefore, a special symbolic meaning accrues to those moments where the ego and its burdens seem to drop away. This trope is first introduced in "Amelia," where Mitchell's attention is repeatedly drawn heavenward, and her visions temporarily dissolve egocentric gravity. In "Hejira," we catch a glimpse of this point of view: "We're only particles of change, I know, I know/Orbiting around the sun." And the cycle concludes with such an image, in its strongest formulation yet. Struck by a photograph on a wall calendar of earth as seen from space, Mitchell emphasizes the feat of her own disappearance:

> And you couldn't see a city
> On that marbled bowling ball
> Or a forest or a highway
> Or me here least of all

Note that this illusion or revelation is made possible through an unusual nesting of different perspectives, as the traveler in a roadside stop is lifted out of her visual orbit courtesy of the view from a lunar module. The same relay of visual perspectives is at work in the concluding image of "Hejira"—the winter moon, reflected in a glass-clad office building, as seen through a hotel window. It is captured as well in the self-portrait collage on the album's cover, where the artist's torso dissolves and recedes into irrational space, revealing a road stretching to the vanishing point and a horizon piled with clouds.

Turning from poetry to music, we also find a remarkable consistency of style. Mitchell has described how she devised a distinct guitar sound for this album:

> On *Hejira* I doubled the guitar and I doubled it in a way that Wayne Shorter and Miles double up on *Nefertiti*. It's like silkscreening—it's not tight doubling. I'm playing the part twice but there's some variations on it so they're not perfectly tight—they're shadowing each other in some places.[21]

This sonic effect—a heterophonic, slightly out-of-phase texture—suggests a sense of echoing space and a haunting, reflective state of mind. Mitchell uses this special sound on her rhythm guitar in combination with bass, lead guitar, and drums to create a basic instrumental palette. Yet she crafts variety within this palette by working with two different drummers and two different bass players, trying out different combinations, and bringing in additional featured instruments (for these and other musical aspects, see Table 7.3). Thus in the end, each song has its own unique instrumentation. The lead guitar, when it appears (particularly in "Amelia," "Strange Boy," and "Black Crow"), extemporizes in such a way as to emphasize space, texture, and the ambient sound environment. Four songs feature the highly unique, unconventional style of bass guitarist Jaco Pastorius. (This is the first album of four on which Mitchell works with Pastorius.) His bass line refuses to stay grounded in the low register or settle for a supporting role; instead it becomes a floating, questing, melodic bass. Its melodic quality is especially sustained in the central, title song, which comes across as a duet between voice and bass guitar. As for rhythmic character, every song except "Blue Motel Room" begins with an instrumental introduction based on a distinct repeating hook with a strong rhythmic profile (Ex. 7.4). These hooks generally serve to initiate propulsive, restless textures (the most propulsive occurring in songs 1, 5, 6, 7, and 9—thus concentrated in the second half). Correspondingly, every song except "Blue Motel Room" ends with a fade-out rather than a cessation of energy. Over these rolling, agitated progressions, Mitchell projects her muted, hovering, elastic melodic spans.

EXAMPLE 7.4. RHYTHMIC HOOKS IN SELECTED INTROS FROM *HEJIRA*

a. "Coyote"

b. "Hejira"

c. "Black Crow"

Songs 3 and 4 are linked by similar open 5th motives in their intros (Ex. 7.5); they are also linked tonally (the concluding D harmony of song 3 matches the initial harmony of song 4). Songs 2, 5, and 9 all end by veering off into the wrong key. ("Amelia" is mainly in G, but ends in F; "Hejira" is in B, but stalls on C♯ minor at the fade-out; "Refuge" is in C, with unstable interludes, eventually settling on A♭ at the end.) A much more pervasive motive, occurring in all but two songs, centers on the special harmonic color of ♭III imported into a major tonic. To take just two examples: the intro to "Coyote" establishes a clear C major, but the opening of the verse is accented by a momentary move to E♭. (The same imported chord also returns at the midpoint of each verse and just before the refrain). In "Hejira," the key of B major is unchallenged during the verse, while the intro and interludes are haunted by D major. "Amelia" incorporates a special treatment of this motive. The verse begins with a direct emblematic move from I to ♭III, in this case, G to B♭ ("I *spotted* six jet planes"). But three bars later ("vapor trails"), the harmony turns to B minor (iii), and for the remainder of the verse it is the B minor color that prevails (with an emphatic appearance on "the *strings* of my guitar"). In this way, the song sets up a dialectic between the imported major chord on ♭III and the intrinsic minor chord on iii (as if commenting on the trickiness of the path—leading to "paradise," or "harm"?). No other song features this particular bifocal harmonic element; but the final song, "Refuge," recalls it by emphasizing the iii chord (E minor) throughout. E minor is the initial sonority of the intro, the second sonority of the verse ("a friend of *spirit*"), and the chord that ushers in the refrain ("I left him then"). In contrast to almost every other song, "Refuge" forgoes the ♭III sonority, and the song's harmonic uniqueness supports its placement as closing song in the cycle.

The ♭III motive has additional significance in the overall tonal plan: the C–E♭ progression salient in song 1 is played out structurally in the sequence of

EXAMPLE 7.5. OPEN 5TH MOTIVES IN *HEJIRA*

a. "Furry Sings the Blues," intro

b. "A Strange Boy," intro

key centers between songs 1 (C), 6 (E♭), 7 (E♭), 8, (C), and 9 (C). This sequence suggests a kind of arch form, which is further heightened by the harsh modulation in song 7 ("Black Crow") from E♭ Dorian to G♭ Dorian—a distorted version of the ♭III motive. In its arrival on G♭ by such a disjunct move, "Black Crow" represents the apogee of the traveler's orbit away from the home key of C. Meanwhile, the preceding song ("Sharon")—in its extended length, its lack of refrain, and its inconclusive final verse—represents the climax of the open-ended cyclic procedures on the album. Where all other songs demarcate their final verses somehow (by alteration, truncation, or partial return to the opening), "Sharon" neglects to differentiate its tenth verse as providing any formal closure. After these two songs, "Blue Motel Room," back in C, with a relaxed, intimate jazz combo instrumentation, stands out as extraordinarily closed and self-contained: the only song without a rhythmic hook, and the only song with a final cadence rather than a fade-out. "Refuge" reaffirms the home key (though veering off at the end, as noted). In a final (fortuitous?) gesture of cyclic return, as the song's coda winds down, the careful listener can hear Pastorius's melodic bass slyly quoting the opening phrase of the title song.

DON JUAN'S RECKLESS DAUGHTER

In certain ways the album that followed *Hejira* presents more overt musical gestures of large-scale coherence than its predecessor. Its key structure is more unified, with side 1 opening in C, side 3 closing in C, and sides 2 and 4 based in C throughout (see Table 7.4).[22] The presentation and grouping of songs implies a sequence of musical "movements" at a level of organization higher than the individual song. Thus the opening song of side 1 is prefaced by a substantial Overture (almost 3 minutes long) whose initiatory function exceeds its immediate context. Song 4 ("Paprika Plains") with its interpolated orchestral passage expands to fill an entire side of the album, thus comprising a distinct movement in itself. The three songs on side 3 are recorded to play without breaks while the first two of these are linked by transitional material. And the final song of side 4 presents conscious echoes of the preceding song while using more intimate performing forces, thus embodying a strong coda function at the album's close.

Connecting motives are also more audible. The primary melodic motive is a three-note figure (rising third, rising second) highlighted in the instrumental refrains of songs 1, 9, and 10. In each of these cases, the motive moves from tonic to subdominant (C-E♭-F; Ex. 7.6a-c). Songs 1 and 9 emphasize the open-endedness of this movement by prolonging F at songs' end without returning

TABLE 7.4. Aspects of Musical Coherence in *Don Juan's Reckless Daughter*

Song	Key	Closure	Motive	Idiom	Instruments
		SIDE 1			
Overture	...C	*segue*		improvisation	gtr, bass
1. "Cotton Avenue"	C polymodal	ends on F; horn coda (ends on C7)	C-Eb-F	R&B	gtr, bass, drums [+ horns]
2. "Talk to Me"	Bb–D (weakly centric)	ends on Am		JM idiolect (strumming)	gtr, bass
3. "Jericho"	D polymodal	ends on Bm		fusion	gtr, bass, drums, bongos, sax
		SIDE 2			
4. "Paprika Plains"	CM	CM cadence	G-B-C; Csus2	ballad→improv. →fusion	pno, bass, drums, sax, orchestra
		SIDE 3			
5. "Otis and Marlena"	EbM–BbM	ends on F; *segue*	C-E♮-F	JM idiolect (figuration)	gtr, electric gtr, drums, pno
6. "The Tenth World"	...Bb...	rhythmic cadence; *attacca*	F-Eb-Bb-C	Afro-Caribbean	percussion
7. "Dreamland"	C Aeol [Eb in drums]	rhy. cadence [Eb]		Afro-Caribbean	percussion
		SIDE 4			
8. "Don Juan's Reckless Daughter"	C Mixolydian	C cadence		JM idiolect (style of *Hejira*)	gtr, bass, percussion
9. "Off Night Backstreet"	C polymodal	ends on F	C-Eb-F	blues	gtr, bass, drums, strings
10. "The Silky Veils of Ardor"	C polymodal	CM cadence	C-Eb-F; Csus2	folk ballad	gtr

to the tonic, while song 10 provides firm tonic closure. The same motive occurs less obviously in transposed form at the very opening of the piano intro to song 4 (without recurring in the body of the song; Ex. 7.6d). In song 5 it is promoted to the vocal melody, at the pivotal moment of the refrain (Ex. 7.6e). The opening phrase of song 7, meanwhile, can be heard to expand on the contour of the primary motive in its inverted form: F-E♭-B♭-[E♭-D]-C (the bracketed segment is variable in pitch from one verse to another). In a secondary motivic connection, the referential, obsessively returning chord of song 4 (Csus2 or C,D,G) returns at the same pitch level as the upper portion of the cadential chord of song 10: C(9) or C,E,G,C,D,G. Consequently, side 2 and side 4 close on related chord structures derived from Csus2: side 2 with a greatly expanded orchestral sonority on C6/9, side 4 with a simple guitar strum on C(9).

Side 3 of the album, already linked by continuous music, is further unified by internal motivic connections (see Table 7.5). Most overtly, each song features vocal tags with the words "Dream on," in acknowledgment of the special sense of a dreamlike excursion sustained in this section. The tags are closely related in pitch. As song 5 comes to a close, the melody dissolves into a spacy tangle of brief vocal curls (at the beginning of track 6 on the CD); blended into the tangle are statements of the tag on F-E♭ and G-F. In the middle of song 6 (at 2:55), Mitchell superimposes the tag over the Spanish-language backup vocals, at the same pitch level, now fused into one double statement: F-E♭-G-F ("Dream on, dream on"). In song 7, the tag becomes a triple statement on G-F, present in backing vocals as rhythmic punctuation at the midpoint and end of each verse. What began as an amorphous musical idea has now been woven throughout the structure of the song. The salient pitches of F and E♭ are further highlighted in

TABLE 7.5. Internal Coherence on Side 3 of *Don Juan's Reckless Daughter*

Song	Motivic Connections: a.	b.	c.
	SIDE 3		
5. "Otis and Marlena"	"Dream on" (coda): collage of fragments—F-E♭, G-F, etc.	B♭-E♭ (intro)	E♭-F (intro, guitar); F-E♭ (coda, piano)
6. "The Tenth World"	"Dream on" (descant): F-E♭-G-F		F-E♭-G-F (descant)
7. "Dreamland"	"Dream on" (refrain): G-F (3x)	B♭-E♭ (drum)	F-E♭-B♭-[...]-C (melody)

EXAMPLE 7.6. THE PRIMARY MOTIVE IN *DON JUAN'S RECKLESS DAUGHTER*

a. "Cotton Avenue," intro

b. "Off Night Backstreet," intro

c. "Silky Veils of Ardor," intro

d. "Paprika Plains," intro

e. "Otis and Marlena," refrain

While Mus - lims stick up   Wash - ing - ton_____

the guitar figuration at the opening of song 5 (Ex. 7.7), the sustained piano pedals in the transition between songs 5 and 6, and the opening melodic gesture of song 7. Finally, the dominant-to-tonic hook that opens side 3 and establishes the key of E♭ for song 5 is paralleled by a similar drum figure undergirding song 7. The music on side 3 is thus not only continuous but tightly interconnected.

And yet these features of musical coherence are supported by no obvious unifying poetic rationale. In contrast to the unity of perspective, tone, and poetic style found on *Hejira, Don Juan* comes across as multifarious and sprawling. Songs of wildly contrasting tone cohabit uncomfortably with one another. "Talk to Me," for instance, is a snapshot of Mitchell in breathless, babbling one-sided conversation with an intriguing silent type. She lets her hair down with a realistic portrayal of awkward, spur-of-the-moment, casually structured language. However, the persona in the song immediately following, "Jericho," is carefully poised and collected, hair back in place, every personal motive scrutinized and every phrase elegantly turned. The song after this, "Paprika Plains," though grounded at first in precise scenic description, gradually floats off into mythic imagery and dreamily expanded horizons, while the following song, "Otis and Marlena," abandons the first person entirely in exchange for distanced satiric commentary. The excursion into Spanish dialect in "The Tenth World" (with guest artist Manolo Badrena taking lead vocals) shows how open Mitchell is in this album to relaxing the effect of a consistent poetic/musical persona. A number of songs conjure up the allusive presence of exterior voices. Thus in the third verse of "Talk to Me," Mitchell cribs from Shakespeare (as she freely confesses: "I stole that!/From Willy the Shake!"), just as Jaco quotes the opening of Stravinsky's ballet *Rite of Spring* in the song's introduction. In the title song, Mitchell incorporates snatches of the American national anthem (as commentary in the backup vocals) as well as overlaying her own singing voice in the first verse with that of a male vocalist to form a composite, double-gendered utterance (representing the numinous speech of a "split-tongued spirit").[23] The lyrics for the final song on the album, "The Silky

EXAMPLE 7.7. "OTIS AND MARLENA," INTRO

Veils of Ardor," present a quodlibet of anonymous preexistent texts, reworking and patching together excerpts from three well-known traditional ballads: "Wayfaring Stranger" (verse 1), "Come All Ye Fair and Tender Ladies" (verses 2, 3 and 4), and "The Water Is Wide" (verse 4).[24]

The music too is more wide ranging in sound and idiom than *Hejira* (see Table 7.4). Instrumentation runs the gamut from solo guitar (song 10) to full orchestra (song 4), though these extremes stand out as exceptional. Songs 6 and 7 resort to Latin percussion ensembles. More commonly, Mitchell works with varied subsets of a fusion combo (guitar, bass, drums, sax), with the addition of piano on songs 4 and 5. The disparate musical dialects include, on the one hand, strong evocations of R&B (song 1), blues rock (song 9), and folk ballad (song 10), and on the other, substyles unique to Mitchell's own artistic development rather than referring to any conventional genre. Song 2, for instance, uses an upbeat, rhythmically accented strumming technique reminiscent of other talkative songs such as "Conversation" (*LC*), "Help Me" (*C&S*), and "Don't Interrupt the Sorrow" (*HSL*). Song 5 employs the motoric, elaborate, registrally stratified figuration that distinguished Mitchell's guitar style since her debut album while introducing a newly heightened, percussive attack. Song 8, meanwhile, is an unmistakable return to the traveling sound prevalent on the previous album.

In tension with this persistent disparity of style and tone, a few important themes provide coherent strands of thought. One such theme is the dual nature of human instincts. Dualism is expressed in various registers. It is spatialized in the thematic contrast between open country and man-made enclosures—a contrast underlying the reverie of "Paprika Plains" ("It's stifling in here . . ./I've got to get some air"), the psychological oppositions of "Don Juan" ("I come from open prairie" in verse 2 set against "Behind my bolt locked door" in verse 4), and the central metaphor of "Jericho": the heart as a constricted, walled city. It is racialized ("Tar baby and the Great White Wonder") and climatized ("On a plane flying back to winter/In shoes full of tropic sand") in the vivid juxtaposed images of "Dreamland." Most pervasively, it is cast as a defining polarity of character motivation: expressed in terms of the wild and the gentle ("Jericho"), the reckless and the coward ("Talk to Me," "Don Juan"), pleasure and pain ("Off Night Backstreet"), and the spirit and the flesh. The latter dichotomy is played out structurally in the tension between the album's Dionysian songs, like "Cotton Avenue," "Talk to Me," and "Tenth World," and the visionary impulse evident in "Paprika Plains," "Don Juan," and "Silky Veils." It is also distilled into an extended meditation in the album's title song.

Here, the dual poles of spirit and flesh are introduced in verse 1 in a schema of counterbalanced but interlaced images. In keeping with the shamanistic teachings popularized by Carlos Castaneda's books at the time (in which "Don Juan" is the medicine man and master of Yaqui spiritual lore),[25] dualism is evoked in the form of animal spirits, which Mitchell superimposes upon artifacts of modern industrial society:

> And [the split tongued spirit] says:
> "Snakes along the railroad tracks"
> He says, "Eagles in jet trails . . .
> Coils around the feathers and talons on scales . . .
> Gravel under the belly plates . . ."
> He says, "Wind in the wings . . ."
> He says, "Big bird dragging its tail in the dust . . .
> Snake kite flying on a string"

In this schema, railway and airplane appear in a double exposure with spirits of earth and sky. The spirits are represented in dynamic terms: racing across the landscape, locked in struggle with each other, and venturing headlong into foreign elements. As the song progresses, the imagery hews resolutely to the same emblematic animals while continuing their motile interplay, first couching it internally (verse 4: "The eagle and the serpent are at war in me/The serpent fighting for blind desire/The eagle for clarity"), then projecting it out into the physical environment of the protagonists (verse 5: "There are rivets up here in this eagle/There are box cars down there on your snake"). In the final verse, the plane in which Mitchell is traveling catches up with the train carrying her lover; she looks down on the landscape as their paths cross. With this image the symbolic thread is resolved in a synthesis that is simultaneously erotic, Jungian, and familial in connotation:

> I touched you on the central plains
> It was plane to train my twin
> It was just plane shadow to train shadow
> But to me it was skin to skin
> [. . .]
> Man to woman
> Scales to feathers
> You and I

In another thematic thread, Mitchell spins out variations on a sense of place. The opening song introduces this theme in its chorus: "If you've got a place like that to go/You just have to go there/If you've got no place special/Then you just go no place special." But over the course of the album, spatial settings split into multiple points of view and switch from one mode of representation to another. "Cotton Avenue" paints a shiny picture of contemporary urban night culture.

"Jericho" alludes to the ancient biblical city in a poetic figure of speech. The mystical geography of "Paprika Plains" is set against the detailed satirical description of a Miami resort in "Otis and Marlena" (which also includes passing references to Washington, D.C., and Iran ["Muslims"]), followed by the sonic tourism of "The Tenth World" and "Dreamland." These disparate points of reference—past and present, real and imaginary—do not connect in a straightforward itinerary as they do in *Hejira*. Even so, though the songs were written separately, Mitchell found that they came together fortuitously to suggest an overall design in the form of a symbolic journey.

> The fact is, even though they were written from other years, miraculously they made this *trip*. It starts off rurally, city lights are in the distance and you're anticipating going to the dance and how wonderful it's going to be—there's a storm brewing. By the time you get down to the dancehall, you get drunk, you come on to somebody, there's no real outcome. Then there's kind of a pledge in the song "Jericho" as to what you will do, what love is—it's a pretty realistic thing, it's not cynical, I don't think. Then "Paprika Plains"—the rain's hit now, the storm comes in. You go to the washroom and the girls are powdering, and that strange smell that women's restrooms have, a combination of perfume, sanitation equipment and barf! And then it gets nostalgic and it goes back to childhood, and that's the flat-land and sky-orientation. And then it returns back to the dancehall. Then the trip is taken to Miami, and from Miami, which is the point of departure into the Third World, you jump off into the Third World countries with the drum piece and the jungle sounds—a purely Latin thing. You get on a plane in "Dreamland" and you head back to New York. The last side of the album could be anywhere, geographically. But up to there it's a journey through a dream world and it's a journey through a real world.[26]

To accommodate the disparate perspectives of individual songs, Mitchell conceives this narrative progression in thoroughly flexible terms, combining movement through time, space, emotions, and imagination. I would add that the sense of an episodic journey is enriched by one's encounters with different natives along the way—for instance, the street hustlers in "Cotton Avenue," the aboriginal Canadians in "Paprika Plains," and the Caribbean islanders in "Dreamland."

The loose narrative progression Mitchell envisions here is also supported in subtle ways by symbolic patterning in the instrumentation. Such an idea—instrumental sequence as a form of, or in service of, narrative—first figures strongly on side 2 of the album, within the large sectional form of "Paprika Plains." This song departs from the prevailing sound of the fusion combo by introducing piano for the first time. At first (from the introduction through verse 1) the solo piano resonates with the lyrical voice to create a special sense of intimacy and introversion. Then, cued by the modal and temporal transition at the end of verse 1 ("I'm floating off in time"), the second verse "goes back to childhood," and this retrogression is registered in sound by the addition of a warm string descant. The transition at the end of verse 2 ("I'm floating into dreams") signals a deeper move into fantasy. At this point—the inception of her dream—Mitchell brings in an entire orchestra (made up of strings, winds, harp, and some percussion). Verse 2 had used the piano and strings in one passage to mimic a child's Indian drum ("I'd beat the drum like war"), and when the orchestra enters ("I dream Paprika Plains"), it does so with two explosive chords, reinforced with a gong, as if channeling the force of a more cosmic drumstroke. After the far-flung orchestral excursion, the entry of verse 3 marks a return to reality and the present tense. The succession of accompanying instruments as the verse progresses is precisely calibrated to achieve a smooth modulation between mental states. The first half of the verse is warmed by strings, prolonging the afterglow of the dream state. At the very moment the speaker reenters the dance hall ("coming back for *more*"), sax and bass subtly make their entrance. A few lines later the drum sneaks in, and we have gradually emerged into the sonic world of the present locale, so that at the verse's conclusion, the full band can launch into an extended jam. The coda thus effects a restoration of the fusion sound of side 1 as well as a symbolic celebration of being in the moment.

This song introduces several timbral motifs that are carried through in the remainder of the album. The special use of the piano as opening a threshold to dream states recurs in side 3, where the piano appears during the transition between songs 5 and 6, interwoven with siren voices crooning "Dream on" (this is the point Mitchell describes as "jumping off" from Miami into the Third World). The special use of percussive piano, gong, and tympani (in the interlude) foreshadows the creation of an exotic sound world made up entirely of percussion instruments in songs 6 and 7. Significant echoes of the intense timbral journey undertaken during sides 2 and 3 appear on the album's concluding side. For instance, the use of ankle bells and shaker in "Don Juan" is a glance back at the percussion soundscape of the previous songs. The addition of a bluesy string section in "Off Night Backstreet" recalls the orchestral commentary in "Paprika Plains." Such retrospective instrumental touches contribute to the preparation for large-scale formal closure found on side 4—the sense that these songs concern the final stages of a journey. (Briefly: the homeward travel in "Don Juan" ["No matter which route home we take"], the relationship postmortem of "Backstreet" ["these sentimental journeys/Late at night"], and the metaphors of death and the promised land in "Silky Veils.")

A third structuring theme is the evocation of dream states. Again, Castaneda's vision of a spirit world hovering just beneath the surface of reality is pertinent here. References to dreams do not appear until song 4, but from then on they are ubiquitous. In general, Mitchell uses the dream experience to represent a kind of integrated, deep knowledge: reconnection with childhood and "mother earth" in "Paprika Plains," restorative transoceanic encounters in "Dreamland," clairvoyant perception of the spirit world in "Don Juan." Yet the moral implications of that knowledge are often ambivalent, exposing uncomfortable truths about personal hypocrisy and fallibility as well as more encompassing histories of racial oppression. In "Otis and Marlena," the symbolic structure is ironically inverted: everyday reality in the upscale beachside hotel is surreal and grotesque ("It's all a dream/She has awake") without leading to any authentic self-knowledge. Mitchell chooses to close the album, in fact, on a precisely ambivalent note—joining two statements of nearly identical wording but opposite moral intent. The first statement is pessimistic and stoic ("It's just in dreams we fly"), summing up a verse about impotent yearning ("I have no wings") and denying the power of dreams to impinge on reality. But her immediate repetition of this line ("In my dreams we fly!") is sung so as to effect a strong reversal, infusing the words with aspiration, a concentrated beauty of tone, and a sense of effortless release.

As mentioned earlier, Mitchell conceived the overall design of this album in terms of a double journey, through real space and imaginative space. The latter is manifest as a recurring gestural pattern of symbolic expansion and return linking the various allusions to dreaming. "Paprika Plains" moves by stages deeper into the imagination, first floating off into nostalgia (and the "wide eyed" openness of childhood), then launching into a spectacular dream sequence. Printed in parentheses on the lyric sheet—but not sung—it reaches to seventy-two lines of poetry, interpolated between the second and third verses and corresponding to the long orchestral interlude.[27] The poetic diction is extremely high flown, leaving realism far behind in a tone of oracular pronouncement in which individual images acquire an ominous weight. Spatial dimensions behave with extreme elasticity, evoking "turquoise skies," then a bomb-burst at the vanishing point of the horizon, then zooming out to the dark vacuums of space. Though unspoken, such images of imaginative exploration are adumbrated in the metaphorical expansion of sonic resources as the solo piano (improvisatory throughout this passage) is enveloped in an orchestral soundscape.[28] Finally, as we have seen, the concluding verse of the song shrinks back to the present moment and real space. Subsequent iterations of this tidal pattern occur over the course of side 3 (jumping off from southern Florida across sonic and linguistic borders, while abandoning realistic description for rhapsodic musical utterance before returning to the familiar north), and, on a smaller scale, within the song "Don Juan" itself, where the prairie again evokes a visionary horizon ("the vast and subtle plains of mystery"). This recurrent spatial pattern spanning the song cycle is shadowed by a secondary, circadian progression of night into day. Thus song 1 takes place at sunset in anticipation of night; songs 2 and 4 are nocturnal; song 5 begins at dawn, moving into full sun for the bulk of side 3; songs 8 and 9 are mainly nocturnal; and song 10 implies a new "daybreak."

In sum, clues to overall formal patterning in *Don Juan's Reckless Daughter* are multifarious and frequently contradictory; it will be useful to attempt to synthesize the foregoing information. Taking a synoptic view, one's perception of large-scale coherence shifts over the course of the album; each of its four sides offers a unique balance of coherence and disparity. Side 1 is consistent in sound but disparate in tone and musical material; it is tonally open-ended in relation to the home key of C. Side 2 (a single song) is tonally and formally closed but episodic and exploratory in its multisectional form. Side 3 has the tightest musical construction but is tonally open in relation to the home key. Side 4 is once again disparate in tone and idiom yet tonally and motivically unified, and tonally closed. In terms of placement within an overall progression (taking into account previously discussed elements of narrative, instrumentation, symbolic patterning, and tonality), side 1 is initiatory, establishing a sense of familiarity in music and conversational tone; side 2 presents far-reaching, progressive modulations, then achieves return and medial closure; side 3 ventures the greatest distance from home; and side 4 returns to the familiar, with retrospective acknowledgment of the journey. Song 4 represents a high point in formal experimentation, song 6 a high point in genre/stylistic experimentation.

One final aspect to be mentioned of the exploratory arc at the heart of the album is the general move from familiar or colloquial language to polished poetic language and dense image construction (that is, deeper into the aesthetic mode). The aesthetic mode is preeminent in songs 4, 5, 7, and 8, perhaps reaching its peak in song 7, "Dreamland." This poem arranges a parade of colorful, evocative images according to an interlocking scheme of polarities: between northern and tropical Americas, First World and Third World culture, and black and white (tires in snow, coconut flesh, flour on skin). Images follow one another with few connectives of narrative or lyrical reflection. Observational detail and collective archetype surrealistically conflate ("Tar baby and the Great White Wonder/ Talking over a glass of rum"). The poem fuses a Dionysian celebration of island night life with a historical awareness of colonialist intervention (in the references to iconic European explorers, slavery, big game hunting, and Hollywood exoticism). Yet even as Mitchell evokes this history in vivid, even tactile ways, she does so with no moral gloss ("I wrapped that flag around me/Like a Dorothy Lamour sarong/And I lay down thinking national/With dreamland coming on"). Thus the listener is suspended in an unresolved double consciousness of holiday indo-lence and cultural domination. In consequence, the "dream" acquires a double edge: equally a fantasy of oblivion sought by the privileged ("As they push the recline buttons down") and a vision of alternative, unspoiled sources of creativity ("Burning on the inside/With the knowledge of things to come"). In this densely constructed poem, Mitchell uses the metaphor of place to explore the intersection of individual and cultural perspectives while illuminating profound rifts within each.[29] The perspectival dialectic embodied in the song is mirrored by its broader context of formal tension between coherence and disparity.

As for the role of visual design in the album's cyclic identity, the three chief themes threading through *Don Juan*—duality, place, and dream—are given visual expression in the art on the cover and record sleeves, which places photographic portraits against a bold two-color backdrop of terra-cotta plains and turquoise skies. The figures juxtapose adults and children, in glamorous evening attire with a glimpse of tennis shoes, bedecked with vaguely Mickey Mouse–shaped balloons and doves in flight. The contemporary fashions on the front cover contrast with the mock-Indian garb on the back as well as with the mythical, nearly featureless abstract Southwestern horizon. All the figures save the young boy are portraits of Joni herself: as a white woman in top hat and stiletto heels; as a dancing, dandi-fied black man; and as an Indian girl, whose thought balloon ("How") humorously portrays her as a beginner on the path to spiritual knowledge.[30] Thus Joni's body is split into multiple personas of different ages, races, and genders. The vision-ary aura of the doves intersects with the frankly sexual symbolism of a female nude, superimposed on the adult Joni's dress at crotch level, from whose pubic area the doves appear to emerge. All three figures on the front look down toward this focal region, the region of the greatest visual density. The adult Joni spreads her arms and mouth wide in a gesture of generosity, as if releasing her offspring to the world in joyous, reckless profusion. On subsequent panels, space becomes emptier, figures more randomly placed. In the image on the second record sleeve, Joni swings away from the camera, gazing at one of her balloons that is getting away. As her self-mocking thought balloon reveals ("In My Dweems We Fwy"), the adult is not entirely free of the child.

But the cover design is not the only artwork connected with this album. "During the period that Mitchell was writing and recording *Don Juan's Reckless Daughter*, she simultaneously worked on a large painting which depicts in pigment some of the same themes, metaphors and imagery of that album."[31] The painting, measuring five feet by six feet and entitled *Axilar Moonrise*, is reproduced in the catalogue of artworks included on Mitchell's official Web site.[32] Its composition features expressionistic nude human figures as well as a half-man/half-eagle figure and a female spirit in war paint and Indian headdress. The background is made up of tropical foliage, multicolored city lights, and a deep blue starscape.[33] Mitchell speaks of this painting as a sibling or outgrowth of the same creative impulse behind the album. In its entirety, then, one might say the *Don Juan* project has a public face (the album) as well as a private face (the appended painting). From this point of view, the musicopoetic form of the cycle is not wholly sufficient unto itself but complemented by (offstage, unseen) thoughts in a different medium— just as the song "Paprika Plains" is complemented by (unspoken) thoughts in an appended poem.

As for this last song, there is practically no model within pop song for such an ungainly media hybrid: three verses of sung lyrics, plus 72 lines of paren- thetical, unsung poetry, corresponding to a seven-and-a-half-minute wordless orchestral interpolation. For most listeners, I imagine, it remains unclear how to approach the appended dream sequence. Are we meant to switch at that moment from simply listening to reading (with grandiose musical accompaniment)? And what is the status of the printed passage: is it a part of the song cycle or not? Is Mitchell sharing a glimpse of private thoughts and hinting that there is more to be said—that the public form of the album is only partially adequate to the themes she invokes? By leaving an evocative gap in the musical form, Mitchell directs the listener to an awareness of something beyond the music, without spell- ing out how to launch into that imagined space or comprehend the implications. This strikes me as a perfect metaphor for the shamanistic education depicted by Castaneda, where the path to knowledge is a leap into the unknown, discerned only by irrational means and only made possible after being faced with one's own ignorance. Just as remarkable, though, is Mitchell's intermingling of the formal and stylistic experiments found on sides 2 and 3 with quite traditional formal elements. One can still clearly recognize the strophic skeleton underlying the extravagant expansions of "Paprika Plains," while both "Otis and Marlena" and "Dreamland" employ standard strophic forms with refrain, however bold their placement within a larger plan. Again, this ambivalence dramatizes the central dialectic between the familiar and the unknown at the level of formal technique.

Whereas in *Hejira* Mitchell presents her material in a well-defined, tightly wrapped package, in *Don Juan* the goods spill out of the basket. In its own way, *Hejira* is as confessional as *Blue*, but the cooler tone and consistently strong pat- terning in *Hejira* offset the cycle's difficult, subjective self-questioning. This clas- sicizing, unifying impulse helps to create the impression of a greater expressive poise and sophistication (compared to the rawness of *Blue*) and a higher degree of conscious artistry. In *Don Juan's Reckless Daughter*, on the other hand, large- scale formal planning is tangible but more precarious, in danger of being under- mined by the cycle's heterogeneous enthusiasm and otherworldly aspirations. In her approach to this work, Mitchell leavens poise and sophistication (connoting adulthood and artistic polish) with spontaneity and receptivity (as in childhood, apprenticeship, improvisation, dream states). The authorial persona comes across as instinctual, uninhibited, and porous ("open to it all") rather than as an imposing, masterful hand thoroughly shaping and arranging the material.[34] Thus *Don Juan* represents a different kind of concept album. Recklessness is key to the overall design. The album's experimental ruptures and disjunctions call for a more flexible, receptive attitude on the part of listeners, who must create their own connections in making sense of the overall concept. Form is not wholly foretold but the result of a process of intellectual and sensuous engagement in the act of listening.[35] In giving freer rein to disparity, while never abandoning an implied coherence, Mitchell is exploiting an ambiguity at the heart of the song cycle genre itself.

8

A TRIBUTE

In one of the few rave reviews of *Don Juan's Reckless Daughter*, critic Blair Jackson offers Joni Mitchell the following tribute:

> The significance of this album is easily explained: it's ambitious as hell; a double-record set of staggering depth, complexity and musical scope from one of the most talented artists working in pop music. It is also the album which will reveal Joni Mitchell's "singer/songwriter" tag to be shamefully inadequate.... There is so much on this record it's going to take months, perhaps even years, to absorb it all.[1]

In praising and legitimizing Mitchell as an artist, Jackson appeals to the high-art standards of value identified at the outset of this book: ambition, depth, complexity, and durability. In particular, he affirms that a long-term relationship with the music is the best way to comprehend its density and rise to its aesthetic challenge.

Tributes may take many different forms. For Mitchell's songwriting peers and followers, "absorbing" and recognizing her musical achievement means learning from her example as a writer—being inspired by her expressive nuance and artistic vision while incorporating and adapting the tricks of her trade. It might also involve covering or resetting gems from her collection. A noteworthy compilation of covers by big-name artists was in the planning stages for many years. Originally announced as *A Case of Joni* (on the Reprise label), the project came to fruition as *A Tribute to Joni Mitchell*, released on the Nonesuch label in 2007.[2] For my concluding thoughts, I would like to offer a few brief impressions about this album.

A Tribute to Joni Mitchell does not denote the final word on the esteem Mitchell enjoys among her peers—merely part of an ongoing conversation. Nevertheless, one gets a sense of the extraordinary scope of her influence from the spectrum of styles represented: jazz (Cassandra Wilson, Brad Mehldau), country (Emmylou Harris), Brazilian Tropicalia (Caetano Veloso) as well as pop of many different stripes (James Taylor, Annie Lennox, k. d. lang, Elvis Costello, Sufjan Stevens). Prince has absorbed "A Case of You" into his own soulful gospel mother tongue. Sarah McLachlan refashions "Blue" in haunting Celtic guise. Björk, true to her image as avant-garde pop artiste, arranges "The Boho Dance" for crystalline celeste with quirky electronic touches, draining it of a beat and using over-deliberate enunciation, "making the song sound like a poem beamed from another planet."[3]

Half of the songs chosen are popular favorites from *Ladies of the Canyon, Blue*, and *Court and Spark*, but there are also three more esoteric choices from *Hissing* and one song from the 1990s, representing the tastes of a connoisseur. In many ways, big and small, the various performers disclose an intimate knowledge of Mitchell's musical style. Annie Lennox alters the refrain in "Ladies of the Canyon" (moving with relish through the lowered seventh degree) in such a way as to heighten the song's Mixolydian flavor. James Taylor sets "River" to a guitar part that bristles with modal clashes. A number of performers (Veloso, Prince, McLachlan, Lennox, lang) create personal variations on Mitchell's trademark multitrack close-harmony backup vocals. Björk's cosmic arrangement of "Boho Dance" calls to mind Mitchell's own experiments with stylized metaphysical pronouncement (especially "Shadows and Light," from the same source album). Brad Mehldau, turning "Don't Interrupt the Sorrow" into a piano solo, still faithfully mimics the distinct verbal rhythms from each verse of Mitchell's original performance.

One challenge of cover versions in general is how to negotiate between strongly personal styles of expression—that is, how to respond to a vivid, idiosyncratic original with an imaginative interpretation of one's own. Success depends on utterly intangible qualities; but one reviewer puts it well when he says, "the key lies in making us believe that this song could be for you, or speak for you." In this light, I understand his enjoyment of "Help Me" as sung by k. d. lang "because it feels close to her skin"; or his appreciation of Emmylou Harris, who "inhabits the pain and the dignity [of 'The Magdalene Laundries'] completely."[4] Such metaphors of bodily familiarity and fit recall Mitchell's evocative image of her music as "a fine cloth."[5]

More specific challenges arise from the high-mindedness and unconventionality of Mitchell's work. Elvis Costello's version of "Edith and the Kingpin" is high-minded in its unusual wind ensemble orchestration, but he pursues taste and decorum at the cost of vitality.[6] Several arrangements polish out certain spiky irregularities of the original numbers. (I think of the Japanese proverb: "The nail that sticks out gets hammered down.") For instance, Veloso removes all tonal ambiguity from "Dreamland" by harmonizing it with sunny, shopworn tonic and dominant chords. Harris, in "Magdalene Laundries," regularizes the strangely uprooted harmonies at the beginning and end of each verse. Lennox opts not to preserve the sharp cross-relation at the melodic peak of "Ladies" (though in exchange she introduces a dramatic phrase extension of her own). k. d. lang's "Help Me" smooths over some of the original metric disruptions. On the other hand, Sufjan Stevens takes up the challenge with a radical, wacky remake of "Free Man in Paris," in which he makes major changes to the melody, harmonic progression, instrumental breaks, and sectional form. This cover treats the original as a point of departure, preserving some aspects but not others, freely prolonging and embellishing the tune with eccentric detail while inventing fresh descants. The tone is manic-depressive, alternating between glitzy horn passages, melancholy vocals, and a campy section of "la la la"s over a suddenly lilting waltz. The chorus is recast harmonically as an intriguing mixed-mode loop over a pedal point, which repeats abundantly while Stevens dismantles and rebuilds his unexpected instrumental textures. "That's the best thing a cover version can offer—a way for longtime listeners to hear new things in songs they thought they knew by heart."[7]

All in all, the collective respect these musicians have to offer Joni Mitchell comes in treating her music as a body of song that bears revisiting, sounding out, and reinterpreting. Music analysis and criticism in their own special way can also be seen as a kind of "covering" or reinterpretation, drawing on an absorbed, long-term relationship with the music. As with *A Tribute*, my own work does not present the final word on analytical insight into Joni Mitchell's music, merely part of an ongoing conversation. In this endeavor too, success depends on certain intangible qualities, in which are mingled respect, intimate knowledge, vivid perceptions, personal fit, and a readiness to take up the challenge.

APPENDIX

Reference Table of Chord Symbols

Chord Type	Symbol	Spelling (relative to major scale)
Major		1, 3, 5
Minor	m	1, ♭3, 5
Diminished	°	1, ♭3, ♭5
Open 5th	5	1, 5
Open 5th, Added 7th	5(7)	1, 5, ♭7
6th	6	1, 3, 5, 6
Minor 6th	m6	1, ♭3, 5, 6
6/9	6/9	1, 3, 5, 6, 9
7th	7	1, 3, 5, ♭7
Major 7th	maj7	1, 3, 5, 7
Minor 7th	m7	1, ♭3, 5, ♭7
Minor 7th, Added 6th	m7(6)	1, ♭3, 5, ♭6, ♭7
Minor/Major 7th	m/maj7	1, ♭3, 5, 7
9th	9	1, 3, 5, ♭7, 9
Major 9th	maj9	1, 3, 5, 7, 9
Minor 9th	m9	1, ♭3, 5, ♭7, 9
Minor/Major 9th	m/maj9	1, ♭3, 5, 7, 9
11th	11	1, 3, 5, ♭7, 9, 11
Major 11th	maj11	1, 3, 5, 7, 9, 11
Minor 11th	m11	1, ♭3, 5, ♭7, 9, 11
13th	13	1, 3, 5, ♭7, 9, 11, 13
Major 13th	maj13	1, 3, 5, 7, 9, 11, 13
Minor 13th	m13	1, ♭3, 5, ♭7, 9, 11, 13
Added 9th	(9)	1, 3, 5, 9
Added 4th	(4)	1, 3, 4, 5
Suspended 4th	sus	1, 4, 5
Suspended 2nd	sus2	1, 2, 5

Chord Type	Symbol	Spelling (relative to major scale)
Suspended 4th and 2nd	sus(2)	1, 2, 4, 5
Suspended 2nd, Added 6th	sus2(6)	1, 2, 5, 6
7th Suspended	7sus	1, 4, 5, ♭7 [or 1, 5, ♭7, 11]
9th Suspended	9sus	1, 5, ♭7, 9, 11
13th Suspended	13sus	1, 5, ♭7, 9, 11, 13
Inversion or "Slash" Chord	X/Y	X = chord; Y = bass note

The root of the chord is in the bass position, except in the case of inverted or "slash" chords. All other chord pitches may be voiced (or doubled) in different octaves (thus 2 = 9, 4 = 11, etc.). Some of the pitches in extended chords (such as 9th, 11th, and 13th chords) may be omitted.

NOTES

1. Introduction

1. A sixteenth album, *Shine*, was released in 2007, too late to be included in this book. See the discography for a complete list.

2. Notable tribute concerts include "Joni's Jazz," Central Park, New York, 1 July 1999; "An All-Star Tribute to Joni Mitchell," Hammerstein Ballroom, New York, 6 April 2000 (televised); and "The Music of Joni Mitchell," Carnegie Hall, New York, 1 February 2006. For information on achievement awards, see Karen O'Brien, *Shadows and Light: Joni Mitchell, The Definitive Biography* (London: Virgin Books, 2001), 12–13; and see chapter 2 of this book.

3. More extended assessments (of varying quality) have also appeared. Chapter-length considerations of Mitchell's work from the standpoint of female artistic production appear in Wilfrid Mellers, *Angels of the Night: Popular Female Singers of Our Time* (New York: Blackwell, 1986), and Sheila Whiteley, *Women and Popular Music: Sexuality, Identity and Subjectivity* (New York: Routledge, 2000). Treatments from within a Canadian context appear in Marco Adria, *Music of Our Times: Eight Canadian Singer-Songwriters* (Toronto: James Lorimer, 1990), and Douglas Fetherling, *Some Day Soon: Essays on Canadian Songwriters* (Kingston, Ont.: Quarry Press, 1991). Larry David Smith focuses on poetic themes and strategies in his disappointing book *Elvis Costello, Joni Mitchell, and the Torch Song Tradition* (Westport, Conn.: Praeger, 2004). Much more careful attention to poetic detail can be found in the chapter on Mitchell in Charles O. Hartman, *Jazz Text: Voice and Improvisation in Poetry, Jazz, and Song* (Princeton: Princeton University Press, 1991).

4. Bernard Gendron, *Between Montmartre and the Mudd Club: Popular Music and the Avant-Garde* (Chicago: University of Chicago Press, 2002), 161. Gendron emphasizes that the high/low distinction is still largely in place: "Rock has gained only a marginal foothold in conservatories, music departments, concert halls, and avant-garde spaces. It has not become part of high culture, nor is it constitutive of any synthesis of 'high' and 'low' that has obliterated the differences. This has been resisted by the rock community as well as by the powers of high culture" (2).

5. Dan Heckman, "Joni Mitchell at a Crossroads," *New York Times*, 8 August 1971.

6. For important sources on the question of the particular challenges facing female artists and critics in popular music, see Evelyn McDonnell and Ann Powers, eds., *Rock She Wrote* (New York: Delta, 1995); Gillian G. Gaar, *She's a Rebel: The History of Women in Rock and Roll*, 2nd ed. (New York: Seal Press, 2002); and Lucy O'Brien, *She Bop II: The Definitive History of Women in Rock, Pop, and Soul* (London: Continuum, 2002). For considerations of this question as it relates to Joni Mitchell's career, see Alice Echols, "Thirty Years with a Portable Lover," *Los Angeles Weekly*, 25 November 1994 (reprinted in Echols, *Shaky Ground: The '60s and Its Aftershocks* [New York: Columbia University Press, 2002], 207–222); and Stuart Henderson, "'All Pink and Clean and Full of Wonder?': Gendering 'Joni Mitchell,' 1966–74," *Left History* 10 (Fall 2005): 83–109.

7. Stephen Holden, "Too Feminine for Rock? Or Is Rock Too Macho?" *New York Times*, 14 January 1996.

8. Polar Music Prize press conference, Stockholm, 7 May 1996, transcribed at http://jmdl.com. In an interview with Morrissey ("Melancholy Meets the Infinite Sadness," *Rolling Stone*, 6 March 1997), Mitchell confirms the idea that separating out the female from the male implies a lower order of achievement:

> MORRISSEY: Do they still refer to you as a female songwriter? it's such a ludicrous title.
>
> JM: It implies limitations.
>
> MORRISSEY: It implies that it's not a real songwriter. To use the term "female songwriter" implies that the word "songwriter" belongs to men.
>
> JM: They tend to lump me always with groups of women. I always thought, "they don't put Dylan with the Men of Rock; why do they do that to me with women?"

9. Interview with Cameron Crowe (1979), in *The Rolling Stone Interviews: Talking with the Legends of Rock & Roll, 1967–1980*, ed. Peter Herbst (New York: St. Martin's Press, 1981), 381.

10. JM: "Folk music [was] where I appeared on the scene, but my roots are in classical music. As a child I lived in a small community in Canada and my playmates were classical music prodigies, and our play involved me leaping around the room while they played prodigious things on the piano.... At the age of eight I dreamed that I could write music beautifully.... The first piece of music I fell in love with was the most beautiful melody I've ever heard, [Rachmaninov's] 'Variations on a Theme by Paganini,' [the theme song] in a movie called *The Story of Three Loves*.... I think my early music has more of that classicism to it than my later music, but I also loved jazz; I was also a rock and roll dancer, so I had a lot of various musics to assimilate" (Polar Music Prize press conference).

11. JM: "None of the songs on my records are folk songs, you know. They're more like German Lieder or something in the beginning. They're more classical than folk" (interview with Liane Hansen, "Weekend Edition," National Public Radio, 28 May 1995). For Debussy, see Jeffrey Pepper Rodgers, "My Secret

Place: The Guitar Odyssey of Joni Mitchell," *Acoustic Guitar*, August 1996, 40–55; see 42; in Stacey Luftig, ed., *The Joni Mitchell Companion: Four Decades of Commentary* (New York: Schirmer, 2000), 221. For the "composer" remark, see Echols, "Thirty Years with a Portable Lover."

12. Anthony Fawcett, "Joni Mitchell—A Search for Clarity," in *California Rock, California Sound* (Los Angeles: Reed Books, 1978), 50–65; see 60.

13. Echols, "Thirty Years with a Portable Lover."

14. "Her first album ... showcased her fine songwriting, soaring soprano, and what could be described as a remarkable lack of desire to court the pop charts—her three most famous songs ('Urge for Going,' 'Both Sides, Now,' and 'The Circle Game,' all made popular by other people) were conspicuously absent from the record" (Henderson, "'All Pink and Clean and Full of Wonder?'" 92).

15. "Mitchell was particularly fortunate to have been signed to Warner-Reprise, a label that by 1968 had come to understand the necessity of allowing its artists creative freedom, and providing a nurturing and patient environment for career growth" (Daniel Sonenberg, "'Who in the World She Might Be': A Contextual and Stylistic Approach to the Early Music of Joni Mitchell" [D.M.A. diss., City University of New York, 2003], 7).

16. Review of *Hejira* by John Rockwell, "Joni Mitchell Recaptures Her Gift," *New York Times*, 12 December 1976.

17. Rockwell, "The New Artistry of Joni Mitchell," *New York Times*, 19 August 1979.

18. Simon Frith, *Performing Rites: On the Value of Popular Music* (Cambridge: Harvard University Press, 1996), 16.

19. Of course in the real world distinctions are rarely as schematic as my two-level grid implies. The broad category of popular music is far from monolithic in attitude, housing internal struggles over which genres are to be accepted as more serious, more authentic, and less commodified, among other things. In North America, the standard of authenticity has been employed to create prestige distinctions between the subcategories of "rock" and "pop." For a discussion of the latter debates, see Keir Keightley, "Reconsidering Rock," in *The Cambridge Companion to Pop and Rock*, ed. Simon Frith, Will Straw, and John Street (Cambridge: Cambridge University Press, 2001), 109–42.

20. JM: "Leonard Cohen was another [influence]; his poetry seemed so much more capable of deeper thought that it made my work seem merely descriptive" (Angela LaGreca, "Joni Mitchell," *Rock Photo*, June 1985).

21. Noel Coppage, "More than a Sprinkling of Symbolism in Joni Mitchell's *The Hissing of Summer Lawns*," *Stereo Review*, February 1976; in Luftig, 78–79.

22. Rockwell, "Joni Mitchell Recaptures Her Gift."

23. To cite just one example, Neil Strauss prefaces an interview (from late in her career) by placing Mitchell's appeals to a fine art model in a highly unsympathetic light: "When it comes to her music, Mitchell can be humorless. People describe her as 'bitter' and a 'loose cannon,' and those are her friends. Over the

course of three days of conversations, Mitchell will compare herself to Mozart, Blake, and Picasso; she will say that the lyrics to one of her songs 'have a lot of symbolic depth, like the Bible' and describe her music as so new it needs its own genre name" (Strauss, "The Hissing of a Living Legend," *New York Times*, 4 October 1998; in Luftig, 210–11).

24. David Brackett, "Music Theory," in *Continuum Encyclopedia of Popular Music of the World*, ed. John Shepherd et al. (London: Continuum, 2003), 1:94–96; see 95.

25. David Brackett, "Music Analysis," in *Continuum Encyclopedia of Popular Music of the World*, 1:86–90; see 88.

26. See Richard Middleton, *Studying Popular Music* (Milton Keynes: Open University Press, 1990); Allan Moore, *Rock: The Primary Text: Developing a Musicology of Rock*, 2nd ed. (Aldershot: Ashgate, 2001); Ken Stephenson, *What to Listen for in Rock: A Stylistic Analysis* (New Haven: Yale University Press, 2002).

27. For a good overview of the controversy, see John Covach, "We Won't Get Fooled Again: Rock Music and Musical Analysis," in *Keeping Score: Music, Disciplinarity, Culture*, ed. David Schwartz, Anahid Kassabian, and Lawrence Siegel (Charlottesville: University Press of Virginia, 1997), 75–89. Richard Middleton details specific criticisms (inappropriate terminology, skewed focus, notational centricity, abstractionism, and monologic listening) in his introduction to *Reading Pop: Approaches to Textual Analysis in Popular Music*, ed. Middleton (Oxford: Oxford University Press, 2000), 4.

28. "Between recent types of popular music and historical traditions of popular, so-called folk, and even bourgeois music stretching back at least as far as the sixteenth century, there are innumerable links and parallels" (Middleton, *Studying Popular Music*, 117).

29. "The challenge then becomes the investigation of popular music along traditional musicological lines while maintaining a careful sensitivity to how popular music may differ from art-music in its specifically musical dimensions" (Covach, "Popular Music, Unpopular Musicology," in *Rethinking Music*, ed. Nicholas Cook and Mark Everist [Oxford: Oxford University Press, 1999], 452–70; see 466). "In seeking to develop alternative approaches to traditional analysis, music scholars have adapted concepts and techniques from music theory for their correspondence to musical values that arise in different contexts of production and reception" (Brackett, "Music Theory," 95).

30. Especially faithful transcriptions in both keyboard and guitar can be found in the songbooks for *FR* and *M*.

31. Moore, *Rock: The Primary Text*, 58.

2. Sound and Style

1. JM: "Separating their personalities from their art, Miles Davis and Picasso have always been my major heroes because we have this one thing in common: They

were restless. I don't know any women role models for that. But Picasso was constantly searching and searching and changing and changing. Even I have favorite periods of Miles, but I would always go to see him in any incarnation. Because he's managed to keep alive" (David Wild, "A Conversation with Joni Mitchell," *Rolling Stone*, 30 May 1991).

2. Barry Kernfeld, "Davis, Miles," *Grove Music Online*, ed. Laura Macy (www.grovemusic.com).

3. See Jeffrey Pepper Rodgers, "My Secret Place: The Guitar Odyssey of Joni Mitchell," *Acoustic Guitar*, August 1996; in Luftig, 228–29.

4. Connor Freff Cochran, "Out of the Quicksand," *Roland Users Group*, October 1996 (www.rolandus.com/rug/), archived at http://jmdl.com.

5. For a complete chronological list of Mitchell's albums, including concert albums and compilations, see the discography.

6. The best source for biographical details is Karen O'Brien, *Shadows and Light: Joni Mitchell, The Definitive Biography* (London: Virgin Books, 2001).

7. A list of thirty-eight early songs never released on commercial recordings is included in the complete listing of lyrics at http://jonimitchell.com/musician/lyrics.cfm. Sheet music arrangements of eight of these songs (dating from 1966 and 1967) were included in the first published songbook, *The Music of Joni Mitchell* (1969), as well as the anthology, *Joni Mitchell Complete* (1971).

8. Formal terms (such as *strophic, verse*, and *chorus*) are defined in chapter 6.

9. It is less common after 1970. Thus one of the stylistic aspects of the song "Little Green" (from *Blue*, released in 1971) that cause it to stand out in its context as an earlier song (written 1967) is its pattern of internal rhymes. For a detailed analysis of the intricate network of rhyme and assonance in the second song on the debut album, "Michael from Mountains," see Charles O. Hartman, "Joni Mitchell: To Whom It May Concern," in his book *Jazz Text: Voice and Improvisation in Poetry, Jazz, and Song* (Princeton: Princeton University Press, 1991), 96–98.

10. Rodgers, "My Secret Place"; in Luftig, 224.

11. Leonore Fleischer, *Joni Mitchell* (New York: Flash Books, 1976), 23–26. On one earlier song, "Night in the City" (*SS*), a piano part was added to embellish the guitar accompaniment.

12. Malka, "Joni Mitchell: Self-Portrait of a Superstar," *Maclean's*, June 1974; in Luftig, 67.

13. Such vocables appear elsewhere in this period, on occasion as rhapsodic melodic discourse (as in the nonverbal coda to "Woodstock" [*LC*]), usually as a response or comment, often in close harmony (as in "Ladies of the Canyon" [*LC*] or "You Turn Me On, I'm a Radio" [*FR*]).

14. The new attention to beauty and consistency of vocal timbre is especially audible in "Trouble Child."

15. Daniel Sonenberg traces such a melodic approach back to "The Last Time I Saw Richard" (*B*); Sonenberg, "'Who in the World She Might Be': A Contextual

and Stylistic Approach to the Early Music of Joni Mitchell" (D.M.A. diss., City University of New York, 2003), 83–104.

16. Metric disruptions are plentiful on *C&S*. Similar patterns of downbeat anticipations being "fixed" by a dropped beat can be found in the instrumental breaks for "Free Man in Paris" and "Down to You." (Mitchell already shows a strong interest in metric disruption on *FR* as well.)

17. Heinrich Wölfflin, *Principles of Art History: The Problem of the Development of Style in Later Art*, trans. M. D. Hottinger (London: G. Bell and Sons, 1932; rept., New York: Dover, 1950), 14. Thanks to Udayan Sen for this insight.

18. Timothy White, *Rock Lives: Profiles and Interviews* (New York: Henry Holt, 1990), 330 (speaking of *C&S*). Compare Wölfflin's description of the painterly as "a perception which is by way of surrendering itself to the mere visual appearance and can abandon 'tangible' design" (*Principles of Art History*, 14).

19. For mixed reviews of *DJRD*, see Stephen Holden, "Madam Joni Almost Pulls It Off," *Village Voice*, 19 December 1977, and Don Heckman, "She Soars, She Orbits, She Never Lands," *High Fidelity*, March 1978; for harsh reviews, see Michael Watts, "Joni: A Fallible Magician," *Melody Maker*, 24 December 1977, and Janet Maslin, "Joni Mitchell's Reckless and Shapeless 'Daughter,'" *Rolling Stone*, 9 March 1978. *Mingus* received a glowing review in *Down Beat* (unsigned review, *Down Beat*, 9 August 1979), a measured positive review in *Village Voice* (Ed Ward, "Charles, Joni, and the Circle Game," *Village Voice*, 30 July 1979; in Luftig, 103–106), a mixed review in *Rolling Stone* (Ariel Swartley, "The Babe in Bopperland and the Great Jazz Composer," *Rolling Stone*, 6 September 1979), and harsh reviews in *Melody Maker* and *Sounds* (Michael Watts, "Joni … er … um," *Melody Maker*, 16 June 1979; Sandy Robertson, "Scared to Dance," *Sounds*, 30 June 1979).

20. Mitchell, "The Lost Years," notes to *The Complete Geffen Recordings* (Geffen B000081902), 2003.

21. White, *Rock Lives*, 338.

22. The title song also contains an implicit reference (especially noticeable in the spoken passage at the end) to the 1966 hit "Wild Thing" by the Troggs.

23. Mitchell returns to this groove throughout periods 3 and 4. The basic pattern is explained under "Triplet Grooves" in the guitar performance notes included in the songbook for *TT*.

24. In classical tonal analysis, this would be considered a secondary dominant (V/V), but that function does not apply here. The progression II-IV, unorthodox in classical music, is common in pop (Ken Stephenson, *What to Listen For in Rock: A Stylistic Analysis* [New Haven: Yale University Press, 2002], 114).

25. Vic Garbarini, "Joni Mitchell Is a Nervy Broad," *Musician*, January 1983; in Luftig, 116–17.

26. Other examples include "Raised on Robbery" (*C&S*) and "Lead Balloon" (*TT*).

27. Notes for this song in *The Complete Geffen Recordings*.

28. Of the ten songs on the album, five are undeniably protest songs, while two more ("Shiny Toys" and "Impossible Dreamer") contain indirect criticism of materialism and social wrongs.

29. See Psalm 115:4–8, decrying the worship of false idols ("Eyes have they, but they see not. They have ears, but they hear not"). While allowances can be made for the self-conscious, dramatic changes Mitchell is undertaking in poetic style and tone, it must be said that beginning with this album one encounters instances where her poetry falls short of its established high quality: patches of knee-jerk alliteration, miscalculations of tone, and raw didactic messages with no attempt at aesthetic modulation (e.g., from "Ethiopia": "A TV star with a P.R. smile/Calls your baby 'It' while strolling/Through your tragic trials").

30. Stephen Holden, "Joni Mitchell Finds the Peace of Middle Age," *New York Times*, 17 March 1991; in Luftig, 152–56; Linda Sanders, "The Grown-Up Game," *Entertainment Weekly*, 1 March 1991.

31. Timothy White, "Billboard Honors Joni Mitchell with Its Highest Accolade," *Billboard*, 9 December 1995.

32. Strongly major-mode songs are already prominent on *DED* ("The Three Great Stimulants," "Shiny Toys" [some modal mixture], "Lucky Girl") and *CMRS* ("My Secret Place" [modal mixture in the bridge], "The Beat of Black Wings" [including secondary dominants]), and become more frequent in the 1990s.

33. For a slightly earlier example of a song based on a scriptural text, see "Love" (*WTRF*), based on I Corinthians 13.

34. It remains to be seen if *Shine* will initiate a new stylistic period.

35. The cover photographs for these collections (by Norman Seeff, responsible for many glamorous portraits of Mitchell in the 1970s) lightheartedly express her aggravation with the whole phenomenon of commercial success. *Hits* has Joni laid out on the road as if the victim of a hit-and-run; on *Misses* she is busy drawing chalk outlines, rear end toward the camera.

36. Mitchell, interview with Josh Simon, *Life*, August 1994.

37. The video of the concert omits "Woodstock"; instead the title song is placed as closing number.

38. In general, the harmonies in the 1979 version are more clearly triadic; however, the guitar breaks between verses strongly retain the suspended, quartal structures of the original.

39. In the 1974 version, the harmonic progression is *more* varied than in 1970. Already in this version, the first section of the refrain is defused by phrase extension to six bars, by resolving the subdominant suspension, and by harmonic release through a half cadence on the minor dominant.

40. In an interview in 1991, Mitchell spoke of the tendency to romanticize the era of Woodstock: "I met a kid the other day who was a self-admitted yuppie. He was in some financial position, and inside this yuppie was this hippie dying to get out. And he was very romantic about the Sixties. He and I had an argument kind of late at night, because he was really praising us. And I kept saying

to him, 'Yeah but we *failed*.' And he kept saying: 'Yeah, but at least you did something. Like, we did *nothing*.' I said: 'Look, the thing is, don't just ape our movement. Don't do hippie poses. Look at us. Admit to yourself that we only took it so far. Build from where we left off.' I know my generation—a lot of them, they're getting old now, and they want to think back fondly, they want to kid themselves. A lot of them think, 'Yeah, we were the best.' That's the kiss of death. That's nongrowth. And also that's very bad for the world" (David Wild, "A Conversation with Joni Mitchell").

41. That is, the concert portion of the video ends with the song. Following the concert, under the closing credits, Mitchell and the band perform "Dreamland" as if in an impromptu jam session in the empty theater.

3. Voices and Personae

1. Larry LeBlanc, "Joni Takes a Break," *Rolling Stone*, 4 March 1971. Her debut album is dedicated "to Mr. Kratzman, who taught me to love words." Mitchell relates more detailed memories about Kratzman's personality and teaching method in an interview with Mary Black, "Both Sides Now," BBC-2, 20 February 1999; quoted in Karen O'Brien, *Shadows and Light: Joni Mitchell, The Definitive Biography* (London: Virgin Books, 2001), 27–28.

2. Marilyn Beker, "Gentle Joni of the Mythical Mood in Folk-Rock," *Toronto Globe and Mail*, 20 April 1968. She confirms this compositional method in an interview from the 1990s. In response to a suggestion that her songs "could almost stand alone as either poetry or prose," she remarks that her songs generally "begin with music" (interview with Merilee Kelly, KCSA-FM, 25 October 1994).

3. Similarly, by compiling her song lyrics under the title *Complete Poems and Lyrics*, Mitchell invites the reader to appreciate them as literary artifacts.

4. Complete lyrics are reproduced on the official website at http://jonimitchell. com/musician/lyrics.cfm. They are also collected in Joni Mitchell, *The Complete Poems and Lyrics* (New York: Crown Publishers, 1997). Note that the latter book perpetuates a number of textual errors due to faulty aural transcription. For instance, the final verse of "Urge for Going" should begin as follows: "I'll ply the fire with kindling now/I'll pull the blankets up to my chin/I'll lock the vagrant winter out and/I'll bolt my wandering in." The *Complete Poems* misprints "I'll ply" as *"Apply"* and "bolt" as *"fold."* In the second verse, "Bully winds" is misprinted as *"Boy* winds."

5. For bibliographies and general surveys of this interdisciplinary field, see Fred Everett Maus, "Narratology, narrativity," *Grove Music Online*, ed. Laura Macy (www.grovemusic.com); Maus, "Classical Instrumental Music and Narrative," in *A Companion to Narrative Theory*, ed. James Phelan and Peter J. Rabinowitz (Oxford: Blackwell, 2005), 466–83. For a well-argued synthesis of linguistic and narrative theory as applied to music analysis, see Philip Rupprecht, *Britten's Musical Language* (Cambridge: Cambridge University Press, 2001).

6. Stephen Holden, "Joni Mitchell Finds the Peace of Middle Age," *New York Times*, 17 March 1991; in Luftig, 156.

7. Jeffrey Pepper Rodgers, "Setting the Stage: The Vocal and Lyrical Craft of Joni Mitchell," *Acoustic Guitar*, February 1997; in Luftig, 259.

8. Jody Denberg, "Taming Joni Mitchell—Joni's Jazz," *Austin Chronicle*, 12 October 1998; in Luftig, 204.

9. The theatrical metaphor is implicit, however, in an interview from 1974: "I feel miscast in some of the songs that I wrote as a younger woman" (Malka, "Joni Mitchell: Self-Portrait of a Superstar," *Maclean's*, June 1974; in Luftig, 67).

10. Interview with Steve Warden, Q107-FM, Toronto, September 1994.

11. For the important formulation of "modes of enunciation," I owe something to Gérard Genette, *The Architext: An Introduction*, trans. Jane E. Lewin (Berkeley & Los Angeles: University of California Press, 1992), 34, 76–77, though I do not adhere to his distinction between modal and thematic categories.

12. By no means am I claiming that the following categories are the only musico-literary modes available. In fact, one could point to another mode that makes rare appearances in Mitchell's work, where the poetic emphasis is almost solely on rhythmic engagement with the audience in the context of dance grooves ("Tenth World" [*DJRD*]) or more abstract vocal chants ("Smokin' [Empty, Try Another]" [*DED*]).

13. M. H. Abrams and Geoffrey Galt Harpham, *A Glossary of Literary Terms*, 8th ed. (Boston: Thomson Wadsworth, 2005), 153.

14. Northrop Frye, *Anatomy of Criticism: Four Essays* (Princeton: Princeton University Press, 1957), 249.

15. Abrams and Harpham, *Glossary of Literary Terms*, 154.

16. Abrams and Harpham, *Glossary of Literary Terms*, 70.

17. Wayne C. Booth, *The Rhetoric of Fiction*, 2nd ed. (Chicago: University of Chicago Press, 1983), 152.

18. Leonard Cohen, *Stranger Music: Selected Poems and Songs* (Toronto: McClelland & Stewart, 1993), 95. The song was first recorded by Judy Collins in 1966 on her album *In My Life*. Mitchell's earliest use of the device dates from that year. On the influence of Cohen, Mitchell has stated, "My lyrics are influenced by Leonard.... We never knew each other in Canada, but after we met at Newport last year we saw a lot of each other. My song 'Marcie' has a lot of him in it, and some of Leonard's religious imagery, which comes from being a Jew in a predominantly Catholic part of Canada, seems to have rubbed off on me, too" (Karl Dallas, "Joni, the Seagull from Saskatoon," *Melody Maker*, 28 September 1968; in Luftig, 7). The Beatles' "For No One" (*Revolver*, 1966) also uses a second-person subject. As for other precedents, I have discovered examples of the device in certain soliloquy songs from the musical theater repertory, including "Hey There" from *The Pajama Game* (1954), "The Party's Over" from *Bells Are Ringing* (1956), and "The Man That Got Away" from the film *A Star is Born* (1954).

19. Note that this song, "Michael from Mountains," uses the second-person subject for the verses, switching to first person in the chorus.

20. Gérard Genette, *Narrative Discourse: An Essay in Method*, trans. Jane E. Lewin (Ithaca: Cornell University Press, 1980), 189.

21. There is a wealth of recent scholarship exploring the diverse uses of second-person narration in postmodern fiction from the late 1950s to the present. Narrative ambiguity is an important aspect of the aesthetic context for such literature. "Second-person fiction (typically) plays with the multifunctionality of the second-person pronoun (*you* as address, as generic "one," or *you* as self-address, etc.) and with the reader's attempt at constructing a situation for the discourse" (Monika Fludernik, "Second-Person Narrative as a Test Case for Narratology: The Limits of Realism," *Style* 28 [1994]: 445–79; see 455).

22. Susan S. Lanser has argued that readers routinely blur the distinction between fictional and autobiographical personas, sometimes equating narrator and historical author even if going against the logic of the text ("The 'I' of the Beholder: Equivocal Attachments and the Limits of Structuralist Narratology," in Phelan and Rabinowitz, *Companion to Narrative Theory*, 206–19).

23. I am referring to analytic insights derived from "speech-act theory," which considers the performative aspect of language; for an extended treatment of this theory as applied to music, see Rupprecht, *Britten's Musical Language*. My point here is to recognize a variety of utterances (or actions performed by poetic speech) without attempting to classify them systematically.

24. Mitchell relates the anecdote in Timothy White, *Rock Lives: Profiles and Interviews* (New York: Henry Holt, 1990), 338–39.

25. The Bible's grand vision of a peaceful kingdom ("they shall beat their swords into plowshares ... neither shall they learn war any more") has been personalized in the spiritual text ("I'm going to lay down my sword and shield/Down by the riverside/Ain't going to study war no more"). Mitchell turns these lines into a general exhortation.

26. David Wild, "A Conversation with Joni Mitchell," *Rolling Stone*, 30 May 1991.

27. Rodgers, "Setting the Stage"; in Luftig, 256.

4. Thematic Threads

1. Thanks to Udayan Sen for this insight.

2. JM: "I never called myself a feminist. I could agree with a lot of the men's point of view. There was something very noble in a woman being willing to swallow her own dreams and devote herself to caring for her husband.... Not that I could ever have done it. I had this talent to feed! ... A Gypsy told me that this is my first life as a woman. In all my previous incarnations I was a man. I'm still getting used to it!" (Bill Flanagan, "Lady of the Canyon," *Vanity Fair*, June 1997).

3. Betty Friedan, *The Feminine Mystique* (New York: Norton, 1963), 44. Jennifer Rycenga has studied the album *Court and Spark* from a similar perspective: namely, as an articulation of woman's experience in terms analogous to concurrent feminist concerns (Rycenga, "Not the Same Situation: Joni Mitchell's Work as a Sonic Document of Feminism," Symposium on the Music and Art of Joni Mitchell, McGill University, 27 October 2004).

4. Interview with Penny Valentine, *Sounds*, 3 June 1972; in Luftig, 46.

5. Barney Hoskyns, "Our Lady of Sorrows," *Mojo*, December 1994; in Luftig, 174–75.

6. The name of her second publishing company, Siquomb, derives from a projected original children's story set in a (Tolkien-inspired) mythical kingdom (Karen O'Brien, *Shadows and Light: Joni Mitchell, The Definitive Biography* [London: Virgin Books, 2001], 52). The first paperback editions of Tolkien's trilogy were issued in 1965.

7. Another expression of such highly romantic, open-ended yearning for the unknown is found in Bilbo's traveling song, "The Road goes ever on and on," from the first chapter of *The Lord of the Rings*.

8. *Crosby, Stills & Nash* (Atlantic Records SD 8229), 1969.

9. Fleischer, *Joni Mitchell*, 58.

10. Edward D. Berkowitz, *Something Happened: A Political and Cultural Overview of the Seventies* (New York: Columbia University Press, 2006), 158.

11. Tom Wolfe, "The Me Decade and the Third Great Awakening," in *Mauve Gloves and Madmen, Clutter and Vine* (New York: Farrar, Straus and Giroux, 1976), 126–67; Christopher Lasch, *The Culture of Narcissism: American Life in an Age of Diminishing Expectations* (New York: Norton, 1979). See also Edwin Schur, *The Awareness Trap: Self-Absorption Instead of Social Change* (New York: Quadrangle, 1976).

12. Flanagan, "Lady of the Canyon," 176. Mitchell described her stay on Crete in more detail in Larry LeBlanc, "Joni Takes a Break," *Rolling Stone*, 4 March 1971.

13. Compare the sentiment in "Night in the City" (*SS*): "we run on laughing with no one to meet." There are embryonic expressions of bohemia such as this (and the alternative community of "Sisotowbell Lane") in the first album, though they have not yet coalesced into a full thematic representation.

14. Compare the same range of economic options in "Barangrill" ("the thumb and the satchel/Or the rented Rolls-Royce"), where she presents it as a dilemma of personal expression.

15. Hoskyns, *Our Lady of Sorrows;* in Luftig, 167.

16. Interview with Cameron Crowe, in *The Rolling Stone Interviews: Talking with the Legends of Rock and Roll, 1967–1980*, ed. Peter Herbst (New York: St. Martin's Press, 1981), 381.

17. For a study that places hippie culture in the context of a long history of bohemian countercultural expression, see Richard Miller, *Bohemia: The Protoculture Then and Now* (Chicago: Nelson-Hall, 1977).

18. Elizabeth Brake, "'To Live Outside the Law, You Must Be Honest': Freedom in Dylan's Lyrics," in *Bob Dylan and Philosophy: It's Alright, Ma (I'm Only Thinking)*, ed. Peter Vernezze and Carl J. Porter (Chicago: Open Court, 2006), 78–89; see 79.

19. Tom Wolfe, *The Painted Word* (New York: Farrar, Straus and Giroux, 1975), 17, 21, 33.

20. Hoskyns, *Our Lady of Sorrows;* in Luftig, 167–68. For a glimpse of the glamorous social scene open to the newly minted musical celebrities, see Barney Hoskyns, *Hotel California: Singer-Songwriters and Cocaine Cowboys in the L.A. Canyons, 1967–1976* (London: Fourth Estate, 2005), 188–90.

21. In a live performance from 1983, Mitchell embellishes the refrain with four extra lines, describing the player himself as a "fallen angel" and a "rising star," thus confirming him as one of her wild rebel characters. See *Refuge of the Roads* (Shout Factory DVD 30352), 2004.

22. O'Brien, *Shadows and Light*, 133–34.

23. JM: "When I retired I felt I never really wanted to do it again—ever.... I gained a strange perspective of performing. I had a bad attitude about it, you know. I felt like what I was writing was too personal to be applauded for" (interview with Penny Valentine, *Sounds*, 3 June 1972; in Luftig, 49).

24. Mitchell sounds this motif again in "Court and Spark": "I couldn't let go of L.A./City of the fallen angels."

25. The visual art associated with this album also projects intense ambivalence regarding the rose imagery. On the inner gatefold of the album, Mitchell includes a felt-tip pen drawing of a woman rapturously smelling flowers in what appears to be a garden setting (though unofficially, the drawing has acquired the title *Judy Collins in the Green Room.*) This suggests yet another interpretation of the song title (shared by the album), namely, the desire to recover a sense of integration with nature. (This is borne out by the cover photography of Joni set within the wild Canadian landscape.) On the other hand, on the cover of the *For the Roses* songbook, Mitchell's drawing depicts a whinnying or smirking horse wreathed with roses, in rear view, on which is superimposed the figures of three "fancy women in thirties evening gowns," so that the rose bouquets they hold aloft appear to emerge from the horse's ass. Inside the songbook, accompanying the printed lyrics to the title song, is a drawing of a bedroom or hotel room interior. A male singer sits on the bed in a despondent, drooping pose, guitar at his side; in the foreground a cut rose in a whiskey bottle rests on the table near an abandoned game of solitaire.

26. Mitchell makes an explicit connection here to a statement by Mingus ("everything I touched turned to gold") included as a rap ("Coin in the Pocket") leading into this song.

27. On Castaneda and the fad for borrowed Indian spirituality, see Philip Deloria, "Counterculture Indians and the New Age," in *Imagine Nation: The American Counterculture of the 1960s and '70s*, ed. Peter Braunstein and Michael William Doyle (New York: Routledge, 2002), 159–88, esp. 174.

28. Mitchell uses these two sites to structure the entire album, prefacing its two parts with lines from this song. Part 1 ("I came to the city") has an urban setting; part 2 ("Out of the city and down to the seaside"), various pastoral settings. The urban, the pastoral, and the visionary horizon are all captured in Mitchell's elaborate cover art for the album; the visionary portion of the cover is set off by its widened focus, lack of color, infinite fan of sunrays, and flight of gulls (more on this album as a whole in chapter 7).

29. Organum is a type of medieval sacred music in which singers harmonize a chant melody in open-sounding intervals (fourths or fifths).

5.   Harmonic Palette

1. John Ephland, "Alternate Tunings," *Down Beat*, December 1996.

2. She did devise her own shorthand system for identifying distinct tunings, specifying the number of half steps separating the pitches of adjacent strings. Thus standard tuning, E A D G B E, would be written as E–5–5–5–4–5; the tuning for "That Song about the Midway" (*C*), E E E F♯ B E, as E–0–12–2–5–5. For more about tunings, see Jeffrey Pepper Rodgers, "My Secret Place: The Guitar Odyssey of Joni Mitchell," *Acoustic Guitar*, August 1996; reprinted in Luftig, 219–30, and in Rodgers, *Rock Troubadours* (San Anselmo, Calif.: String Letter Publishing, 2000), 33–55.

3. At an early point in Mitchell's career, Joel Bernstein took on the role of her musical archivist, transcribing tunings and fingerings for each song (O'Brien, *Shadows and Light*, 50, 92). He was involved in the production of sheet music for a limited number of albums, namely *FR, M, NRH, TI, TT, Hits,* and *Misses,* as well as the recent anthology *Joni Mitchell Complete (Guitar Songbook Edition)*.

4. John Rockwell, "The New Artistry of Joni Mitchell," *New York Times*, 19 August 1979.

5. JM: "According to the guy who wrote a book on jazz, Victor Feldman, he defined it and locked it into harmonic laws. Victor Feldman apparently wrote a technical teaching book or some kind of book on jazz harmony [*Musicians Guide to Chord Progression*]. We were playing on a date. What was it? 'Moon at the Window' [*WTRF*]. Victor was playing vibes. Well, on this one, he got really uptight.... I said, 'Are the words bothering you?' He said, 'I hate the harmony and the harmonic movement.' I had to stop and send him home. I said, 'You can't play on something that you hate!' " (Ephland, "Alternate Tunings").

6. Joe Jackson, "The Second Coming of Joni Mitchell," *Hotpress*, 26 April 2000.

7. Daniel Levitin, "A Conversation with Joni Mitchell," *Grammy Magazine*, Spring 1996; in Luftig, 186–87.

8. Robin Eggar, "Both Sides Now," *The Word*, April 2007 (referring to *CMRS*).

9. Vic Garbarini, "Joni Mitchell Is a Nervy Broad," *Musician*, January 1983; in Luftig, 115.

10. Ethan Brown, "Influences: Joni Mitchell," *New York Magazine*, 9 May 2005. "Drawing from classical composers and the great pre–World War II pop songwriters such as Gershwin, she came up with original and complex chord structures" (interview with Robert Hilburn, *Los Angeles Times*, 20 September 2004).

11. The anecdote about Rachmaninov is ubiquitous; see, e.g., O'Brien, *Shadows and Light*, 20; Stephen Holden, "Joni Mitchell Finds the Peace of Middle Age," *New York Times*, 17 March 1991; in Luftig, 155.

12. Interview with Chris Douridas, "Morning Becomes Eclectic," KCRW-FM, 12 September 1994.

13. Interview with Tony Hale, "Rock Master Class," Capitol 95.8FM, London, 29 December 1985.

14. Kristine McKenna, "Lady of the Canyon," *Spin*, May 1988. The following quotation (discussing tritone motion) also highlights the notion of a critical perspective through harmony: "The church forbade it. You know why? Because it evokes doubt. Every chord must be designed to keep the eyes lifted up to the cathedral ceiling, and somehow or other this . . . makes the heart tilt. . . . It takes your eyes off the cathedral ceiling and makes them look at your toes" (interview with Chris Douridas, "Morning Becomes Eclectic").

15. She never uses minor mode as the basis for a song, preferring Aeolian or Dorian.

16. On modal usage in pop/rock, with a focus on the lowered $\hat{7}$, see Allan Moore, "The So-Called 'Flattened Seventh' in Rock," *Popular Music* 14 (1995): 185–201.

17. The following modes are less common in popular music: Lydian (corresponding to the scale from F to F on the white piano keys), Phrygian (E to E), and Locrian (B to B).

18. Ken Stephenson, *What to Listen for in Rock: A Stylistic Analysis* (New Haven: Yale University Press, 2002), especially chap. 5, "Harmonic Succession." For discussion of increased harmonic options, see 103; for relaxed goal orientation, see 119; for deemphasis of tonic cadence, see 111–12. Stephenson goes so far as to propose a new "rock standard" of harmonic movement (defined 103–104), but this position is weakened by his acknowledgment of the persistence of the older standard alongside the new one, as well as their hybridization (108)—not to mention his failure to define the precise scope of the term "rock."

19. On modal mixture in pop/rock generally, see Walter Everett, "Confessions from Blueberry Hell, or, Pitch Can Be a Sticky Substance," in *Expression in Pop-Rock Music: A Collection of Critical and Analytical Essays*, ed. Everett (New York: Garland, 2000), 269–345; specifically 326–30. Elsewhere, Everett proposes a typology of tonal systems active in rock ("Making Sense of Rock's Tonal Systems," *Music Theory Online* 10/4 [December 2004]). The five categories I will be using in this chapter exhibit some apparent overlap with his types (thus my modal category parallels his Type 2, my polymodal category his Type 3a,

my polytonal category his Type 3b), but the two methods of classification are at odds in other ways. First, in contrast to Everett, whose aim is a systematic theory of syntactic principles, I am describing collections of harmonic resources without making categorical claims about syntax. (Thus my chromatic category he would divide according to whether the syntax is tonal, pentatonic, or free.) Second, whereas Everett posits "common-practice tonality" and its "ageless principles" as his harmonic standard, I am positing modal usage as the standard for Joni Mitchell, allowing for a less strict sense of syntactic "norms." (Thus for my purposes, the major mode is one mode among others, with no priority as to functional behavior, while for Everett, major/minor tonality is a separate, primary, normative category.)

20. The chord charts and harmonic reductions in this book are my own transcriptions, with reference to the songbooks incorporating Joel Bernstein's notations. Most of the other published songbooks are unreliable.

21. In traditional tonal practice, this chord would suggest a secondary dominant of Em (V/ii); but the chord does not resolve to Em. Stephenson offers numerous examples of such chords appearing in popular music as coloristic alternatives to an underlying mode, without functioning as secondary dominants (*What to Listen for in Rock*, 114–17).

22. Walter Everett includes a discussion of songs with multiple tonal centers in "Confessions from Blueberry Hell," 311–12; he uses the term "progressive tonality." Elsewhere he states that the Beatles' exploration of progressive tonality began with *Revolver* (1966), in the songs "Good Day Sunshine" (B-A) and "Doctor Robert" (A-B). "Lucy in the Sky with Diamonds," from *Sgt. Pepper's Lonely Hearts Club Band* (1967) is in A-Bb-G (Everett, *The Beatles as Musicians*: Revolver *through the* Anthology [New York: Oxford University Press, 1999]).

23. Interview with Tony Hale, "Rock Master Class." See the analysis of "Amelia" in chapter 4 (Ex. 4.6).

24. In assigning dual keys to such songs, one should not disregard the modal character of each tonal pole. Thus the keys of "Let the Wind Carry Me" could be more fully described as F♯ Aeolian/A Aeolian. But since Mitchell's modal usage is so often ambiguous or mixed, I have resisted being too specific about naming modes in the polytonal category.

25. This song shares a tuning, key, and similar chord progressions with "Cactus Tree" (*SS*) and "Conversation" (*LC*), though the effects she aims for in the three songs are quite different.

26. Judy Collins, *Wildflowers* (Elektra 74012-2, 1967); arrangement by Joshua Rifkin.

27. Note that some songs from other categories also exploit a similar polarity, for example, the polymodal "For Free" (*LC*) (CM/Mixolydian/Am).

28. JM: "The principle of the game was that ... C was home and that then you could venture out anywhere, and if you were meandering out there and you felt like you were lost, you wandered home to C. And then you departed again. So

we sat down and we recorded three of these improvisational flights [on piano]. From that we edited together a piece of music which was to become the medallion, the insert, in 'Paprika Plains'" (interview with Tony Hale, "Rock Master Class").

29. In a few later songs, Mitchell experiments with pedals laid down on a separate rhythm track, such as the cricket chirping on a tonic C in "Night Ride Home" (*NRH*). "The Three Great Stimulants" (*DED*) is notable for using an E pedal in the key of CM/Am.

30. Ephland, "Alternate Tunings."

31. Interview with Chris Douridas, "Morning Becomes Eclectic."

6. Melodic Turns

1. Richard Middleton points out the historical derivation of strophic ("stanzaic") form from folk traditions (Middleton, "Song Form," in *Continuum Encyclopedia of Popular Music of the World*, ed. John Shepherd et al. [London: Continuum, 2003], 2:513–19; see 515).

2. John Covach calls this 'AABA form,' relating it historically to one of the common forms in Tin Pan Alley songs. His example of AABA (verse-bridge) form from Tin Pan Alley is "Over the Rainbow" (Arlen-Harburg); his examples from the 1960s include Carole King's "Will You Love Me Tomorrow?" and the Beatles' "I Want to Hold Your Hand" (Covach, "Form in Rock Music: A Primer," in *Engaging Music: Essays in Music Analysis*, ed. Deborah Stein [Oxford: Oxford University Press, 2005], 65–76). I will avoid the use of AABA in referring to song form, reserving such alphabetic shorthand for the analysis of phrase structure.

3. The original sheet music prints a double bar line at this point to denote a chorus.

4. Some later songs contain sections whose function lies somewhere between bridge (i.e., modulation/contrast) and chorus (i.e., return/culmination), for example, "Good Friends" (*DED*), "Number One," and "Snakes and Ladders" (both *CMRS*). The formally ambiguous "Sweet Sucker Dance" (*M*) is a special case, since Mitchell wrote the text to preexisting music by Charles Mingus. The sixteen-bar section beginning and ending in A♭ (first appearing at the words, "We move in measures") behaves musically like a chorus, though Mitchell doesn't consistently give it the same text; she does, however, always give it the same end refrain ("... only a dance"). The unconventional order of sections can be diagrammed as follows (choruses in bold have identical text): V1 Ch **Ch** B Ch V2 Ch B **Ch**.

5. Middleton, "Song Form," 516. He also identifies the Rolling Stones' "Satisfaction" as strongly favoring continuity over sectionalism.

6. In these three songs, the instrumental refrain is not used for the introduction.

7. Given the threefold repetition within the verse, the IR is not used as punctuation between every verse in this song, only after the bridge. The sequence of

sections is as follows: (IR) V1 V2 B1 (IR) V3 B2 (IR) V4. Mitchell also varies the length (5mm.) of the IR pattern for flexibility: verse 1 repeats the pattern in versions of 4mm. (phrase 1), 5mm. (phrase 2), and 7mm. (phrase 4).

8. This IR also parallels phrases 2 and 4 of the verse.

9. Walter Everett, "Confessions from Blueberry Hell, or, Pitch Can Be a Sticky Substance," in *Expression in Pop-Rock Music: A Collection of Critical and Analytical Essays*, ed. Everett (New York: Garland, 2000), 269–345; see 293. "There is no difficulty in finding phrases and subphrases of [irregular length] in the Beatles' work after 1962, but very few appear before then" (Everett, *The Beatles as Musicians: The Quarry Men through* Rubber Soul [New York: Oxford University Press, 2001], 64).

10. Mitchell has written some completely foursquare songs, but they are in the minority. For instance, *SS* contains none, *C* one ("I Don't Know Where I Stand"), *LC* five ("Morning Morgantown," "Conversation," "Ladies of the Canyon," "Big Yellow Taxi," "The Circle Game"), and *B* two ("My Old Man," "The Last Time I Saw Richard"). Some songs, like "Both Sides, Now" (*C*) and "This Flight Tonight" (*B*), are mostly foursquare but include a single carefully placed irregularity.

11. See Ken Stephenson's discussion of phrase overlaps in *What to Listen for in Rock: A Stylistic Analysis* (New Haven: Yale University Press, 2002), 9–14.

12. A well-known example from the Beatles is "Eleanor Rigby," whose irregular lines (in poetic meter: 2 beats/5 beats/2 beats) call for five-bar musical phrases. When asked whether she composes melody or lyrics first, Mitchell has consistently stated that the melody generally comes first, and she works the lyrics out afterward, though I presume there is some musical adjustment as the lyrics take shape. Nevertheless, in specific analyses I try to sidestep the question of which element (melody or lyrics) is prior and which is a subsequent response, preferring to understand the two as mutually supportive and constitutive.

13. The measure numbers in this song are inexact due to frequent changes of meter and irregular bar lengths.

14. Middleton traces such patterns to nineteenth-century commercial popular song ("Song Form," 514), and develops a class-based interpretation, according to which the formal symmetries of so-called bourgeois song reflect deep-seated ideological values (individualism, self-sufficiency) (Middleton, *Studying Popular Music* [Milton Keynes: Open University Press, 1990], 10, 16–17). I will not be subscribing to such an argument here, preferring to relate formal characteristics to social function (leisure, aesthetic contemplation, etc.) rather than class ideology, and seeking signs of individuation at a higher structural level.

15. Middleton, "Song Form," 514; quoting János Maróthy, *Music and the Bourgeois, Music and the Proletarian* (Budapest: Akadémiai Kiado, 1974).

16. In my phrase structure diagrams, sequential letters refer to distinct melodic material. Open phrases are notated with a subscript o; other phrases are closed. I have taken harmonic cadence as primary sign of closure; not all phrases marked as closed have a linear arrival on $\hat{1}$.

17. Two well-known traditional songs with period structure are "Greensleeves" and "Home Sweet Home." In these cases the phrases fall into two successive periods, each member comprising a single phrase ($a_o a'b_o b''$). There is a great deal of disagreement and confusion in the use of the term *period* in both classical and popular music studies. Allen Forte uses it merely to describe any grouping of two four-bar phrases, with no specificity of function (Forte, *The American Popular Ballad of the Golden Era, 1924–1950* [Princeton: Princeton University Press, 1995], 36–37). Others use it to describe a complementary phrase pair with or without parallel musical material (such usage occurs in Deborah Stein and Robert Spillman, *Poetry into Song: Performance and Analysis of Lieder* [New York: Oxford University Press, 1996], 175; and Ken Stephenson, *What to Listen for in Rock*, 55). Allan Moore introduces a definition proposed by Arnold Schoenberg, then seems to disregard Schoenberg's precise criteria (Moore, *Rock: The Primary Text*, 58). I will follow the narrow usage of the term (a complementary phrase pair with parallel musical material) as defined by William E. Caplin, *Classical Form: A Theory of Formal Functions for the Instrumental Music of Haydn, Mozart, and Beethoven* (New York: Oxford University Press, 1998), 12. According to my usage, the period is a special kind of open/closed pair; songwriters can exploit open/closed relationships without recourse to period structures.

18. Ken Stephenson points out how in rock music, tonal closure is often relocated from the end of formal (phrase or hypermetric) units to the beginning of formal units. "As a result, many rock songs proceed through a series of overlapping propelling gestures"—for example, phrases that begin in the tonic and end harmonically open (Stephenson, *What to Listen for in Rock*, 21). From this sound observation, he proceeds to make the blanket claim that period structures never apply in rock (60, 111). Unfortunately, he is indiscriminate in his use of the term "rock," including pop artists and singer-songwriters in that overarching category without allowing for any distinctions in practice. Richard Crawford, in his analysis of this song, is more precise in linking phrase structure to subgenre: "Too free in form, redundant in material, and scarce in vocal melody to pass in 1965 as a standard pop, country, or folk song, *Like a Rolling Stone* is an early example of a rock song" (Crawford, *America's Musical Life: A History* [New York: Norton, 2001], 792). Richard Middleton attributes the incorporation of short open-ended musical loops ("musematic repetition") in songs such as this to African American influence (Middleton, *Studying Popular Music*, 269–84). It should be mentioned that melodies consisting entirely of open phrases can also be found in European folksong traditions.

19. As Stephenson explores in useful detail, harmonic practice in pop/rock differs in significant ways from common tonal practice in classical music. One crucial area of difference involves the treatment of dominant and subdominant chords and their arrangement in a syntactic hierarchy. The difference in syntax means that rules developed for cadential hierarchies in classical music (e.g., "half," "imperfect," "authentic" cadences) are not generally applicable in pop. It also

means that the notion of "cadence" itself needs to be conceived differently. I follow Stephenson's pragmatic guidelines, identifying cadences primarily by rhythmic and textual criteria: "A cadence occurs when the melody comes to rest at the end of a textual line on [or near] the fourth downbeat of a four-bar hypermeasure" (Stephenson, *What to Listen for in Rock*, 57). Thus cadence is equivalent to phrase articulation; cadences have a wide spectrum of conclusiveness; and "open cadences can occur on almost any chord" (58).

20. Mitchell rarely uses period structure. One exception is the verse of "Big Yellow Taxi" (*LC*). The first phrase, while it does end on a tonic chord, is melodically open (ending on $\hat{3}$); the second phrase ends on $\hat{1}$ with stronger harmonic closure (**aa'**). The rudimentary period structure is appropriate to the song's artless character. Another example is found in the verse of "The Circle Game" (*LC*) (**aa'$_o$ + a''$_o$b**). Like "Blowin' in the Wind," this song is designed to be suitable for communal singing.

21. "Continuation" is a neutral designation, encompassing a variety of more specific medial functions (such as "contrast," "development," etc.). Richard Crawford glosses the standard **aaba** phrase pattern of Tin Pan Alley in terms of the functional sequence "statement, restatement, contrast, and return" (*America's Musical Life*, 657–58). Walter Everett describes the sequence in terms of statement, restatement, departure, and conclusion (**aaba** or **aabc**), stating that the model is "the basis of most of the Beatles' verses throughout their career" (Everett, *The Beatles as Musicians*: Revolver *through the* Anthology [New York: Oxford University Press, 1999], 16). Steven Huebner identifies similar functional models at work in melodies from nineteenth-century Italian opera ("Lyric Form in *Ottocento* Opera," *Journal of the Royal Musical Association* 117 (1992): 123–47), a repertory that had a strong influence on American popular song of the time (see Nicholas E. Tawa, *Sweet Songs for Gentle Americans: The Parlor Song in America, 1790–1860* [Bowling Green, Ohio: Bowling Green University Popular Press, 1980], 163–64). My terminology is indebted to William Caplin's theory of formal function in instrumental music, particularly his sentence model (*Classical Form*, 9–12), though the correspondence between repertories is not exact.

22. This song has dual tonal centers; the **b** phrases close on G, the **d** phrase on A.

23. According to Ex. 5.13, the **a** phrases appear to be harmonically open, but in fact, completion of these melodic phrases only occurs upon the following downbeat, coinciding with tonic arrival.

24. A traditional song using this pattern is "Scarborough Fair": **ab$_c$d**.

25. For a traditional example of this asymmetrical distribution of open/closed, see the Stephen Foster song "Jeanie with the Light Brown Hair" (**a$_o$a'$_o$b$_o$a''**). For examples from Tin Pan Alley, see George Gershwin, "A Foggy Day" (**a$_o$b$_o$a$_o$c**), and Cole Porter, "Ev'ry Time We Say Goodbye" (**a$_o$b$_o$a$_o$b'**).

26. While the first three **c** phrases are clearly two bars long with pickup, the wordy fourth **c** phrase is tricky to measure, since its "pickup" constitutes virtually an entire bar, sounding like an overlap with the previous phrase.

27. "Edith and the Kingpin" (*HSL*) also has an open second half; its first half is periodic: $a_o b_o c_o + a_o b_o c/d_o e_o$ (see Ex. 6.6).

28. Models of open-ended phrase structure occur in the folksong repertory. Judy Collins included her own adaptations of two examples on her first albums: "I Know Where I'm Going" ($a_o b_o$) on *A Maid of Constant Sorrow* (1961), and the ravishing "Golden Apples of the Sun" ($a_o b_o a_o c_o/d_o a_o b_o c_o$) on the album of that title (1962).

29. Philip Tagg provides a useful survey of melodic typologies, based on various factors such as scale, rhythm, motivic/phrase structure, and so on. He cites a standard ethnomusicological method of melodic classification by pitch contour, in which basic types are labeled according to rather impressionistic gestural categories: rising, falling, arched, terraced, oscillatory, wavy, and so on (Tagg, "Melody," in *Continuum Encyclopedia of Popular Music of the World*, 2:567–84; see 569). A similar typology of melodic contour is introduced in Middleton, *Studying Popular Music*, 203–207.

30. The sense of formal extension, as described by terms like **aabc** or statement/restatement/departure/conclusion, I have covered under the heading of phrase structure.

31. See the assorted definitions and extended discussion in Gary Burns, "A Typology of 'Hooks' in Popular Records," *Popular Music* 6 (1986): 1–20.

32. To be precise, the iii chord should be spelled as a Imaj7 with $\hat{3}$ in the bass (Bmaj7/D♯). This progression allows Mitchell to exploit the $\hat{3}$–$\hat{2}$–$\hat{1}$ bass motion while sustaining the tonic B as a pedal in the middle of the texture, where it interacts poignantly with the A♯ of the first chord. The progression (Imaj7/$\hat{3}$–ii7–I) also appears prominently in "Morning Morgantown" (*LC*) (at the end of the **b** phrases) and "The Circle Game" (*LC*) (intro and end of chorus).

33. Vic Garbarini, "Joni Mitchell Is a Nervy Broad," *Musician*, January 1983; in Luftig, 116.

34. JM: "After *Court and Spark* I got fed up with four beats to the bar, and by the time I hit the Mingus project I was having the rhythm section play totally up in the air.... Then at a certain point I began to crave that order again. So doing this album [*WTRF*] was a natural reentry into it" (Garbarini, "Joni Mitchell Is a Nervy Broad"; in Luftig, 115).

35. Stephen Holden, review of *HSL*, *Rolling Stone*, 15 January 1976; Ariel Swartley, "The Siren and the Symbolist," *Rolling Stone*, 10 February 1977; Kristine McKenna, "Bleak Visions of Life in the Fast Lane," *Los Angeles Times*, 25 December 1977; Michael Watts, "Joni: A Fallible Magician," *Melody Maker*, 24 December 1977; Janet Maslin, "Joni Mitchell's Reckless and Shapeless 'Daughter,'" *Rolling Stone*, 9 March 1978; Holden, "Madam Joni Almost Pulls It Off," *Village Voice*, 19 December 1977. Watts prefaces his review by pointing out how "on her previous two albums she patently stopped building songs upon attractive hooks and became more interested in textures and rhythms, to the point where *Hejira*, her last record, was recitative in tone."

36. An exception is the thoroughly mean-spirited review of *Hejira* by Perry Meisel: "Usually, Mitchell's melodies have been so compelling that her songs stand up on purely musical grounds, at least until her last LP, *The Hissing of Summer Lawns*, which sounded so aimless that it put off many of Joni's oldest fans.... The predominance of the verbal and vocal on *Hejira* is largely the result of its simple dearth of melody" ("An End to Innocence: How Joni Mitchell Fails," *Village Voice*, 24 January 1977; in Luftig, 79).

37. Don Heckman pointed this out at the time in a review of *DJRD*: "Very few other artists make such intense demands upon such a large audience: Dylan does, of course, even though the rudimentary qualities of his composing skills make his music both more obvious and more accessible. [He mentions a few other artists.] As with Mitchell, their audiences usually gravitate toward the more accessible, lightweight cuts than the acute, penetrating ones" (Heckman, "She Soars, She Orbits, She Never Lands," *High Fidelity*, March 1978).

38. See her comments on appropriate text declamation in Jeffrey Pepper Rodgers, "Setting the Stage: The Vocal and Lyrical Craft of Joni Mitchell," *Acoustic Guitar*, February 1997; in Luftig, 257.

39. Joe Jackson, "The Second Coming of Joni Mitchell," *Hotpress*, 26 April 2000.

40. Daniel Sonenberg, "'Who in the World She Might Be': A Contextual and Stylistic Approach to the Early Music of Joni Mitchell" (D.M.A. diss., City University of New York, 2003), 87.

41. Mitchell subjects the descending triad and subsequent rising two-note tag to motivic development in the refrain phrases. Note that the IR features repetitions of motive *j* high in the keyboards.

7. Collections and Cycles

1. Vic Garbarini, "Joni Mitchell Is a Nervy Broad," *Musician*, January 1983; in Luftig, 128. Further details can be found in O'Brien, *Shadows and Light*, 124–26.

2. Ruth O. Bingham, "The Early Nineteenth-Century Song Cycle," in *The Cambridge Companion to the Lied*, ed. James Parsons (Cambridge: Cambridge University Press, 2004), 101–19; see 104.

3. Allan F. Moore, *The Beatles: Sgt. Pepper's Lonely Hearts Club Band* (Cambridge: Cambridge University Press, 1997), 70–73.

4. For instance, see David Brackett, *The Pop, Rock, and Soul Reader: Histories and Debates* (New York: Oxford University Press, 2005), 209. For a discussion of concept albums in Zappa's output, see James Borders, "Form and the Concept Album: Aspects of Modernism in Frank Zappa's Early Releases," *Perspectives of New Music* 39 (2001): 118–60.

5. A critic made this connection at the time: "The album [*Song to a Seagull*] is one of the few I can think of—the others that spring to mind are *Sgt. Pepper* and the Mothers of Invention LPs—which successfully hangs together as a complete

whole" (Karl Dallas, "Joni, the Seagull from Saskatoon," *Melody Maker*, 28 September 1968; in Luftig, 7).

6. See Robert W. Butts, "More Than a Collection of Songs: The Concept Album in Country Music," *Mid-America Folklore* 16 (Fall 1988): 90–99.

7. Deena Weinstein identifies several Pink Floyd albums unified by central themes ("Progressive Rock as Text: The Lyrics of Roger Waters," in *Progressive Rock Reconsidered*, ed. Kevin Holm-Hudson [New York: Routledge, 2002], 91–109; see 100).

8. Systematic attention to the musical construction of coherence stems from Arthur Komar's analysis of Schumann song cycles (Komar, "The Music of *Dichterliebe*: The Whole and Its Parts," in *Robert Schumann: Dichterliebe*, ed. Komar [New York: Norton, 1971], 63–94). His enumeration of analytical categories (see 63–66) has been influential; Komar's influence is discussed in David Ferris, *Schumann's Eichendorff* Liederkreis *and the Genre of the Romantic Cycle* (New York: Oxford University Press, 2000), 11–12. But note John Daverio's comment: "Even Arthur Komar's criteria for establishing 'song cyclehood'—unity of poetic content, shared thematic, harmonic, and rhythmic figures, continuity between adjacent songs, coherent tonal planning—represent less a set of prescriptions than a series of possibilities" (Daverio, "The Song Cycle: Journeys through a Romantic Landscape," in *German Lieder in the Nineteenth Century*, ed. Rufus Hallmark [New York: Schirmer, 1996], 279–312; see 281).

9. Robert Gauldin diagrams a tightly organized internal grouping of this kind according to a "double-tonic" complex (A/C) on side 2 of the Beatles' *Abbey Road* (Gauldin, "Beethoven, *Tristan*, and the Beatles," *College Music Symposium* 30 [1990]: 142–52; see 150).

10. Beethoven's *An die ferne Geliebte* (1816) is anomalous in its strongly coherent tonal structure; the Romantic cycles that followed allowed for much more ambiguity in their harmonic plan.

11. "The association of Part I of the narrative with the complex ballad and Part II with the simpler genres [such as gospel and blues] helps convey the two sides of the protagonist's personality" (Peter Kaminsky, "The Popular Album as Song Cycle: Paul Simon's 'Still Crazy after All These Years,'" *College Music Symposium* 32 [1992]: 38–54; see 44).

12. Borders, "Form and the Concept Album." The Beatles' *Abbey Road* features a partial recapitulation of "You Never Give Me Your Money" (Gauldin, "Beethoven, *Tristan*, and the Beatles," 150–51).

13. "There has been a definite thread in the last few albums that Joni has created—in *The Hissing of Summer Lawns, Hejira* and especially in *Don Juan's Reckless Daughter*. Joni feels that in a sense she is trying to make movies within the concept of an album, rather than it being a collection of individual songs. 'The music is the score,' she says, 'the voice speaks as characters speak—but also sets up the scene—it's also the camera. And the music is background music, also it is shading, framing it, it is also visual in a way. Sometimes it's

merely accompaniment, but from time to time it paints too. The last three albums—involuntarily I have seen the whole thing visually: cast, costumed, moving. It's like I've seen it with the clarity of a dream'" (Anthony Fawcett, "Joni Mitchell—A Search for Clarity," in *California Rock, California Sound* [Los Angeles: Reed Books, 1978], 50–65; see 63).

14. *Song to a Seagull* was the originally intended title (spelled out in gull shapes on the album cover), dropped through a misunderstanding during production. The album was released under the title *Joni Mitchell* (see O'Brien, *Shadows and Light*, 81).

15. "Sisotowbell Lane" has a riverside setting, amid woodlands and grasslands, although the reference to Noah in the rain calls up the subliminal image of an ark surviving the flood.

16. "Mitchell says *Hejira*'s songs were written during or after three journeys she took in late 1975 and the first half of 1976": touring with Bob Dylan's Rolling Thunder Revue, a concert tour for *Hissing*, and a cross-country automobile trip to Maine, on the return journey of which she was traveling alone (Doug Fischer, "The Trouble She's Seen," *Ottawa Citizen*, 8 October 2006; see O'Brien, *Shadows and Light*, 158–68). Since the album is so markedly autobiographical, I will not be making a strong distinction in this section between the poetic speaker and Mitchell herself.

17. "The word is used in Islam to refer to Mohammed's flight from persecution in the seventh century, when he fled Mecca to reach safety in Medina, where he founded the first Moslem community" (O'Brien, *Shadows and Light*, 167).

18. For another concentrated example of mercurial discourse, see the third verse of "Furry Sings the Blues," which begins with evocative description of the neighborhood location, then plunges into fragmentary impressions in an unstable mingling of past and present: "Diamond boys and satin dolls/Bourbon laughter—ghosts—history falls/To parking lots and shopping malls/As they tear down old Beale Street/Old Furry sings the blues."

19. For details about the production of the cover photography, see O'Brien, *Shadows and Light*, 165–67. The published songbook contains additional photographic collages from the same session. The recent compilation *Songs of a Prairie Girl* also uses images from the earlier session for its cover.

20. The line in "Hejira" in fact refers to a "ballroom girl"; in the live performance included in *S&L*, Mitchell changes the phrase to "bridal girl."

21. Interview with Chip Stern, *Musician*, January/February 1995. In the same interview, Mitchell claims that her desire to reproduce this sound in live performance led to the invention of the Roland Jazz Chorus amp.

22. This interpretation depends on hearing song 7, "Dreamland," as in C Aeolian, which has always been my experience. I know of others, however, who hear its melody as favoring a B♭ center. I grant that Mitchell is using the tonal ambiguity of unaccompanied chant to full advantage in this song.

23. The role of the Split-Tongued Spirit was spoken by Boyd Elder (credited as "El Bwyd"), artist and mystic from Texas, an associate of the Eagles in the early 1970s (Fawcett, *California Rock, California Sound*, 52, 64, 130).

24. Some versions of "Come All Ye Fair and Tender Ladies" include the following verse: "I wish I had known before I courted/That love had been so hard to gain/ I'd of locked my heart in a box of golden/And fastened it down with a silver chain." Many versions also include the following lines: "I wish I were some little sparrow/And I had wings and I could fly/[...]But I am not some little sparrow/I have no wings nor can I fly."

25. Castaneda's first book, *The Teachings of Don Juan: A Yaqui Way of Knowledge* (Berkeley & Los Angeles: University of California Press), appeared in 1968. By 1977 (when *DJRD* was being written), five books in the series had been published in trade editions.

26. JM interview in Fawcett, *California Rock, California Sound*, 61.

27. JM: "In the dream world on the album there's a printed dream, which is a dream I had on the Rolling Thunder Tour, about Paprika Plains—it's not sung but this is a real dream" (Fawcett, *California Rock, California Sound*, 61).

28. JM: "The piano—all of a sudden I went through a breakthrough period last year where I sat down and off the top of my head, I couldn't play anything wrong. What I mean by that is that if I hit what would be called a wrong note, a dissonance, I would repeat it and it would sound fantastic—like where a dissonance was simply another statement and was not a wrong note. You know, lay on it; you hit a dissonance—well lay on it! ... The instrumental passage in the middle [of "Paprika Plains"] just poured out" (Fawcett, *California Rock, California Sound*, 60). "What I'd done was give myself a freeing lesson and said to myself, 'Everything resolves to C; no matter where you go you can't hit a wrong note, just go home to C.' We went in the studio and cut this thing four times.... From those four [improvisations] I edited together a piece that was to become the bridge for 'Paprika Plains'" (Garbarini, "Joni Mitchell Is a Nervy Broad"; in Luftig, 121–22).

29. Compare Michael Watts on "Don Juan": "The title song is a dazzling, metaphorical piece which uses images of snakes/trains and eagles/planes to express not just personal inner conflict but the sense of a riven America" (Watts, "Joni: A Fallible Magician").

30. Karen O'Brien explains the genesis of Mitchell's black drag character, Art Nouveau (*Shadows and Light*, 174–75).

31. Fawcett, *California Rock, California Sound*, 52.

32. It is also reproduced on the back cover of Gilles Hébert, ed., *Voices: The Work of Joni Mitchell* (Saskatoon, Sask.: Mendel Art Gallery, 2000).

33. For detailed discussion of the painting's genesis, symbolism, and relation to the album, see Mitchell's remarks in Fawcett, *California Rock, California Sound*, 64 (archived at http://jmdl.com).

34. JM: "I remember they wrote, 'What is she trying to say [by donning black drag]—that blacks have more fun?' Regardless of what I was trying to say— because a lot of it is instinct—the important point is the chain of events. I was just going on the hottest impulses I had, the creative ideas" (Angela Greca, "Joni Mitchell," *Rock Photo*, June 1985).

35. Compare Jennifer Rycenga's remarks on experimental large-scale form in albums by Yes and PJ Harvey: "These fragmentary narratives hint at—even beg for—interconnection; . . . tendrils of relational possibility hover around the whole album, creating a prismatic, morphing sense of form. Obvious as it is that the songs belong together, the questions of how and why grow and shift rather than resolve, driving repeated listenings. . . . It was exactly this kind of compositional construction—in which formal markers are everywhere, but the form as an abstract external entity remains inscrutable—that annoyed rock critics" ("Endless Caresses: Queer Exuberance in Large-Scale Form in Rock," in *Queering the Popular Pitch*, ed. Sheila Whiteley and Jennifer Rycenga [New York: Routledge, 2006], 235–47; see 238, 240). Such deliberate exploitation of formal ambiguity is a hallmark of the Romantic cycles of Robert Schumann, as theorized by David Ferris: "The context that the cycle sets up is provocative; it implies structural connections and hints at larger meanings, but it never makes them explicit or definitive. . . . Schumann flirts with incoherence as he experiments with fragmentary and discontinuous musical structures" (Ferris, *Schumann's Eichendorff* Liederkreis, 6, 17).

8. A Tribute

1. Review of *DJRD* by Blair Jackson, *BAM*, January 1978; in Luftig, 85–86.
2. *A Tribute to Joni Mitchell* (Nonesuch 2 122620), 2007. Karen O'Brien includes a preliminary playlist for *A Case of Joni* in her 2001 biography (*Shadows and Light*, 334). Five of the originally announced covers made it onto the eventual album. Dropped from the slate were P. M. Dawn, Stevie Wonder, Janet Jackson, Duncan Sheik, Chaka Khan, Etta James, Elton John, Lindsey Buckingham, and Mick Fleetwood.
3. Bradley Bambarger, "Both Sides Again," *New Jersey Star-Ledger*, 22 April 2007.
4. Review of *A Tribute*, Bernard Zuel, *The Guardian*, 20 April 2007.
5. For another reviewer, lang's cover song "fits her like a tailored suit" (Ray Mark Rinaldi, "A Tough Act to Follow," *Denver Post*, 23 April 2007).
6. Much more successful and vibrant, to my ears, is the cover of "Edith and the Kingpin" on the recent album by Herbie Hancock, *River: The Joni Letters* (2007), with Tina Turner as vocalist.
7. Jim Farber, "Echoing the Lady of the Canyon," *New York Daily News*, 23 April 2007.

BIBLIOGRAPHY

Works by Joni Mitchell

Discography

Song to a Seagull. Reprise RS 6293. 1968.
Clouds. Reprise RS 6341. 1969.
Ladies of the Canyon. Reprise RS 6376. 1970.
Blue. Reprise MS 2038. 1971.
For the Roses. Asylum SD 5057. 1972.
Court and Spark. Asylum 7E 1001. 1974.
Miles of Aisles. (Live.) Asylum AB 202. 1974.
The Hissing of Summer Lawns. Asylum 7E 1051. 1975.
Hejira. Asylum 7E 1087. 1976.
Don Juan's Reckless Daughter. Asylum BB 701. 1977.
Mingus. Asylum 5E 505. 1979.
Shadows and Light. (Live.) Asylum BB 704. 1980.
Wild Things Run Fast. Geffen GHS 2019. 1982.
Dog Eat Dog. Geffen GHS 24074. 1985.
Chalk Mark in a Rain Storm. Geffen GHS 24172. 1988.
Night Ride Home. Geffen GEFD 24302. 1991.
Turbulent Indigo. Reprise 9 45786-2. 1994.
Hits. (Compilation.) Reprise 9 46326-2. 1996.
Misses. (Compilation.) Reprise 9 46358-2. 1996.
Taming the Tiger. Reprise 9 46451-2. 1998.
Both Sides Now. (Standards.) Reprise 9 47620-2. 2000.
Travelogue. (Compilation in orchestral arrangements.) Nonesuch 79817-2.
    2002.
Complete Geffen Recordings. (Reissue.) Geffen B000081902. 2003.
The Beginning of Survival. (Compilation.) Geffen B000283602. 2004.
Dreamland. (Compilation.) Asylum/Reprise/Nonesuch/Rhino WTVD
    76520. 2004.
Songs of a Prairie Girl. (Compilation.) Asylum/Reprise/Nonesuch/Rhino R2
    74634. 2005.
Shine. Hear Music HMCD-30457. 2007.

Instrumental/Vocal Scores

The Music of Joni Mitchell. New York: Charles Hansen, 1969.

Ladies of the Canyon. New York: Charles Hansen, 1970.

Blue. New York: Charles Hansen, 1971.

Joni Mitchell Complete. New York: Charles Hansen, 1972.

For the Roses. New York: Warner Bros. Publications, 1973.

Court and Spark. New York: Warner Bros. Publications, 1974.

Joni Mitchell Songbook: Complete Volume Number 1 *(1966–1970).* New York: Warner Bros. Publications, 1974.

Joni Mitchell Songbook: Complete Volume Number 2. New York: Warner Bros. Publications, 1975.

The Hissing of Summer Lawns. New York: Warner Bros. Publications, 1976.

Hejira. New York: Warner Bros. Publications, 1977.

Don Juan's Reckless Daughter. New York: Warner Bros. Publications, 1978.

Mingus. New York: Warner Bros. Publications, 1979.

Wild Things Run Fast. New York: Warner Bros. Publications, 1983.

Chalk Mark in a Rain Storm. Secaucus, N.J.: Warner Bros. Publications, 1988.

Night Ride Home. Transcribed and arranged for piano by John Curtin; special guitar transcriptions by Joel Bernstein. Secaucus, N.J.: Warner Bros. Publications, 1991.

Turbulent Indigo. Transcribed and arranged by John Curtin; special guitar transcriptions by Joel Bernstein. Miami: Warner Bros. Publications, 1995.

Hits. Arrangements by Hemme Luttjeboer and Dylan Schorer based on transcriptions by Joel Bernstein. Miami: Warner Bros. Publications, 1997.

Misses. Arrangements by Hemme Luttjeboer based on transcriptions by Joel Bernstein. Miami: Warner Bros. Publications, 1997.

Taming the Tiger. Arranged and edited by Ethan Neuburg, John Curtin, and Joel Bernstein; guitar notes by Howard Wright. Miami: Warner Bros. Publications, 1999.

Joni Mitchell Complete (Guitar Songbook Edition). Transcriptions by Joel Bernstein and Daniel Libertino. Van Nuys, Calif.: Alfred Publishing, 2006. [Released and quickly withdrawn by the publisher in anticipation of a corrected edition.]

Video Recordings

Shadows and Light. (Live.) Shout Factory DVD 30161. (1980) 2003.

Refuge of the Roads. (Live.) Shout Factory DVD 30352. (1984) 2004.

Come In from the Cold. (Video collection.) Geffen GEFV-39512. 1991.

Painting with Words and Music. (Live.) Eagle Rock EE39035-9. (1998) 2004.

Books

The Complete Poems and Lyrics. New York: Crown Publishers, 1997.
Voices: The Work of Joni Mitchell. [*Voices: Joni Mitchell.*] Ed. Gilles Hébert.
   Saskatoon, Sask.: Mendel Art Gallery, 2000.

Web sites devoted to Joni Mitchell

The Joni Mitchell Discussion List. http://jmdl.com. Fan-oriented site
   includes guitar tunings and tablature transcriptions, and a vast searchable
   archive (Library) of journalistic sources (as of fall 2007).
The Joni Mitchell Home Page. http://jonimitchell.com. Official web site
   includes a biographic essay, a comprehensive chronology of appearances,
   discographic information, a searchable database of the complete lyrics, a
   compiled list of Mitchell songs covered by other artists, and selections of
   Mitchell's visual art. The JMDL Library is also duplicated here (as of fall
   2007).

Other References

Abrams, M. H., and Geoffrey Galt Harpham. *A Glossary of Literary Terms*,
   8th ed. Boston: Thomson Wadsworth, 2005.
Adria, Marco. *Music of Our Times: Eight Canadian Singer-Songwriters.* Toronto:
   James Lorimer, 1990.
Anonymous. Review of *Mingus. Down Beat*, 9 August 1979.
Bambarger, Bradley. "Both Sides Again." *New Jersey Star-Ledger*, 22 April 2007.
Beker, Marilyn. "Gentle Joni of the Mythical Mood in Folk-Rock." *Toronto
   Globe and Mail*, 20 April 1968.
Berkowitz, Edward D. *Something Happened: A Political and Cultural Overview
   of the Seventies.* New York: Columbia University Press, 2006.
Bingham, Ruth O. "The Early Nineteenth-Century Song Cycle." In *The
   Cambridge Companion to the Lied*, ed. James Parsons, 101–19. Cambridge:
   Cambridge University Press, 2004.
Black, Mary. Interview with Joni Mitchell. "Both Sides Now." BBC-2,
   20 February 1999.
Booth, Wayne C. *The Rhetoric of Fiction*, 2nd ed. Chicago: University of
   Chicago Press, 1983.
Borders, James. "Form and the Concept Album: Aspects of Modernism
   in Frank Zappa's Early Releases." *Perspectives of New Music* 39 (2001):
   118–60.
Brackett, David. "Music Analysis." In *Continuum Encyclopedia of Popular
   Music of the World*, ed. John Shepherd et al., 1:86–90. London:
   Continuum, 2003.

————. "Music Theory." In *Continuum Encyclopedia of Popular Music of the World*, ed. John Shepherd et al., 1:94–96. London: Continuum, 2003.

————. *The Pop, Rock, and Soul Reader: Histories and Debates*. New York: Oxford University Press, 2005.

Brake, Elizabeth. " 'To Live Outside the Law, You Must Be Honest': Freedom in Dylan's Lyrics." In *Bob Dylan and Philosophy: It's Alright, Ma (I'm Only Thinking)*, ed. Peter Vernezze and Carl J. Porter, 78–89. Chicago: Open Court, 2006.

Brown, Ethan. "Influences: Joni Mitchell." *New York Magazine*, 9 May 2005.

Burns, Gary. "A Typology of 'Hooks' in Popular Records." *Popular Music* 6 (1986): 1–20.

Butts, Robert W. "More Than a Collection of Songs: The Concept Album in Country Music." *Mid-America Folklore* 16 (Fall 1988): 90–99.

Caplin, William E. *Classical Form: A Theory of Formal Functions for the Instrumental Music of Haydn, Mozart, and Beethoven*. New York: Oxford University Press, 1998.

Castaneda, Carlos. *The Teachings of Don Juan: A Yaqui Way of Knowledge*. Berkeley and Los Angeles: University of California Press, 1968.

Cochran, Connor Freff. "Out of the Quicksand." *Roland Users Group*, October 1996. www.rolandus.com/rug/. Archived at http://jmdl.com.

Cohen, Leonard. *Stranger Music: Selected Poems and Songs*. Toronto: McClelland & Stewart, 1993.

Collins, Judy. *Wildflowers*. Elektra 74012-2. 1967.

Coppage, Noel. "More than a Sprinking of Symbolism in Joni Mitchell's *The Hissing of Summer Lawns*." *Stereo Review*, February 1976. [Reprinted in Luftig, 77–79.]

Covach, John. "Form in Rock Music: A Primer." In *Engaging Music: Essays in Music Analysis*, ed. Deborah Stein, 65–76. Oxford: Oxford University Press, 2005.

————. "Popular Music, Unpopular Musicology." In *Rethinking Music*, ed. Nicholas Cook and Mark Everist, 452–70. Oxford: Oxford University Press, 1999.

————. "We Won't Get Fooled Again: Rock Music and Musical Analysis." In *Keeping Score: Music, Disciplinarity, Culture*, ed. David Schwartz, Anahid Kassabian, and Lawrence Siegel, 75–89. Charlottesville: University Press of Virginia, 1997.

Crawford, Richard. *America's Musical Life: A History*. New York: Norton, 2001.

Crosby, Stills & Nash. *Crosby, Stills & Nash*. Atlantic Records SD 8229. 1969.

Crowe, Cameron. Interview with Joni Mitchell (1979). In *The Rolling Stone Interviews: Talking with the Legends of Rock & Roll, 1967–1980*, ed. Peter Herbst, 376–91. New York: St. Martin's Press, 1981.

Dallas, Karl. "Joni, the Seagull from Saskatoon." *Melody Maker*, 28 September 1968. [Reprinted in Luftig, 6–8.]

Daverio, John. "The Song Cycle: Journeys through a Romantic Landscape." In *German Lieder in the Nineteenth Century*, ed. Rufus Hallmark, 279–312. New York: Schirmer, 1996.

Deloria, Philip. "Counterculture Indians and the New Age." In *Imagine Nation: The American Counterculture of the 1960s and '70s*, ed. Peter Braunstein and Michael William Doyle, 159–88. New York: Routledge, 2002.

Denberg, Jody. "Taming Joni Mitchell—Joni's Jazz." *Austin Chronicle*, 12 October 1998. [Reprinted in Luftig, 197–209.]

Douridas, Chris. Interview with Joni Mitchell. "Morning Becomes Eclectic." KCRW-FM, 12 September 1994.

Echols, Alice. "Thirty Years with a Portable Lover." *Los Angeles Weekly*, 25 November 1994. [Reprinted in Echols, *Shaky Ground: The '60s and Its Aftershocks*. New York: Columbia University Press, 2002.]

Eggar, Robin. "Both Sides Now." *The Word*, April 2007.

Ephland, John. "Alternate Tunings." *Down Beat*, December 1996.

Everett, Walter. *The Beatles as Musicians*: Revolver *through the* Anthology. New York: Oxford University Press, 1999.

———. *The Beatles as Musicians: The Quarry Men through* Rubber Soul. New York: Oxford University Press, 2001.

———. "Confessions from Blueberry Hell, or, Pitch Can Be a Sticky Substance." In *Expression in Pop-Rock Music: A Collection of Critical and Analytical Essays*, ed. Everett, 269–345. New York: Garland, 2000.

———. "Making Sense of Rock's Tonal Systems." *Music Theory Online* 10/4 (December 2004).

Farber, Jim. "Echoing the Lady of the Canyon." *New York Daily News*, 23 April 2007.

Fawcett, Anthony. "Joni Mitchell—A Search for Clarity." In *California Rock, California Sound*, 50–65. Los Angeles: Reed Books, 1978.

Ferris, David. *Schumann's Eichendorff* Liederkreis *and the Genre of the Romantic Cycle*. New York: Oxford University Press, 2000.

Fetherling, Douglas. *Some Day Soon: Essays on Canadian Songwriters*. Kingston, Ont.: Quarry Press, 1991.

Fischer, Doug. "The Trouble She's Seen." *Ottawa Citizen*, 8 October 2006.

Flanagan, Bill. "Lady of the Canyon." *Vanity Fair*, June 1997.

Fleischer, Leonore. *Joni Mitchell*. New York: Flash Books, 1976.

Fludernik, Monika. "Second-Person Narrative as a Test Case for Narratology: The Limits of Realism." *Style* 28 (1994): 445–79.

Forte, Allen. *The American Popular Ballad of the Golden Era, 1924–1950*. Princeton: Princeton University Press, 1995.

Friedan, Betty. *The Feminine Mystique*. New York: Norton, 1963.

Frith, Simon. *Performing Rites: On the Value of Popular Music*. Cambridge: Harvard University Press, 1996.

Frye, Northrop. *Anatomy of Criticism: Four Essays*. Princeton: Princeton University Press, 1957.

Gaar, Gillian G. *She's a Rebel: The History of Women in Rock and Roll*, 2nd ed. New York: Seal Press, 2002.

Garbarini, Vic. "Joni Mitchell Is a Nervy Broad." *Musician*, January 1983. [Reprinted in Luftig, 113–33.]

Gauldin, Robert. "Beethoven, *Tristan*, and the Beatles." *College Music Symposium* 30 (1990): 142–52.

Gendron, Bernard. *Between Montmartre and the Mudd Club: Popular Music and the Avant-Garde*. Chicago: University of Chicago Press, 2002.

Genette, Gérard. *The Architext: An Introduction*. Trans. Jane E. Lewin. Berkeley & Los Angeles: University of California Press, 1992.

―――. *Narrative Discourse: An Essay in Method*. Trans. Jane E. Lewin. Ithaca: Cornell University Press, 1980.

Hale, Tony. Interview with Joni Mitchell. "Rock Master Class." Capitol 95.8FM, London, 29 December 1985.

Hansen, Liane. Interview with Joni Mitchell. "Weekend Edition." National Public Radio, 28 May 1995.

Hartman, Charles O. *Jazz Text: Voice and Improvisation in Poetry, Jazz, and Song*. Princeton: Princeton University Press, 1991.

Heckman, Dan. "Joni Mitchell at a Crossroads." *New York Times*, 8 August 1971.

―――. "She Soars, She Orbits, She Never Lands." *High Fidelity*, March 1978.

Henderson, Stuart. "'All Pink and Clean and Full of Wonder?': Gendering 'Joni Mitchell,' 1966–1974." *Left History* 10 (Fall 2005): 83–109.

Hilburn, Robert. Interview with Joni Mitchell. *Los Angeles Times*, 20 September 2004.

Holden, Stephen. "Joni Mitchell Finds the Peace of Middle Age." *New York Times*, 17 March 1991. [Reprinted in Luftig, 152–56.]

―――. "Madam Joni Almost Pulls It Off." *Village Voice*, 19 December 1977.

―――. Review of *The Hissing of Summer Lawns*. *Rolling Stone*, 15 January 1976.

―――. "Too Feminine for Rock? Or Is Rock Too Macho?" *New York Times*, 14 January 1996.

Hoskyns, Barney. *Hotel California: Singer-Songwriters and Cocaine Cowboys in the L.A. Canyons, 1967–1976*. London: Fourth Estate, 2005.

―――. "Our Lady of Sorrows." *Mojo*, December 1994. [Reprinted in Luftig, 161–75.]

Huebner, Steven. "Lyric Form in *Ottocento* Opera." *Journal of the Royal Musical Association* 117 (1992): 123–47.

Jackson, Blair. Review of *Don Juan's Reckless Daughter*. *BAM*, January 1978. [Reprinted in Luftig, 85–86.]

Jackson, Joe. "The Second Coming of Joni Mitchell." *Hotpress*, 26 April 2000.

Kaminsky, Peter. "The Popular Album as Song Cycle: Paul Simon's 'Still Crazy after All These Years.'" *College Music Symposium* 32 (1992): 38–54.

Keightley, Keir. "Reconsidering Rock." In *The Cambridge Companion to Pop and Rock*, ed. Simon Frith, Will Straw, and John Street, 109–42. Cambridge: Cambridge University Press, 2001.

Kelly, Merilee. Interview with Joni Mitchell. KCSA-FM, 25 October 1994.

Kernfeld, Barry. "Davis, Miles." *Grove Music Online*, ed. Laura Macy. www. grovemusic.com.

Komar, Arthur. "The Music of *Dichterliebe*: The Whole and Its Parts." In *Robert Schumann: Dichterliebe*, ed. Komar, 63–94. New York: Norton, 1971.

Lacy, Susan, dir. *Woman of Heart and Mind: Joni Mitchell, A Life Story*. Eagle Vision EV300399. 2003. DVD.

LaGreca, Angela. "Joni Mitchell." *Rock Photo*, June 1985.

Lanser, Susan S. "The 'I' of the Beholder: Equivocal Attachments and the Limits of Structuralist Narratology." In *A Companion to Narrative Theory*, ed. James Phelan and Peter J. Rabinowitz, 206–19. Oxford: Blackwell, 2005.

Lasch, Christopher. *The Culture of Narcissism: American Life in an Age of Diminishing Expectations*. New York: Norton, 1979.

LeBlanc, Larry. "Joni Takes a Break." *Rolling Stone*, 4 March 1971.

Levitin, Daniel. "A Conversation with Joni Mitchell." *Grammy Magazine*, Spring 1996. [Reprinted in Luftig, 177–87.]

Luftig, Stacey, ed. *The Joni Mitchell Companion: Four Decades of Commentary*. New York: Schirmer, 2000.

Malka. "Joni Mitchell: Self-Portrait of a Superstar." *Maclean's*, June 1974. [Reprinted in Luftig, 66–74.]

Maslin, Janet. "Joni Mitchell's Reckless and Shapeless 'Daughter.'" *Rolling Stone*, 9 March 1978.

Maus, Fred Everett. "Classical Instrumental Music and Narrative." In *A Companion to Narrative Theory*, ed. James Phelan and Peter J. Rabinowitz, 466–83. Oxford: Blackwell, 2005.

―――. "Narratology, narrativity." *Grove Music Online*, ed. Laura Macy. www.grovemusic.com.

McDonnell, Evelyn, and Ann Powers, eds. *Rock She Wrote*. New York: Delta, 1995.

McKenna, Kristine. "Bleak Visions of Life in the Fast Lane." *Los Angeles Times*, 25 December 1977.

———. "Lady of the Canyon." *Spin*, May 1988.

Meisel, Perry. "An End to Innocence: How Joni Mitchell Fails." *Village Voice*, 24 January 1977. [Reprinted in Luftig, 79–85).

Mellers, Wilfrid. *Angels of the Night: Popular Female Singers of Our Time*. New York: Blackwell, 1986.

Middleton, Richard. "Song Form." In *Continuum Encyclopedia of Popular Music of the World*, ed. John Shepherd et al., 2:513–19. London: Continuum, 2003.

———. *Studying Popular Music*. Milton Keynes: Open University Press, 1990.

———, ed. *Reading Pop: Approaches to Textual Analysis in Popular Music*. Oxford: Oxford University Press, 2000.

Miller, Richard. *Bohemia: The Protoculture Then and Now*. Chicago: Nelson-Hall, 1977.

Moore, Allan. *The Beatles: Sgt. Pepper's Lonely Hearts Club Band*. Cambridge: Cambridge University Press, 1997.

———. *Rock: The Primary Text: Developing a Musicology of Rock*, 2nd ed. Aldershot: Ashgate, 2001.

———. "The So-Called 'Flattened Seventh' in Rock." *Popular Music* 14 (1995): 185–201.

Morrissey. "Melancholy Meets the Infinite Sadness." *Rolling Stone*, 6 March 1997.

O'Brien, Karen. *Shadows and Light: Joni Mitchell, The Definitive Biography*. London: Virgin Books, 2001.

O'Brien, Lucy. *She Bop II: The Definitive History of Women in Rock, Pop, and Soul*. London: Continuum, 2002.

Polar Music Prize press conference, Stockholm, 7 May 1996. Transcribed at http://jmdl.com.

Rinaldi, Ray Mark. "A Tough Act to Follow." *Denver Post*, 23 April 2007.

Robertson, Sandy. "Scared to Dance." *Sounds*, 30 June 1979.

Rockwell, John. "Joni Mitchell Recaptures Her Gift." *New York Times*, 12 December 1976.

———. "The New Artistry of Joni Mitchell." *New York Times*, 19 August 1979.

Rodgers, Jeffrey Pepper. "My Secret Place: The Guitar Odyssey of Joni Mitchell." *Acoustic Guitar*, August 1996, 40–55. [Reprinted in Luftig, 219–30; and in Rodgers, *Rock Troubadours*. San Anselmo, Ca.: String Letter Publishing, 2000.]

————. "Setting the Stage: The Vocal and Lyrical Craft of Joni Mitchell." *Acoustic Guitar*, February 1997. [Reprinted in Luftig, 255–59.]

Rupprecht, Philip. *Britten's Musical Language.* Cambridge: Cambridge University Press, 2001.

Rycenga, Jennifer. "Endless Caresses: Queer Exuberance in Large-Scale Form in Rock." In *Queering the Popular Pitch*, ed. Sheila Whiteley and Jennifer Rycenga, 235–47. New York: Routledge, 2006.

————. "Not the Same Situation: Joni Mitchell's Work as a Sonic Document of Feminism." Symposium on the Music and Art of Joni Mitchell, McGill University, 27 October 2004.

Sanders, Linda. "The Grown-Up Game." *Entertainment Weekly*, 1 March 1991.

Schur, Edwin. *The Awareness Trap: Self-Absorption Instead of Social Change.* New York: Quadrangle, 1976.

Simon, Josh. Interview with Joni Mitchell. *Life*, August 1994.

Smith, Larry David. *Elvis Costello, Joni Mitchell, and the Torch Song Tradition.* Westport, Conn.: Praeger, 2004.

Sonenberg, Daniel. "'Who in the World She Might Be': A Contextual and Stylistic Approach to the Early Music of Joni Mitchell." D.M.A. diss., City University of New York, 2003.

Stein, Deborah, and Robert Spillman. *Poetry into Song: Performance and Analysis of* Lieder. New York: Oxford University Press, 1996.

Stephenson, Ken. *What to Listen for in Rock: A Stylistic Analysis.* New Haven: Yale University Press, 2002.

Stern, Chip. Interview with Joni Mitchell. *Musician*, January/February 1995.

Strauss, Neil. "The Hissing of a Living Legend." *New York Times*, 4 October 1998. [Reprinted in Luftig, 209–16.]

Swartley, Ariel. "The Babe in Bopperland and the Great Jazz Composer." *Rolling Stone*, 6 September 1979.

————. "The Siren and the Symbolist." *Rolling Stone*, 10 February 1977.

Tagg, Philip. "Melody." In *Continuum Encyclopedia of Popular Music of the World*, ed. John Shepherd et al., 2:567–84. London: Continuum, 2003.

Tawa, Nicholas E. *Sweet Songs for Gentle Americans: The Parlor Song in America, 1790–1860.* Bowling Green, Ohio: Bowling Green University Popular Press, 1980.

A Tribute to Joni Mitchell. Various artists. Nonesuch 2 122620. 2007. Compact disc.

Valentine, Penny. Interview with Joni Mitchell. *Sounds*, 3 June 1972. [Reprinted in Luftig, 45–50.]

Ward, Ed. "Charles, Joni, and the Circle Game." *Village Voice*, 30 July 1979. [Reprinted in Luftig, 103–106.]

Warden, Steve. Interview with Joni Mitchell. Q107-FM, Toronto, September 1994.

Watts, Michael. "Joni: A Fallible Magician." *Melody Maker*, 24 December 1977.

————. "Joni ... er ... um." *Melody Maker*, 16 June 1979.

Weinstein, Deena. "Progressive Rock as Text: The Lyrics of Roger Waters." In *Progressive Rock Reconsidered*, ed. Kevin Holm-Hudson, 91–109. New York: Routledge, 2002.

White, Timothy. "Billboard Honors Joni Mitchell with Its Highest Accolade." *Billboard*, 9 December 1995.

————. *Rock Lives: Profiles and Interviews*. New York: Henry Holt, 1990.

Whiteley, Sheila. *Women and Popular Music: Sexuality, Identity and Subjectivity*. New York: Routledge, 2000.

Wild, David. "A Conversation with Joni Mitchell." *Rolling Stone*, 30 May 1991.

Wolfe, Tom. "The Me Decade and the Third Great Awakening." In *Mauve Gloves and Madmen, Clutter and Vine*, 126–67. New York: Farrar, Straus and Giroux, 1976.

————. *The Painted Word*. New York: Farrar, Straus and Giroux, 1975.

Wölfflin, Heinrich. *Principles of Art History: The Problem of the Development of Style in Later Art*. Trans. M. D. Hottinger. London: G. Bell and Sons, 1932. Rept., New York: Dover, 1950.

Zuel, Bernard. Review of *A Tribute to Joni Mitchell*. *The Guardian*, 20 April 2007.

INDEX

communal voice. *See under* voice

compositional method, 41, 160, 239n2, 246n28, 248n12, 255n28

concept albums, 13, 195–226, 252n5, 253n13; and cover art, 195, 199, 200–201, 206, 209–210, 224. *See also* coherence, cyclic; song cycles

confinement. *See under* themes, musico-poetic

Coppage, Noel, 9

Costello, Elvis, 228

counterculture. *See* youth movement/ counterculture

Covach, John, 11

critic persona. *See* personae, poetic

critical reception, 25, 30. *See also* popular reception

Crosby, Stills, Nash & Young, 33–34

"Cruel Mother, The," 119

dance, 5, 26, 40, 92, 164, 233n10, 240n12. *See also under* imagery, poetic

Davis, Miles, 15, 210, 235n1; *Nefertiti,* 210

Debussy, Claude, 6, 118

diction, poetic: ordinary, 23, 29, 41, 56–57, 59, 99, 112, 217, 223; heightened, 23, 29, 41–42, 56, 57–59, 106, 142, 222, 223

disillusionment. *See under* themes, musico-poetic

dramatic mode. *See under* mode, poetic

Drifters, 157

"Drunken Sailor," 119

dulcimer, 91, 142–43

Dunaway, Faye, 43

Dylan, Bob, 4, 77, 92–93, 185, 252n37, 254n16; "Blowin' in the Wind," 47, 164, 250n20; "Bob Dylan's 115th Dream," 92; "It Ain't Me, Babe," 149; "It's All Over Now, Baby Blue," 149; "Like A Rolling Stone," 74, 151, 165, 249n18; "Mr. Tambourine Man," 93, 151; "North Country Blues," 45; "Positively 4th Street," 74, 77, 153; "Subterranean Homesick Blues," 49, 149; "Visions of Johanna," 92

Earhart, Amelia, 46, 109–111

Everett, Walter, 157, 245n19

explicit poetic speakers, 50–53; dramatized, 52; undramatized, 52, 56. *See also* implicit poetic speakers; person, grammatical; personae, poetic

fan behavior, 15–16, 194

"Father and Son" (Cat Stevens), 45

Feldman, Victor, 244n5

female authorship, undervaluing of, 4–5, 14, 233n8. *See also* feminism; woman's perspective

feminism, 82, 241n2, 242n3. *See also* female authorship, undervaluing of; gender roles; woman's perspective

focalization. *See* person, grammatical; perspective, poetic

form. *See* coherence, cyclic; phrase structure; poetic structure; song forms

fortune. *See under* themes, musico-poetic

Franklin, Aretha, 26, 39

free spirit. *See* personae, poetic

freedom. *See under* themes, musico-poetic

Friedan, Betty, 82

Frith, Simon, 8

Frye, Northrop, 46

Galatea, 53, 81

gender roles, 58, 64, 80–84, 89. *See also* female authorship, undervaluing of; feminism; woman's perspective

Gendron, Bernard, 4

Genette, Gérard, 53

genre. *See* song genres

Gershwin, George, 118, 245n10; "A Foggy Day," 250n25

"God Rest Ye, Merry Gentlemen," 119

"Golden Apples of the Sun," 251n28

"Greensleeves," 126, 249n17

Guerin, John, 82

"Guinnevere" (David Crosby), 49, 85

guitar performance, characteristics, 15, 17–18, 36, 134, 218

guitar tunings, 6, 11, 15, 107, 117, 118, 197, 244n2

Guy, Buddy, 30

harmonic categories: chromatic, 13, 138, 146–47; modal, 13, 127–130, 146; pedal point, 13, 79, 86, 91, 104, 142–47, 202–3, 229, 247n29; polymodal, 13, 18, 19, 131–38, 143, 146, 246n27; polytonal, 13, 22, 81, 110–111, 139–42, 146, 246n22, 250n22

harmony: cadence, 250n19; pivot chords, 22, 131, 133, 136; quartal, 18, 34, 104, 133,

202–3; quintal, 131, 202; "slash" chords, 19, 107–108, 136; suspended chords, 18, 19, 36, 130, 133, 134, 136, 202. *See also* coherence, cyclic: tonal planning; modes, musical

Harris, Emmylou, 228

Harrison, George, 30

Heckman, Dan, 4, 252n37

hemiola, 26, 28

Hendrix, Jimi, 15, 39

high/low art distinction, 4, 5–10, 11, 39–40, 232n4. *See also* art song; classical music; song cycles; value systems

hippies. *See* themes, musico-poetic: bohemia; youth movement/counterculture

Holden, Stephen, 4, 30, 184, 185

"Home Sweet Home" (Bishop), 249n17

hooks, 9, 23, 27–28, 40, 179, 182, 185, 186, 187, 188, 192, 211, 217, 251n35

hypermeter, 176, 249n18, 250n19

"I Know Where I'm Going," 251n28

"If You Could Read My Mind" (Gordon Lightfoot), 127

imagery, poetic, 24, 49–50, 58, 60, 69, 70, 71, 73, 98, 103, 135–36, 223–24; animals, 58, 88, 90, 100, 103–9, 112, 157, 206, 207, 219; clothing, 80, 81, 95, 200; color, 129, 196; dance, 48, 72, 78, 115, 220–21; flying, 103–15, 143, 201; matriarchal figures, 83–84; seafaring, 49, 85–86, 103, 131, 135, 200; stone, 81, 83–84, 105, 115; treasure, 87–90, 131, 200, 208; vanishing, 104–14, 210; vehicles, 58, 86, 88, 109, 204, 219; weaving, 96–97, 98, 115, 204. *See also* coherence, cyclic: recurrent imagery; themes, musico-poetic

"Imagine" (John Lennon), 47

implicit poetic speakers, 50, 53–56, 57, 203. *See also* explicit poetic speakers; person, grammatical; personae, poetic

ingenue. *See* personae, poetic

instrumentation, 21–22, 25, 26, 31–32, 34, 39, 95, 107, 112, 154, 155, 177, 187, 210–11, 213, 218, 220–21, 222, 228–29

Jackson, Blair, 227

"Jeanie with the Light Brown Hair" (Stephen Foster), 250n25

Joel, Billy, 30

"Johnny Angel" (Shelley Fabares), 115

Kaminsky, Peter, 198

Kerouac, Jack, 94

Khan, Chaka, 119

Klein, Larry, 25, 29

L. A. Express, 21, 34

Landau, Mike, 28

lang, k. d., 228–29

Lasch, Christopher, 90

"Leader of the Pack" (Shangri-Las), 45

Lennox, Annie, 228–29

Lewis, C. S., 84–85

Lieder. *See* art song

Los Angeles, 3, 19, 54, 94, 127, 204

lyric mode. *See under* mode, poetic

McKenna, Kristine, 184

McLachlan, Sarah, 228

Maslin, Janet, 184

Mays, Lyle, 34

Mehldau, Brad, 228

melodic contour, 13, 19, 34, 86, 91, 97, 105, 107, 137, 145, 165, 171, 175, 178–93, 251n29; nodal pitches, 182, 186

melodic style: first period, 25, 181, 185–86, 188; second period, 23, 25, 94, 97, 182–87, 211; third period, 183–84, 187–89; fourth period, 31, 189–92. *See also* style periods

Mendoza, Vince, 39

metaphorical language, to describe music, 117–118

Metheny, Pat, 34

metric disruption, 13, 23, 108, 130, 154, 157, 161–63, 173, 229, 237n16, 248n13

Middleton, Richard, 11, 152, 164

Mingus, Charles, 3, 21, 46, 51, 59, 101–2, 103, 196, 243n26, 247n4

Mitchell, Chuck, 16

Mitchell, Joni (works)

Albums:

Beginning of Survival, The, 33, 199

Blue, 13, 19, 62, 99, 142, 146, 148, 185, 186, 194, 196, 199, 204, 209, 225, 228; review, 4

Both Sides Now, 33, 196, 199

Chalk Mark in a Rain Storm, 31, 42

"Urge for Going" (*Hits*), 85, 159, 234n14
"Wild Things Run Fast" (*WTRF*), 26, 29, 149
"Willy" (*LC*), 17, 19, 61, 70, 155, 158–59, 164, 175, 197–98
"Windfall, The" (*NRH*), 156
"Wizard of Is, The," 52
"Wolf That Lives in Lindsey, The" (*M*), 59, 149, 153, 155, 162
"Woman of Heart and Mind" (*FR*), 46, 56, 69, 74, 133, 153, 178, 196
"Woodstock" (*LC*), 12, 14, 19, 33–38, 46, 68, 103, 154, 158, 165–66, 236n13; CSN&Y cover version, 34, 38; *MA* version, 34; *Painting with Words and Music* (video) version, 38–39; *Refuge of the Roads* (video) version, 38–39; *S&L* version, 34–39, 61, 238n37; *Travelogue* version, 39
"You Dream Flat Tires" (*WTRF*), 26, 27–29, 40, 167
"You Turn Me On, I'm a Radio" (*FR*), 153, 167, 236n13
"Yvette in English" (*TI*), 166
mixing. *See* studio production and mixing
modality. *See* harmonic categories; modes, musical
mode, poetic: dramatic, 43, 44–45, 46, 51, 62, 64, 111; dramatic lyric, 47–48; hybrid, 45, 47–48, 52; incantatory, 240n12; lyric, 43, 46, 47, 50, 52, 59–60, 68, 73, 75, 80, 81, 98, 101, 134, 154, 203, 204; narrative, 43, 45–46, 50, 52, 54, 59–60, 63–65, 99, 154, 185; political, 47–48, 63, 64
modes, musical, 118, 119, 126–27; mixed, 126–29, 131–33, 142, 143, 146, 175, 179, 202–3, 228, 229; pure, 31, 127. *See also* harmonic categories; harmony
Moore, Allan, 10
mortality. *See under* themes, musico-poetic
motives, 179–81, 182, 187, 196–97, 202–3, 212–17, 252n41. *See also under* coherence, cyclic
Mozart, Wolfgang Amadeus, 235n23
music industry, 4, 6–7, 42, 92, 98–101
musical styles: Afro-Caribbean, 32, 184, 214; blues, 26, 34, 97, 102–3, 138, 142, 145, 208, 253n11; blues rock, 218, 221; Celtic, 228; country, 228, 249n18; folk,

3, 4, 5, 12, 15, 16, 19, 42, 45, 85, 86, 118, 119, 142, 218, 233n10, 233n11, 247n1, 249n18, 251n28; folk rock, 7, 9, 85; funk, 34; fusion (jazz-rock), 15, 21, 218, 220–21; gospel, 228, 253n11; jazz, 12, 15, 21–23, 26, 32, 36, 38, 50, 62, 94, 101, 118, 147, 184, 185, 186, 213, 228, 233n10, 244n5; new wave, 25–26; pop ballad, 26; reggae, 26; rhythm and blues, 26, 218; rock, 4, 28, 34, 38, 72, 95, 153, 234n19, 249n18; rock 'n' roll, 26, 27, 77, 90, 233n10; spiritual, 64, 241n25; Tin Pan Alley, 26, 118, 166, 247n2, 250n21, 250n25; Tropicalia, 228; world music, 15, 146. *See also* classical music; singer-songwriter
mystic persona. *See* personae, poetic
mythic representation. *See under* representation

narrative mode. *See under* mode, poetic
Nash, Graham, 19
New Orleans Jazz and Heritage Festival, 15–16
New York City, 3, 50, 59, 89, 200–201, 204, 208, 220
nonconformity. *See* themes, musico-poetic: bohemia
notation, music, 117. *See also* transcription, musical

"O Come, O Come, Emmanuel," 119
"Operator" (Jim Croce), 48
"Over the Rainbow" (Arlen-Harburg), 247n2

"P. S. I Love You" (Jenkins-Mercer), 48
Pastorius, Jaco, 34, 103, 117, 186, 211, 213, 217
pedal points. *See* harmonic categories
person, grammatical: first-person subject, 50–52, 55, 73, 204; first-person reflexive address, 51; second-person address, 50, 51, 55, 65, 74, 94, 153, 179; second-person focal character, 54–56; second-person subject, 52–53, 55, 86–87, 240n18, 241n19; third-person focal character, 50, 53–54, 61, 63, 74, 81, 203; third-person object, 51–52. *See also* explicit poetic speakers; implicit poetic speakers
personae, poetic, 12, 15, 41–77, 202, 217, 226; critic, 64, 73–77, 157, 217; free

U2, 30
"Unchained Melody" (North-Zaret), 26, 146, 156
utterance types, 59–60, 65, 204, 241n23, 254n18

value systems, 5–10, 185; fine art, 5–10, 40, 194, 227, 234n23; popular art, 6–9, 40. *See also* high/low art distinction
Van Gogh, Vincent, 6
Veloso, Caetano, 228
vocal performance: characteristics, 16, 19, 21–22, 26, 28, 29–30, 34–36, 60–63, 94, 187, 188–89; conceived as dramatic roles, 42–43, 240n9. *See also under* personae, poetic
voice: autobiographical, 46, 51, 54, 55, 63, 75, 89, 109, 140, 204, 241n22, 254n16; communal, 47, 50; various meanings distinguished, 42

"Water Is Wide, The," 218
Watts, Michael, 184
"Wayfaring Stranger," 218
"We Shall Overcome," 47

"Wedding Bell Blues" (Laura Nyro), 149
"What Wondrous Love," 119
"Wild Thing" (Troggs), 237n22
"Will You Love Me Tomorrow?" (Goffin-King), 26, 149, 247n2
Williams, Tennessee, 105
Wilson, Cassandra, 228
Wolf, Hugo, 9
Wolfe, Tom, 90, 93–94
Wölfflin, Heinrich, 24, 237n18
woman's perspective, 3, 42, 65, 72, 82–84, 85–86, 91–92, 242n3. *See also* female authorship, undervaluing of; feminism; gender roles
Woodstock festival, 33, 38, 89
Wordsworth, William, 24, 46–47
"Wreck of the Edmund Fitzgerald, The" (Gordon Lightfoot), 119

Yeats, W. B., 31, 39, 69, 147
youth movement/counterculture, 3, 38, 39, 89, 103, 238n40

Zappa, Frank, 7, 198; *Freak out!* 196, 252n5